# SPEAK, HEAR & BELIEVE

## BIBLE MEDITATION:

### A workbook for spiritual growth, maturity, health, wealth and wisdom.

By

**Michael Dean Haller**

INFINITY PUBLISHING

Copyright © 2011 by Michael Dean Haller

ISBN 0-7414-6422-5

Printed in the United States of America

Published  March 2011

INFINITY PUBLISHING
1094 New DeHaven Street, Suite 100
West Conshohocken, PA 19428-2713
Toll-free (877) BUY BOOK
Local Phone (610) 941-9999
Fax (610) 941-9959
Info@buybooksontheweb.com
www.buybooksontheweb.com

# BIBLE VERSES MEMORIZED

| Week 1 | | Week 2 | | Week 3 | | Week 4 | | Week 5 | |
|--------|--------|--------|--------|--------|--------|--------|--------|--------|--------|
| BOOK | VERSE | BOOK | VERSE | BOOK | VERSE | BOOK | VERSE | BOOK | VERSE |
| Psalm | 14:1 | Rom. | 1:20 | Rom. | 1:21 | Rom. | 1:22 | Psalm | 19:1 |
| Psalm | 119:130 | | | | | | | | |
| | | | | | | | | | |
| | | | | | | | | | |
| | | | | | | | | | |
| | | | | | | | | | |
| | | | | | | | | | |
| | | | | | | | | | |
| | | | | | | | | | |
| | | | | | | | | | |
| | | | | | | | | | |
| | | | | | | | | | |
| | | | | | | | | | |
| | | | | | | | | | |
| | | | | | | | | | |
| | | | | | | | | | |
| | | | | | | | | | |
| | | | | | | | | | |
| | | | | | | | | | |
| | | | | | | | | | |
| | | | | | | | | | |
| | | | | | | | | | |
| | | | | | | | | | |
| | | | | | | | | | |
| | | | | | | | | | |
| | | | | | | | | | |
| | | | | | | | | | |
| | | | | | | | | | |
| | | | | | | | | | |
| | | | | | | | | | |
| | | | | | | | | | |
| | | | | | | | | | |
| | | | | | | | | | |

All Scripture quotations are taken from the King James Version of the Bible.

All Hebrew Words are taken from: *A Consise Dictionary of the Words in the Hebrew Bible; with their renderings in the Authorized English Version*; by James Strong, S.T.D., LL.D., Copyright 1890.

All Greek Words are taken from: *A Consise Dictionary of the Words in the Greek Testament; with their renderings in the Authorized English Version*; by James Strong, S.T.D., LL.D., Copyright 1890.

# FOREWORD

CAN TWO WALK TOGETHER, EXCEPT THEY BE AGREED?
AMOS 3:3

If you are anything like me, and I believe every human being on earth is like me, you have lived a great deal of your life in total bewilderment. You have wondered why there is evil and trouble in the world. You have wondered whether there was a way to control your circumstances.

How many times have you heard someone say something like this? "When things start going too good for too long, I know some trouble is just around the corner."

It seemed to me that something was always going wrong. If I was healthy, I would have some financial problem. If my finances were in good shape, I would have a health problem. If both my finances and health were in good condition, I would have some relationship problem. Sometimes it seemed that I was sick, broke, and without any friends, all at the same time. There always seemed to be something going wrong somewhere in my life at any one time. I wondered if there was a way to stop evil and troubles from impacting my life. I wondered if there was a way to control my own selfish and self-destructive impulses.

As I read the New Testament, the Apostle Paul uses a term that indicates there is a Christian process of self control, or should I say spirit control. In Paul's writings he uses a term that indicates that mature Christians should have control over his or her circumstances and control over his or her appetites and desires. The term Paul used was, "*Walk in the Spirit*".

THIS I SAY THEN, WALK IN THE SPIRIT, AND YE SHALL NOT FULFILL THE LUST OF THE FLESH.
GALATIANS 5:16

I earnestly prayed to God, "Show me how to *walk in the spirit* Father!." This book is what He has shown me.

*Walking in the spirit* is simply agreeing with the Spirit of God. If you wish to walk with God, you must start by agreeing with God. I found out that I cannot change God's mind, but God's spoken Word, through His Holy Spirit, can and did change my mind and my circumstances. This book is a step by step treatise on how you, by speaking and agreeing with God's Word, can begin to believe the Word of God and increase your faith. This book explains how to *walk in the spirit*.

I hope and pray you will read it with an enlightened spirit and revelation from God.

# CONTENTS

# PART 1

## THE BEGINNING

*"Although affliction cometh not forth of the dust,*
*Neither doth trouble spring out of the ground;*
*Yet man is born unto trouble,*
*As the sparks fly upward."*

*Job 5:6-7*

# CHAPTER 1

## THE MEANING OF OUR EXISTENCE IN THE WORLD

Why does mankind suffer? Why did God make us so weak and fragile? Why did God allow us to be placed in such seemingly hopeless circumstances?

God wants to teach us a simple lesson, a lesson that will stay with us throughout eternity. We only have a very short time to learn the lesson.

THE VOICE SAID, CRY. AND HE SAID, WHAT SHALL I CRY? ALL FLESH IS GRASS, AND ALL THE GOODLINESS THEREOF IS AS THE FLOWER OF THE FIELD:
THE GRASS WITHERETH, THE FLOWER FADETH: BECAUSE THE SPIRIT OF THE LORD BLOWETH UPON IT: SURELY THE PEOPLE IS GRASS.
ISAIAH 40:6-7

I remember when my dad turned eighty years old. I asked him if he had ever thought that he would reach eighty years old when he was a boy. He answered me saying, "It doesn't seem that long ago that I was fifteen years old."

I replied, "It doesn't seem that long ago that I was fifteen years old either." At the time, I was over forty years old, half an average person's life span was over, and it was then that I realized just how fast time was passing me by. It was then that I realized how fleeting my life really is, and if we ask any older person, time seems to go faster and faster the older we get. I realized that someday, if God blessed me, I would live to be an old man breathing my last breath, and while looking back over a very long life, all my time on earth would only have been a blink of an eye.

If we fail to learn *one* lesson, we will be forever lost and separated from God. However, if we learn this one lesson, we will be joined with God forever, and we will have all eternity before us!

I am not going to keep you in suspense. The one lesson we must learn before we die is this:

**GOD LOVES US ... AND HIS "WORD" WAS, IS, AND FOREVER WILL BE, ABSOLUTELY RELIABLE!**

THE GRASS WITHERETH, THE FLOWER FADETH: BUT THE WORD OF OUR GOD SHALL STAND FOR EVER.
ISAIAH 40:8

We suffer hurt because we have left the protection of God's everlasting arms. The reason for all the suffering in the world is mankind's *unbelief*, or lack of trust, in God and His Word. It would appear that any child could learn this lesson: *THE WORD OF OUR GOD SHALL STAND FOREVER*; however, it is the most difficult lesson in the world to learn. The whole purpose of this book is to show you how to learn this one lesson or how to *walk in the spirit* and believe God's Word.

My hope and desire is that by the end of this book, you will begin travelling on a journey of excitement, wonder and faith, and by the end of your journey, you will be radically transformed into the very image of Jesus Christ, who is in Himself, the express image of God the Father. *See* 2 Corinthians 3:18 and Hebrews 1:3. You will learn how to agree with God, you will learn how to believe God, and you will walk with God.

Many modern day Christians tend to believe that after a person accepts Jesus Christ as LORD and Savior, the battle is over. They are right in one respect. Our battle against God is over! Once we confess the LORD Jesus as our Savior, we have passed the biggest hurdle in our relationship with God. We are no longer in outright rebellion and battle against God. We have seen the light. God has delivered us from the bondage of our enemy the devil. It is the first step on our journey to the land of promise, and like the ancient Chinese proverb states: *Every journey of a thousand miles begins with one step.*

However, even though we are no longer in outright rebellion against God, we are involved in a battle, and we still have a long journey ahead of us. We have simply switched sides and directions. We now have acquired an evil adversary and our war is with our flesh and against the Devil. The Devil will stop at nothing to prevent us from reaching our ultimate destination.

There are literally armies of angels and devils battling over every soul. We have taken the first step on our journey, and we have a long road ahead of us, we have a specific destination. Like the children of Israel, who fled Egypt, escaping bondage is not the end of the journey, it is just the beginning. We still must reach the Promised Land. Listen to Moses' description of the Promised Land:

AND IT SHALL BE, WHEN THE LORD THY GOD SHALL HAVE BROUGHT THEE INTO THE LAND WHICH HE SWARE UNTO THY FATHERS, TO ABRAHAM, TO ISAAC, AND TO JACOB, TO GIVE THEE GREAT AND GOODLY CITIES, WHICH THOU BUILDEST NOT,
AND HOUSES FULL OF ALL GOOD THINGS, WHICH THOU FILLEDST NOT, AND WELLS DIGGED, WHICH THOU DIGGEDST NOT, VINEYARDS AND OLIVE TREES, WHICH THOU PLANTEST NOT; WHICH THOU SHALL HAVE EATEN AND BE FULL;
DEUTERONOMY 6:10-11

If our own salvation was the end of our journey, I expect that once we publically declare that Jesus Christ is our LORD, and we believe that God has raised Him from the dead, a fiery chariot would come sweep us away and take us to heaven. However, we know that is not how it works. After we are saved, God expects us to bear fruit, not of our own works, but by trusting in His Word and relying totally on the life generating work of the Holy Spirit in our lives. The destination for all believers is a place of perfect peace, perfect rest, and perfect trust in God. The end of our journey is our perfect and absolute assurance of God's *love*, His might and our total reliance on His power, sustenance and the absolute authority of Jesus Christ.

FOR THE EYES OF THE LORD RUN TO AND FRO THROUGHOUT THE WHOLE EARTH, TO SHOW HIMSELF STRONG IN THE BEHALF OF THEM WHOSE HEART IS PERFECT TOWARD HIM.
2 CHRONICLES 16:9

The Promised Land is a place where God provides us perfect protection. It is a place where God provides for our every need. It is *not* a place where we earn our living by the sweat of our brow. It is a place of abundance. It is a place of faith, joy, hope and love. It is a place where we stop relying on ourselves and start relying totally on God. It is a place where God gives us the desires of our heart. It is a place where we have a deep and intimate relationship with the Father, the Son and the Holy Ghost.

FOR GOD SO LOVED THE WORLD, THAT HE GAVE HIS ONLY BEGOTTEN SON, THAT WHOSOEVER "BELIEVETH" IN HIM SHOULD NOT PERISH, BUT HAVE EVERLASTING LIFE.
JOHN 3:16

We see that the action verb required in order to attain everlasting life is *believing*!

Believing in What? *Believing in the Son*! We must believe that God gave His Son for the world because He loves us! Who did God give His Son too? Whosoever *believeth*!

GREATER LOVE HATH NO MAN THAN THIS, THAT A MAN LAY DOWN HIS LIFE FOR HIS FRIENDS.
JOHN 15:13

We understand that God loved us enough to give His only begotten Son, and we also see Jesus Christ loved us enough to lay down His life for us.

What more evidence do we need of God's love?

We need to have an absolute belief in God's perfect love for us. The beginning of Wisdom is the fear (reverence) of the Lord, but the end of Wisdom is the love of the LORD. Once we understand the perfect love of God, we can boldly approach Him and request the desires of our heart. Our final destination is the very throne room of the Almighty. Our final destination is *total reliance on God*! Our final destination is the *Holy of Holies*. It is the place where our own spirit and the Holy Spirit co-habit for eternity.

The destination where we are walking is not a physical place, it is a spiritual place; however, arriving at this spiritual place will absolutely change our physical circumstances. Our physical situation will mirror our spiritual situation. When we *walk in the spirit*, we will reach our spiritual promised land in many different physical places and among many different peoples. We will reach the Promised Land whether we are living in Asia, Australia, South America, Africa, Europe or North America. Listen to the Word of God:

IF YE "WALK" IN MY STATUTES, AND KEEP MY COMMANDMENTS, AND DO THEM;
THEN I WILL GIVE YOU RAIN IN DUE SEASON, AND THE LAND SHALL YIELD HER
INCREASE, AND THE TREES OF THE FIELD SHALL YIELD THEIR FRUIT.
AND YOUR THRESHING SHALL REACH UNTO THE VINTAGE, AND THE VINTAGE SHALL
REACH UNTO THE SOWING TIME: AND YE SHALL EAT YOUR BREAD TO THE FULL, AND
DWELL IN YOUR LAND SAFELY.
AND I WILL GIVE PEACE IN THE LAND, AND YE SHALL LIE DOWN, AND NONE SHALL
MAKE YOU AFRAID: AND I WILL RID EVIL BEASTS OUT OF THE LAND, NEITHER SHALL
THE SWORD GO THROUGH YOUR LAND.
AND YE SHALL CHASE AN HUNDRED, AND AN HUNDRED OF YOU SHALL PUT TEN
THOUSAND TO FLIGHT; AND YOUR ENEMIES SHALL FALL BEFORE YOU BY THE SWORD.
FOR I WILL HAVE RESPECT UNTO YOU, AND MAKE YOU FRUITFUL, AND MULTIPLY YOU,
AND ESTABLISH MY COVENANT WITH YOU.
AND YE SHALL EAT OLD STORE, AND BRING FORTH THE OLD BECAUSE OF THE NEW.
AND I WILL SET MY TABERNACLE AMONG YOU: AND MY SOUL SHALL NOT ABHOR YOU.
AND I WILL WALK AMONG YOU, AND WILL BE YOUR GOD, AND YE SHALL BE MY
PEOPLE.
LEVITICUS 26:3-12

WALK. H3212. Yaw-lak': a primitive root. To walk (literally or figuratively); causatively
to carry (in various senses): - x again, away, bear, bring, carry (away), come (away)
depart, flow, + follow (-ing), get, (away, hence, him), (cause to, made) go (away, -ing, -
ne, one's way, out), grow, lead (forth), let down, march, prosper, + pursue, cause to run,
spread, take away ((-journey)), vanish, (cause to) walk (-ing), wax, x be weak.

Do you see that we must *walk* in God's commandments? We must *carry* God's
commandments. We must *get* God's commandments.

Is this some type of legalism, does it mean if we carry a Bible every place we go, we are
safe?

No ... God wants us to have an intimate relationship with Him. God wants a deep,
personal relationship with everyone. God want everyone to trust Him. Listen to what
God says:

AND THESE WORDS, WHICH I COMMAND THEE THIS DAY, SHALL BE "IN" THINE HEART:
AND THOU SHALT TEACH THEM DILIGENTLY UNTO THY CHILDREN, AND SHALT TALK OF
THEM WHEN THOU SITTEST IN THINE HOUSE, AND WHEN THOU WALKEST BY THE WAY,
AND WHEN THOU LIEST DOWN, AND WHEN THOU RISEST UP.
DEUTERONOMY 6:6-7

Do you see how we *walk* in God's commandments? We must keep God's Word "in" our
heart. We must be constantly *speaking* God's Word to ourselves, to our family, to our
friends, to strangers we meet. How can we teach them to our children or talk of them
when we are sitting, walking, lying and rising if we do not *know* God's Word intimately?

6

**LET US HEAR THE CONCLUSION OF THE WHOLE MATTER: FEAR GOD, AND "KEEP" HIS COMMANDMENTS: FOR THIS IS THE WHOLE DUTY OF MAN. ECCLESIASTES 12:13**

KEEP. H8104. Shaw-mar': to hedge about (as with thorns), i.e. guard; generally to protect, attend, to, etc.: - beware, be circumspect, take heed (to self), keep (-er, self), mark, look narrowly, observe, preserve, regard, reserve, save (self), sure, (that lay) wait (for), watch (-man).

COMMANDMENTS. H4687. Mits-vah': a command, whether human or divine (collect the Law): - which was) commanded (-ment), law, ordinance, precept.

In case you begin thinking that I am just another legalist trying to put you under the law, and trying to make you forsake the liberty and grace of Jesus Christ. Let me reassure you, I definitely do not want to put anybody under the law. I want to show you how a Christian can stop trying to obey the law, and can begin trusting in the total sufficiency of God's Word, and the perfect atonement of Jesus Christ, which is *walking in the spirit*.

# CHAPTER 2

## SPEAKING AND BELIEVING THE WORD OF GOD = WALKING IN THE SPIRIT

WORD. G3056. **Logos**, log'-os: from 3004; SOMETHING **SAID** [emphasis added] (including the thought); by implication, a topic (subject of discourse), also reasoning (the mental faculty) or motive; by extension. A computation; specially concerning doctrine, fame, x (with the article in John) the Divine Expression (i.e. Christ): - account, cause, communication, x have to do, intent, matter, mouth, preaching, question, reason, + reckon, remove, say (-ing), shew, x speaker, speech, talk, thing, + none of these things move me, tidings, treatise, utterance, word, work.

The Word *Logos* jumped out at me. I have read the meaning of *Logos* in my Strong's Concordance many times, but now I had a *revelation* about this most important and KEY Word for the first time. Logos is the cornerstone, Logos is the key that unlocks the mysteries of God, Logos is Jesus Christ. *Logos* is the *spoken Word, Logos* is not the written word. I want to repeat it again... *Logos* is the *spoken Word... Logos* is not the written word.

IN THE BEGINNING WAS THE **LOGOS** (SPOKEN WORD), AND THE **LOGOS** (SPOKEN WORD) WAS WITH GOD, AND THE **LOGOS** (SPOKEN WORD) WAS GOD.
THE SAME WAS IN THE BEGINNING WITH GOD.
ALL THINGS WERE MADE BY HIM; AND WITHOUT HIM WAS NOT ANYTHING MADE THAT WAS MADE.
IN HIM WAS LIFE; AND THE LIFE WAS THE LIGHT OF MEN.
AND THE LIGHT SHINETH IN DARKNESS; AND THE DARKNESS COMPREHENDED IT NOT.
JOHN 1:1-5

When we *speak*, it is a manifestation of our spirit life. God's *spoken* Word is the physical manifestation of God's Spirit in, to, and on His creation. Fallen mankind can only *speak* death, darkness, lies and selfishness, because fallen mankind has been contaminated by sin. Fallen mankind will always *speak* who and what he is on the inside. Fallen man will *speak* what is dwelling in his spirit. However, God *speaks* only life, light, truth and love. God cannot speak opposite of who and what He is. Our *spoken* Word is the same as our *spirit*.

A GOOD MAN OUT OF THE GOOD TREASURE OF THE HEART BRINGETH FORTH GOOD THINGS: AND AN EVIL MAN OUT OF THE EVIL TREASURE BRINGETH FORTH EVIL THINGS.
MATTHEW 12:35

If we desire to transform into His image, we must begin *speaking* truth, light, life and love, we must begin *speaking God's Word. Speaking* God's Word is the only way we can approach God and appropriate His promises. Jesus Christ (God's *spoken* Word) is the light that shines in darkness and the darkness cannot understand or comprehend Him because he is the opposite of darkness. Only the children of the light can comprehend Him and be transformed into His perfect image.

**I AM THE "WAY", THE TRUTH, AND THE LIFE; NO MAN COMETH UNTO THE FATHER, BUT BY ME.**
**JOHN 14:6**

WAY. G3598. Hod-os': apparently a primary word; a road; by implication a progress (the route, act or distance); figuratively a mode or means; - journey, (high-) way.

Jesus Christ (the Logos or *spoken* Word) is the *only way* or the *only route* to the Father. The children of darkness cannot comprehend or apprehend Jesus Christ; therefore, they reject Him (God's *spoken* Word), and they are lost and forever separated; wandering lost from the Father. However, the children of God walk the way Jesus walked and talk the way Jesus talked. Even as Jesus Christ is the manifestation of our Heavenly Father in the flesh, the children of God are the manifestation of Jesus Christ (God's *spoken* Word) in the flesh, but only if we *speak* the Word of God. There is no other entrée to the Father except by *speaking* and *believing* His Word. We must *confess* the LORD Jesus and *believe* in our heart that God has raised Him from the dead before we can be saved.

Often times we know things *intuitively*. We know, but we do not understand how we know. Most of the time we acquire knowledge through experience, sometimes we have knowledge because someone we trust explains it to us and we believe them, and sometimes we just know. *Intuition* is when we *know*, without explanation or experience.

*Intuition* is the method the Holy Spirit uses to communicate to our spirit. Therefore, we can know something without being able to explain how we know something. If we trusted our *intuition*, we would stay out of a lot of trouble. Listening and being obedient to our *intuition* is all part of *Walking in the Spirit*.

I am reminded of the second temptation of Jesus Christ:

**THEN THE DEVIL TAKETH HIM UP INTO THE HOLY CITY, AND SETTETH HIM ON A PINNACLE OF THE TEMPLE.**
**AND SAITH UNTO HIM, IF THOU BE THE SON OF GOD, CAST THYSELF DOWN: FOR IT IS WRITTEN, HE SHALL GIVE HIS ANGELS CHARGE CONCERNING THEE: AND IN THEIR HANDS THEY SHALL BEAR THEE UP, LEST AT ANY TIME THOU DASH THY FOOT AGAINST A STONE.**
**JESUS SAID UNTO HIM, IT IS WRITTEN AGAIN, THOU SHALT NOT TEMPT (TEST) THE LORD THY GOD.**
**MATTHEW 4:5-7**

Could not the LORD Jesus Christ, who walked on the water and raised the dead, have jumped off the pinnacle of the temple without harm?

I dare say he could have, but then Jesus would have been disobedient to the *intuition* that God gave to all of us for our safety. One of the reasons that Jesus *walked in the spirit* was because he trusted and obeyed his *intuition*. He listened to his *intuition* and did what he knew was right, *all the time*!

Our *intuition* and our *conscience* are the sensing methods the Holy Spirit uses to communicate to our spirit. The Holy Spirit uses our *intuition* and *conscience* to lead us towards God and Life, and away from Hell and Death. *Intuition* and *conscience* are spiritual senses similar to our physical senses: sight, sound, taste, smell and touch, but the *intuition* and *conscience* are spiritual senses. There is a difficulty with this type of communication. We can *intuitively* know when something is wrong or right, but we cannot explain how or why we know.

*Intuition* is how God communicates to our spirit, we must simply trust and obey. A person who *intuitively* knows a thing can no more explain it to a person that does not use their *intuition,* than a sighted person can explain the colors red and blue to a person who has been blind all of their life. The main difficulty with our *intuition* and *conscience* is that we can ignore using them and eventually they will cease to work. This is similar to someone who has been bedridden for a long period of time; if their feet and leg muscles are not exercised, eventually their muscles will atrophy and they will lose their ability to walk. Listen to what the Apostle Paul had to say about this:

NOW THE SPIRIT SPEAKETH EXPRESSLY, THAT IN THE LATTER TIMES SOME SHALL DEPART FROM THE FAITH, GIVING HEED TO SEDUCING (DECEIVING) SPIRITS, AND DOCTRINES OF DEVILS;
SPEAKING LIES IN HYPOCRISY; HAVING THEIR "CONSCIENCE" SEARED WITH A HOT IRON;
FORBIDDING TO MARRY, *AND COMMANDING* TO ABSTAIN FROM MEATS (FOODS), WHICH GOD HATH CREATED TO BE RECEIVED WITH THANKSGIVING OF THEM WHICH BELIEVE AND KNOW THE TRUTH. (I TIMOTHY 4:1-3)

If you continually ignore your *conscience*, it will eventually stop working. The Apostle Paul compares it to having a part of your body seared with a hot iron. Imagine searing your eyes, ears, nose, or tongue with a hot iron. It would cause great damage to these sense organs, and they would become forever useless. This is why it becomes progressively harder for someone to be saved after years of hearing the gospel. It is not impossible because God can miraculously cause the blind to see, and He can miraculously cause the deaf to hear. God can also miraculously save those who everyone else would believe were hopelessly lost sinners.

We can repair a damaged conscience by *speaking* God's Word to ourselves. The sensitivity we once possessed as children can be ours again. After we begin *walking in the spirit*, our conscience will gradually become more and more sensitive to the Holy Spirit. We will begin to desire the right things again, and the wrong things will give us a feeling of dread. Our desires will begin to align with God's perfect will for our life.

**Faith cometh by hearing and hearing by the** *spoken* **WORD OF GOD**. *See* Romans 10:17. You will never *hear* the *Word* of God prior to being saved unless somebody *speaks* it to you. Your loved ones will never be saved unless you or somebody else *speaks* God's *Word* to them. People are not saved by mans wisdom or by clever arguments, people are saved by *hearing* God's living, *spoken Word*! You will not become a mature Christian, and you will be of no value to the Kingdom of God unless you *speak, hear* and *believe* the *Word* of God.

Mankind was created in the image of God. We have God's attributes. Being saved is the easy part for us, even though being saved requires a miracle from God. As a matter of fact, Jesus has already done all the work for our salvation, but maturing into a mature Christian takes some work. In order to be saved, all we have to do is *hear* the gospel and accept the saving work of Jesus on the cross at Calvary, *confess* Jesus is LORD, and *believe* that God has raised Him from the dead. *See* Romans 10:9. Repent from our dead works (deeds, labors). *See* Hebrews 6:1.

In the spirit dimension, immediately after being saved, we become spiritual newborn babies. Maturing in the spirit dimension takes time, just like maturing in the physical dimension takes time. After being saved, we are still greatly limited by our physical bodies. Most important, we are severely limited by the memory of our past sinful natures, and our past sin filled life. Sin has made us spiritual cripples. Actually, the Bible says sin made us spiritually dead, our spirits were totally separated from the Spirit of God until our salvation. The Spirit of God created physical reality by the *spoken Word* (Jesus Christ). We can also re-create our physical realty by *speaking God's Word*.

EXAMPLE:
**AND GOD SAID, LET THERE BE LIGHT: AND THERE WAS LIGHT.**
**GENESIS 1:3**

The Apostle Paul explained creative faith in the Book of Hebrews.

**NOW FAITH IS THE "SUBSTANCE" OF THINGS HOPED FOR, THE EVIDENCE OF THINGS NOT SEEN.**
**FOR BY IT THE ELDERS OBTAINED A GOOD REPORT.**
**THROUGH FAITH WE UNDERSTAND THAT THE WORLDS WERE FRAMED BY THE WORD OF GOD, SO THAT THINGS WHICH ARE SEEN WERE NOT MADE OF THINGS WHICH DO APPEAR.**
**HEBREWS 11:1-3**

SUBSTANCE . G5287. Hoop-os'-tas-is: a setting under (support), i.e. (figuratively) concretely, essence, or abstractly assurance (objectively or subjectively): - confidence, confident, person, substance.

We understand from the Bible that *speaking* God's Word and mixing His Word with *faith* is what makes his Word become real in the physical world, not only for God, but for us. God always has faith because He knows that whatever He speaks will come to pass. Throughout eternity God spoke and what He has spoken has come to pass. God knows the end from the beginning. God does not doubt His own Word because He never has reason to.

Do you know there is something God cannot do?

You might say, "Hold on, God can do anything!" No, there is one thing God cannot do. *God cannot lie*!

FOR MEN VERILY SWEAR BY THE GREATER; AND AN OATH FOR CONFIRMATION IS TO THEM AN END OF ALL STRIFE.
WHEREIN GOD, WILLING MORE ABUNDANTLY TO SHOW UNTO THE HEIRS OF PROMISE THE IMMUNITABILITY OF HIS COUNSEL, CONFIRMED IT BY AN OATH:
THAT BY TWO IMMUNTABLE THINGS, IN WHICH IT WAS "IMPOSSIBLE FOR GOD TO LIE", WE MIGHT HAVE A STRONG CONSOLATION, WHO HAVE FLED FOR REFUGE TO LAY HOLD UPON THE HOPE SET BEFORE US:
WHICH HOPE WE HAVE AS AN ANCHOR OF THE SOUL, BOTH SURE AND STEDFAST, AND WHICH ENTERED INTO THAT WITHIN THE VEIL.
HEBREWS 6:16-19

So we must learn that we can lay hold of God's Word as an anchor. Once we have taken hold of God's Word, once it is committed to memory, once we have confidence in God's Word, once our spirit has matured, then our soul (mind) will be un-moveable as surely as God's Word is un-moveable. When a sailing ship ceases from travelling, it must find a safe harbor. In order to remain in the harbor and not be dragged back out to sea by a raging storm, it must drop its anchor. Jesus Christ is our safe harbor and God's Word is our anchor. A Christian without God's Word is like a ship without an anchor.

When the storms of life come, if a Christian does not have God's Word committed to memory, he or she will be dragged out of the safe harbor of his or her trust and reliance in Jesus Christ, right back out into the tempests and storms of the World. We must have God's Word abiding in our hearts (minds) if we want to escape the many dangers and storms that everybody in the World eventually must face. We must have the Word of God written on the tables of our hearts if we desire to remain safe in the cleft of the rock.

AND THE WORD WAS MADE FLESH...
JOHN 1:14

Jesus Christ is the Word of God made flesh. The *spoken Word of God* is the most powerful thing in heaven, in the earth and under the earth. The *spoken Word of God is everlasting life*!

VERILY (TRULY), VERILY (TRULY), I "SAY" UNTO YOU, HE THAT "HEARETH" MY WORD, AND BELIEVETH ON HIM THAT SENT ME, HATH EVERLASTING LIFE, AND SHALL NOT COME INTO CONDEMNATION; BUT IS PASSED FROM DEATH UNTO LIFE.
VERILY, VERILY, I SAY UNTO YOU, THE HOUR IS COMING, AND NOW IS, WHEN THE DEAD SHALL "HEAR" THE VOICE OF THE SON OF GOD: AND THEY THAT "HEAR" SHALL LIVE.
JOHN 5:24-25

Kenneth Copeland has an excellent group of teaching Compact Discs (CDs) called, *You are the Prophet of Your Own Life*, I highly recommend listening to them. I remember hearing Mr. Copeland say, "When you hear Jesus say verily, verily, in the scriptures, you should pay special attention because He's saying something very important. So important, you should probably memorize it."

Jesus said in John 5:24-25, that *hearing* His Word was the way to everlasting life, I think everlasting life is a pretty important subject and deserves a verily (truly), verily (truly) preface! Prior to being Born Again, we are dead people. We are similar to a branch that has recently been cut off from a tree trunk. The leaves might be green, after it has been cut off from the tree, the sap may even continue running through the branch. The branch may appear alive for a short time. However, even though a dead branch may appear alive, it cannot bear fruit. Eventually the branch dries up completely and become un-mistakenly dead. Unsaved people are the same way.

When Adam and Eve sinned, they were cut off from God and they became dead, they ceased bearing the fruit of the spirit. They, and their descendants, kept on walking and talking, but eventually everything cut off from God will become un-mistakenly dead. Only God is the source of life! However, there is a way to save a branch that has been cut off from a vine. We can graft the dead branch back onto the vine before it is too late. As long as someone is alive and kicking it is *not too late*! The life giving Spirit can start flowing through that dead branch and give it life again.

A dead branch cannot bear fruit until after it has been grafted back into the living vine. Jesus is telling us that "*Hearing His Word* and *believing on Him that sent Him*" is the key to everlasting life. By *hearing* and *believing* God's Word, we can nurture the branch and it can begin bearing spiritual fruit. The Bible is very clear, all of the dead branches cut off from God are reserved for fire! Only the branches grafted back into the living vine and bearing fruit will live forever.

**AND NOW ALSO THE AXE IS LAID UNTO THE ROOT OF THE TREES: THEREFORE EVERY TREE WHICH BRINGETH NOT FORTH GOOD FRUIT IS HEWN DOWN, AND CAST INTO THE FIRE.**
**MATTHEW 3:10**

The *spoken word* is how our spirit communicates and impacts our physical reality. Like God, we have the power to dictate physical reality by our *spoken Word*. The physical world is malleable, we can change our circumstances by *speaking* God's Word to the creation. We can *speak* wealth into existence, we can *speak* health into existence, we can *speak* wisdom, love, hope, faith and joy into existence. If you are interested in learning about how your own spoken words impact your circumstances, I recommend that you read *The Tongue: A Creative Force* by Charles Capps.

We are creative beings, we are spirits created in the image of God. Don't you believe me? Hopefully you will believe Jesus:

THEN CAME THE DISCIPLES TO JESUS APART, AND SAID, WHY COULD NOT WE CAST HIM OUT?

AND JESUS SAID UNTO THEM, BECAUSE OF YOUR UNBELIEF: FOR VERILY (TRULY) I SAY UNTO YOU, IF YE HAVE FAITH AS A GRAIN OF MUSTARD SEED, YE SHALL "SAY" UNTO THIS MOUNTAIN, REMOVE HENCE TO YONDER PLACE; AND IT SHALL REMOVE; AND "NOTHING" SHALL BE IMPOSSIBLE UNTO YOU.

MATTHEW 17:19-20

Jesus wanted his disciples to understand that if they would *speak* with faith, *nothing is impossible*! Wow!

The problem is, how do we *speak with faith*?

I was visiting with my brother and his wife one day and I told them, "We have power over all of creation ... if we have faith." I believe I was speaking by *intuition* and *revelation*. I knew that what I said was true, but I did not know the biblical basis for what I said. If we do not have a biblical basis for something we say or teach, we should diligently search the scriptures until we find that biblical basis or not say and teach it. When I was driving home from my brother's house, I spoke to God. I said, "God, I know Jesus taught that we have power over creation if we have faith, but how do we acquire the kind of faith that moves mountains?"

Then the following bible story came to me:

AND WHEN JESUS WAS ENTERED INTO CAPERNAUM, THERE CAME UNTO HIM A CENTURION, BESEECHING HIM,

AND SAYING, LORD, MY SERVANT LIETH AT HOME SICK OF THE PALSY, GRIEVOUSLY TORMENTED.

AND JESUS SAITH UNTO HIM, I WILL COME AND HEAL HIM.

THE CENTURION ANSWERED AND SAID, LORD, I AM NOT WORTHY THAT THOU SHOULDEST COME UNDER MY ROOF: BUT "SPEAK" THE WORD ONLY, AND MY SERVANT SHALL BE HEALED.

FOR I AM A MAN UNDER "AUTHORITY", HAVING SOLDIERS UNDER ME; AND I "SAY" TO THIS MAN, GO, AND HE GOETH; AND TO ANOTHER, COME, AND HE COMETH; AND TO MY SERVANT, DO THIS, AND HE DOETH IT.

WHEN JESUS HEARD IT, HE MARVELLED, AND SAID TO THEM THAT FOLLOWED, VERILY (TRULY) I SAY UNTO YOU, I HAVE NOT FOUND SO "GREAT FAITH", NO, NOT IN ISRAEL.

MATTHEW 8:5-10

We know from the rest of the story, Jesus did *speak* the Word, and the centurion's servant was healed. When this bible story came to me, I suddenly had a rush of revelation from the Holy Spirit.

# CHAPTER 3

## FAITH IS BASED ON OUR BELIEF IN GOD'S VERACITY AND "AUTHORITY"!

AUTHORITY. G1849. ex-oo-see'-ah: privilege, i.e. (subjectively) force, capacity, competency, freedom, or (objectively) mastery (concretely magistrate, superhuman, potentate, token of control), delegated influence: - authority, jurisdiction, liberty, power, right, strength.

The main questions we need to ask ourselves are: *Does Jesus speak truth? Does Jesus have all authority? Can God keep His Word?* We need to have the same faith as the centurion. I want to explain my understanding and experience with authority.

I graduated from the University of Oregon, School of Law, and I work for the Bureau of Indian Affairs, an agency of the Department of the Interior, a department of the United States federal government. Most people understand that the United States Constitution is a delegation of specific authorities from the people of the United States to the Federal Government. The U.S. Constitution established specific responsibilities for the Congressional Branch (to pass laws under the constitution), for the Executive Branch (to enforce laws under the constitution), and for the Judicial Branch (to interpret laws under the constitution).

The President of the United States has been delegated the authority by the people of the United States to enforce all laws and regulations passed by Congress. The President of course is only human and cannot enforce all the laws and regulations by himself. Therefore, he in turn delegates that authority to the people who run the different departments and agencies in the federal government. God by His sovereign will has also delegated His authority to the Church.

I am an employee of the Bureau of Indian Affairs (BIA). Employee(s) of the BIA have the responsibility and the delegated authority (the jurisdiction) to make decisions and enforce the laws of the United States on Indian lands under the BIA's jurisdiction. There are millions of acres of tribal and individual Indian lands in the United States and trespass is a fairly common occurrence. Sometimes a neighboring rancher's cattle will enter tribal lands and eat the grass because cows are not very good at understanding boundaries, and cows have no ethical problem with crossing a boundary line if a fence is down. Cows will eat grass on land that does not belong to their owners. Cows had sense enough not to eat fruit from the tree of the knowledge of good and evil.

First, we deal with trespassing by finding out who owns the cows, and then we tell the owner to remove their cows. The rancher always removes their cows, but if the owner did not remove their cows, we would write a trespass letter and cite Title 25 United States Code (the authority delegated by Congress to the Executive Branch) concerning trespass and demand damages. If the owner refused to move their cows or pay damages, we would not get a shot gun and baseball bat in order to put the fear of God into the cows and their owner.

Why not? Although we have jurisdiction and authority over the property, it is not our responsibility to physically punish the owners of trespassing cows!

In the United States, in our various states, and in most other countries of the world, there is a huge governmental organization (called a bureaucracy) that will begin to move into action against people who defy the laws of the government. God, by His sovereign will, has delegated His authority to the Church, and God has a much greater spiritual governmental organization in the spiritual realm, which will begin to move into action against people who defy God's authority. There are angels, archangels, cherubim, seraphim, principalities, powers, etc. All of them are ready, willing and able to enforce God's Word after a believer *speaks* the Word of God to God's creation.

**BUT TO WHICH OF THE ANGELS SAID HE AT ANY TIME, SIT ON MY RIGHT HAND, UNTIL I MAKE THINE ENEMIES THY FOOTSTOOL?**
**ARE THEY NOT ALL MINISTERING SPIRITS, SENT FORTH TO MINISTER (DO SERVICE) FOR (FOR THE SAKE OF) THEM WHO SHALL BE HEIRS OF SALVATION?**
**HEBREWS 1:13-14**

There is a vast host of angels ready, willing and able to enforce every Word of God if we will *believe* and *speak* His Word. They are servants of God just like us, but with different governmental responsibility. The Church is God's delegated authority in the world. Our responsibility is simply to *speak* God's Word. Jesus Christ gave all Christian's His authority. God made us stewards over the earth, similar to an ambassador, a town mayor, a state governor, or a king.

**NOW THEN WE ARE "AMBASSADORS" FOR CHRIST, AS THOUGH GOD DID BESEECH YOU BY US: WE PRAY YOU IN CHRIST'S STEAD, BE YE RECONCILED TO GOD.**
**FOR HE THAT MADE HIM TO BE SIN FOR US, WHO KNEW NO SIN; THAT WE MIGHT BE MADE THE RIGHTEOUSNESS OF GOD IN HIM.**
**2 CORINTHIANS 5:20-21**

There is nobody in the world that doubts that Condoleezza Rice or Hillary Clinton can walk boldly into any dictator's office, read them the riot act, and walk out again safely.

Why? Is it because Ms. Rice and Ms. Clinton are the meanest, scariest people that the United States can find to confront the world's worst dictators? No, it is because, as the United States Secretary of State, these women have the full power of the United States Government backing them up.

Christians are in a similar position, we are ambassadors for Christ. We do not command devils to leave by our own power or strength, but by the Word of God and in the name of Jesus Christ. Jesus Christ has the power, strength and authority to enforce His every Word. The angels are responsible for enforcing God's Word, similar to policemen or

soldiers. There are many stories in the Bible describing the actions of angels, but one especially terrifying story occurs in the Book of 2 Kings.

The King of Assyria sent a great army against Jerusalem. The Assyrians were the terrors of the ancient world for several hundred years. They would conquer cities, remove whole populations, and replace them with peoples from other parts of their empire. The Assyrians did not take kindly to resistance. The scary part of this story is that when Jerusalem resisted the Assyrian host, the King of Assyria committed a very foolish mistake: He threatened God's people, blasphemed God and questioned God's ability to save Jerusalem. Listen to what God said concerning the King of Assyria and his mighty army.

THEREFORE, THUS SAITH THE LORD CONCERNING THE KING OF ASSYRIA. HE SHALL NOT COME INTO THIS CITY, NOR SHOOT AN ARROW THERE, NOR COME BEFORE IT WITH SHIELD, NOR CAST A BANK AGAINST IT.
BY THE WAY THAT HE CAME, BY THE SAME SHALL HE RETURN, AND SHALL NOT COME INTO THIS CITY, SAITH THE LORD.
FOR I WILL DEFEND THIS CITY, TO SAVE IT, FOR MINE OWN SAKE, AND FOR MY SERVANT DAVID'S SAKE.
AND IT CAME TO PASS THAT NIGHT, THAT THE ANGEL OF THE LORD WENT OUT, AND SMOTE IN THE CAMP OF THE ASSYRIANS AN HUNDRED FOURSCORE AND FIVE THOUSAND: AND WHEN THEY AROSE EARLY IN THE MORNING, BEHOLD, THEY WERE ALL DEAD CORPSES.
2 KINGS 19:32-35

The Angel of the Lord smote and killed 185,000 soldiers in one night. In comparison, during World War II, it is estimated that between 130,000 and 160,000 allied soldiers landed at Normandy, France, on D-day, and there were approximately 183,000 United States and British invasion forces during the invasion of Okinawa, Japan.

Can you imagine every one of the Allied invasion forces that landed on D-day or every one of the Allied invasion forces at Okinawa being killed in one night by *one* Angel? Do you think it probably would have been a cataclysmic loss for the Allied war effort during World War II?

BLESS THE LORD, YE HIS ANGELS, THAT EXCEL IN STRENGTH, THAT DO HIS COMMANDMENTS, HEARKENING UNTO THE VOICE OF HIS "WORD".
PSALM 103:20

We are commanded to *speak* God's *Word* and to subdue the earth. Christians represent God's delegated authority on the earth. The Angels *do* God's commandments and hearken to the voice of His *Word*!

How can Angels hearken to the voice of God's *Word* unless somebody with delegated authority on the earth *speaks* God's *Word*?

If we can begin to comprehend the awesome power of one Angel, perhaps we can begin to comprehend the power at our disposal if we are truly servants of the Most High. God has many Angels serving Him, and each child of God probably has a multitude of Angel looking after him or her.

**FOR HE SHALL GIVE HIS ANGELS CHARGE OVER THEE, TO KEEP THEE IN ALL THY WAYS, THEY SHALL BEAR THEE UP IN THEIR HANDS, LEST THOU DASH THY FOOT AGAINST A STONE.**
**PSALMS 91:11-12**

When I hear somebody say, God *damn* this, or God *damn* that, it makes me cringe. People, especially the people of God, should probably get a needle and thread, and sew their lips shut. Also, a word of warning, watch out how you treat children or you might end up regretting your actions.

**TAKE HEED THAT YE DESPISE NOT ONE OF THESE LITTLE ONES; FOR I SAY UNTO YOU, THAT IN HEAVEN THEIR ANGELS DO ALWAYS BEHOLD THE FACE OF MY FATHER WHICH IS IN HEAVEN.**
**MATTHEW 18:10**

Just like most people, kids can be rude sometimes, and you might want to let them have it, but do not lose your temper. God has a special regard for the weak and defenseless. I truly believe that there have been many adults snatched from the jaws of destruction by the prayers of a child.

**AND I JOHN SAW THESE THINGS, AND HEARD THEM. AND WHEN I HAD HEARD AND SEEN, I FELL DOWN TO WORSHIP BEFORE THE FEET OF THE ANGEL WHICH SHEWED ME THESE THINGS.**
**THEN SAITH HE UNTO ME, SEE THOU DO IT NOT: FOR I AM THY FELLOW SERVANT, AND OF THY BRETHREN THE PROPHETS, AND OF THEM WHICH KEEP THE "SAYINGS" OF THIS BOOK: WORSHIP GOD.**
**REVELATION 22:8-9**

Do you see that the Angel that speaks with John identifies himself with the servants of God, which *keep the sayings* of this Book.
How do you keep sayings? Don't you have to memorize or remember them?
How would you keep a person's sayings?
I guess you could write them down and keep them in your pocket, but the easiest way is just to remember them. God's servants should *know (keep, memorize)* God's *Word.*

# CHAPTER 4

## SPEAKING GODS WORD IS BASED ON AUTHORITY, NOT MAGIC!

Speaking and believing God's Word has sometimes been confused with magic. The Devil often attempts to counterfeit God for two important reasons. First, because people are created spiritual beings, we have a natural inclination to seek out and use spiritual authority. Therefore, the Devil must create a substitute for God's Word and His spiritual authority.

Second, the Devil desires to lead people away from God's Word because he knows that God's Word is the source of mankind's authority on the earth, and God's Word is the weapon that will ultimately destroy and defeat the Devil. The Devil's substitute for God's Word is *magic*.

The Devil is the father of lies; therefore, he promises that magic will help us attain our desires. He promises that magic will give us authority over people and over the elements. He promises that magic will make us wise. However, magic is everything opposite to the Word of God.

The Word of God's meaning is plain ... Magic is unintelligible and often uses secret incantations, spells, and words, such as *abracadabra* or *hocus pocus*.

The Word of God is available to everyone ... Magic is a hidden mystery only available to a few select.

The Word of God is available immediately after salvation ... Magic is available only after a long initiation period.

The Word of God is based on God's supreme authority ... Magic is based on associations with devils.

Everything that magic promises, the Word of God delivers. When we *speak* the Word of God, we exercise authority over demons and devils. When we *speak* the Word of God, we exercise authority over the elements. When we *speak* God's Word, we can exercise authority over poverty, sickness and death. When we *speak* God's Word, we exercise authority over our rebellious and sin infected flesh. When we *speak* the Word of God, we attain the desires of our heart. When we *speak* the Word of God, we save the lost and set the captive free.

One important point about authority, if a rancher's cows are on his own land, I do not have authority to tell him to remove his cattle, this is a principal that is very important to understand. We have to understand the extent and the limits of our authority in Jesus Christ. Although, as I have illustrated, Christians have a lot of authority and power at their disposal, there are some limits to a Christian's authority. Also, if you are not a Christian, I would be very careful about attempting to use the authority of Jesus Christ to gain advantage in the world.

People always ask, "Why does God allow so much suffering in the world?" The answer is very simple, people have been given a free will by God. People can decide whether or not they will serve God or whether they will serve the Devil. People can decide to hurt other people. People can decide to take advantage of other people. People can decide to use other people. Therefore, if somebody decides they would rather serve their flesh, and remain in bondage and service to Satan, all we can do is pray for them. Have you heard the story concerning the sons of Sceva in the Book of Acts?

THEN CERTAIN OF THE VAGABOND JEWS, EXORCISTS, TOOK UPON THEM TO CALL OVER THEM WHICH HAD EVIL SPIRITS THE NAME OF THE LORD JESUS, SAYING, WE ADJURE YOU BY JESUS WHOM PAUL PREACHETH.
AND THERE WERE SEVEN SONS OF ONE SCEVA, A JEW, AND CHIEF OF THE PRIESTS, WHICH DID SO.
AND THE EVIL SPIRIT ANSWERED AND SAID, JESUS I KNOW, AND PAUL I KNOW; BUT WHO ARE YE?
AND THE MAN IN WHOM THE EVIL SPIRIT WAS LEAPED ON THEM, AND OVERCAME THEM, AND PREVAILED AGAINST THEM, SO THAT THEY FLED OUT OF THAT HOUSE NAKED AND WOUNDED.
ACTS 19:13-16

The sons of Sceva thought the name of Jesus was some type of *magic* word. *Speaking* the Word of God is not based on magic; *speaking* the Word of God is based on *authority*. You must have a relationship with God before you can *speak* the name of Jesus and expect to be obeyed.

There are many people who believe that speaking verses out of the Bible, and speaking the name of Jesus is some type of magic. They believe that it doesn't matter whether they have a relationship with Jesus Christ or not. If they speak the name of Jesus, they must be obeyed. As the story about the sons of Sceva illustrates, they are dangerously wrong. If you begin to attack spiritual forces without a clear understanding of your authority in Jesus Christ, and you do not have Angels backing you up, you can get into serious trouble.

Every once in a while, we hear stories of a layman who pretends to be a policeman, or a doctor, or a lawyer, and then goes around getting into all kinds of mischief. When someone uses the name of Jesus without being a Christian, they are doing the same thing, except they are treading on much more dangerous ground. This is the main reason why we need to confess that Jesus is our Lord, and why we need to be well versed in the Word of God.

Would you want somebody who has thumbed through a medical book to perform open heart surgery on you?

I hope not! Somebody who has thumbed through the Bible and claims to be a teacher, a preacher, a pastor, or a priest is very dangerous, not only to the church, but to themselves.

**THESE ARE SPOTS IN YOUR FEASTS OF CHARITY WHEN THEY FEAST WITH YOU, FEEDING THEMSELVES WITHOUT FEAR: CLOUDS THEY ARE WITHOUT WATER, CARRIED ABOUT OF WINDS; TREES WHOSE FRUIT WHITHERETH, WITHOUT FRUIT, TWICE DEAD, PLUCKED UP BY THE ROOTS.**
**JUDE 1:12**

Authority is still the same today as it was when the centurion was telling his soldiers to come and to go. The centurion simply *spoke* his order and he expected to be obeyed. If the centurion was not obeyed, you can be sure the consequences were very bad for the disobedient soldier under his command.

Why? Because the centurion was delegated authority from Caesar and the Roman Senate, the centurion could meet out punishment, up to and including death, to a disobedient soldier.

If a rancher refused to remove his or her cows from Indian land when a Bureau of Indian Affairs employee orders him to remove them, eventually they will end up paying a lot of money for court costs and fines for trespass damages. Actually, I have never even heard of a rancher that refused to remove their cows after being notified of trespass.

# CHAPTER 5

## THE DEVIL HAS AUTHORITY OVER THE REBELLIOUS

**FOR REBELLION IS AS THE SIN OF WITCHCRAFT, AND STUBBORNNESS IS AS INIQUITY AND IDOLATRY. BECAUSE THOU HAS REJECTED THE WORD OF THE LORD, HE HAS ALSO REJECTED THEE FROM BEING KING.**
**I SAMUEL 15:23**

God rejected Saul as king of Israel because Saul rejected the Word of God.

Why do Christian's think that God will accept them when they reject God's Word?

You cannot accept Jesus Christ as your savior and simultaneously reject God's Word. Jesus Christ *is* the Word of God. When you accept Jesus Christ as Savior, you must also accept the authority of God's Word. They are both one and the same.

If you do not submit to God's authority, you are destined to be in bondage your entire life. Not only you, but your children, and your children's children will be in bondage. If you disrespect authority, you are in rebellion against God. The only way you can wield God's authority is to first be under submission to authority, otherwise you will be a slave to your own passions. You will end up becoming a tyrant if you have any power at all. God gives His authority only to those who are willing to be servants, and He allows the rebellious to be under the curse of bondage.

That is what the curse of Canaan was all about. Ham disrespected Noah, who possessed authority over him as his father. When God cursed Canaan, it was because the rebellion in Ham was going to be manifested in his descendants. The curse of bondage always follows rebellion against authority. If you cannot control yourself, God will make sure that somebody else will!

Rebellion against God is the reason why Adam and Eve were cast out of the Garden of Eden. After Adam and Eve ate the fruit from the tree of the knowledge of good and evil, something God specifically told them not to do, they immediately came under bondage to sin and the Devil. All the descendants of Adam and Eve are born in bondage to sin and the Devil. However, we do not have to continue in bondage because God has made a way of escape for us.

**CURSED BE CANAAN; A SERVANT OF SERVANTS SHALL HE BE UNTO HIS BRETHREN.**
**GENESIS 9:25**

I am trying to make the following point. If we are Christians and know God's Word, we will also know the glorious liberty God has prepared for us. We will begin *speaking* God's Word of Truth to our circumstances and to our sinful flesh until we bring every thought under obedience to God's Word and under the authority of Jesus Christ. We can be assured that if we mortify our flesh by *speaking* God's Word, God will send His

Angels to enforce His Word to His creation. If we are Christians, we are officers of God's kingdom and ambassadors for Christ.

We are designated kings and priests by God, and we are responsible to know God's Word, and to let other people know this rebellious world, and the rebellious people in it, are in danger of judgment. There is a mighty deliverer named Jesus Christ (the Word of God). We are the children of God, and possess delegated authority just as surely as Jesus Christ is the Son of God and possesses all authority.

**AND IT CAME TO PASS, WHEN JESUS HAD ENDED THESE SAYINGS, THE PEOPLE WERE ASTONISHED AT HIS DOCTRINE.**
**FOR HE TAUGHT THEM AS ONE HAVING AUTHORITY, AND NOT AS THE SCRIBES.**
**MATTHEW 7:28-29**

Jesus knew who He was and He knew where the Words He spoke came from. He did not doubt that the authority of His Father's Word was available to Him. *All things were possible to Him*! Christians need to have the same mind set. We need to know who we are in Jesus Christ. We *speak* in the name of Jesus Christ and all other authority pales in comparison with His authority. We are subjects of the King of kings. We are heirs of God, and joint-heirs with Christ! We do not have to quietly take being humiliated by the world and the devil. I remember when I was a young man and I saw another man being physically bullied.

I remembered thinking to myself, why doesn't he fight back?

Even if you fight and lose, the bully is going to think twice about messing with you again. The same goes for the world and the devil. If sickness comes, if doubt comes, if negative thoughts come, *speak* the Word of God! Fight back! Do not just passively take whatever the devil dishes out!

*And having done all to stand... STAND! Put on the WHOLE ARMOR of God!*

**GOD RESISTETH THE PROUD, BUT GIVETH GRACE UNTO THE HUMBLE.**
**SUBMIT YOURSELVES THEREFORE TO GOD, RESIST THE DEVIL, AND HE WILL FLEE FROM YOU.**
**DRAW NIGH TO GOD, AND HE WILL DRAW NIGH TO YOU.**
**JAMES 4:6-8**

Pride = I can do it all on my own! My dead works are sufficient.
Humble = I cannot do anything on my own, but **I CAN DO ALL THINGS THROUGH CHRIST WHICH STRENGTHENETH ME.**
**PHILIPIANS 4:13**

God will resist us if we attempt to solve a problem or difficulty with our own strength, or our own knowledge, or our own wisdom, but God gives grace (unmerited favor) to those who rely on Jesus Christ (the WORD of GOD). If we have a problem, we must not try to figure it out on our own, or go to some expert in the field, we *must* always go the Word of God. Draw nigh to God and He will draw nigh to you.

We resist the devil by *speaking* God's Word. We do not have to get a shot gun and baseball bat in order to put the fear of God into people or demons. We simply find what God's Word says about the problem, *speak* God's Word to the situation, and let God take care of our problem. I promise you, God has the authority and the power to take care of any and every problem, situation or circumstance!

FOR AS THE RAIN COMETH DOWN, AND THE SNOW FROM HEAVEN, AND RETURNETH NOT THITHER, BUT WATERETH THE EARTH, AND MAKETH IT BRING FORTH AND BUD, THAT IT MAY GIVE SEED TO THE SOWER, AND BREAD TO THE EATER;
SO SHALL MY WORD BE THAT GOETH FORTH OUT OF MY MOUTH: IT SHALL NOT RETURN UNTO ME VOID, BUT IT SHALL ACCOMPLISH THAT WHICH I PLEASE, AND IT SHALL PROSPER IN THE THING WHERETO I SENT IT.
FOR YE SHALL GO OUT WITH JOY, AND BE LED FORTH WITH PEACE: THE MOUNTAINS AND THE HILLS SHALL BREAK FORTH BEFORE YOU INTO SINGING, AND ALL THE TREES OF THE FIELD SHALL CLAP THEIR HANDS. *Hallelujah!*
ISAIAH 53:10-12

Do you understand that God has the power to accomplish his Word?

If we are faithful to *speak* his Word to the lost, the blind, the poor, the sick, the sinner, and all those in bondage to the Devil, God will be faithful to make His Word produce fruit in its season. God may not take care of a certain situation according to our timetable, but God will always take care of the situation, if we are faithful to *speak* His Word.

# CHAPTER 6

## JESUS IS LORD!

"Jesus is Lord" is the beginning of every Christian's *walk in the spirit*. One thing is very curious in the New Testament. There were several occasions when even the LORD Jesus Christ could not heal people.

If Jesus is really God incarnate, why couldn't Jesus heal everyone?

One clue occurs in the Book of Mark when Jesus visits His hometown:

BUT JESUS SAID UNTO THEM, A PROPHET IS NOT WITHOUT HONOUR, BUT IN HIS OWN COUNTRY, AND AMONG HIS OWN KIN, AND IN HIS OWN HOUSE.
AND HE COULD THERE DO NO MIGHTY WORK, SAVE THAT HE LAID HIS HANDS UPON A FEW SICK FOLK, AND HEALED THEM.
AND HE MARVELLED BECAUSE OF THEIR "UNBELIEF". AND HE WENT ROUND ABOUT THE VILLAGES, TEACHING.
MARK 6:5-6

The people in Jesus' hometown knew Him and His family, or they thought they knew Him. They could not comprehend that somebody they were associated with could be the Messiah. Their perspective was clouded by preconceptions. They lived in Jesus' home town. They knew Jesus their whole lives.

"How can Jesus of Nazareth be the Savior of Israel?"

"Everybody might be making a big fuss over Jesus in Jerusalem, but he is the son of Mary. he is just a carpenter. We know his brothers and sisters."

"How can Jesus be the Lord Messiah, the Son of David? It can't be!"

Many people have also refused to acknowledge Jesus Christ as Lord because of their preconceptions. They refuse to acknowledge that Jesus is Lord because of what they know or because of what they think they know. Jesus Christ will not interject Himself into a person's life, if He is unwelcomed. God wants people to willingly acknowledge the supremacy and Lordship of Jesus Christ. Listen to the petitions of those who received their requests from Jesus in the Gospels:

AND, BEHOLD, THERE CAME A LEPER AND WORSHIPPED HIM, SAYING, "LORD", IF THOU WILT, THOU CANST MAKE ME CLEAN.
MATTHEW 8:2

AND, BEHOLD, A WOMAN OF CANAAN CAME OUT OF THE SAME COAST, AND CRIED UNTO HIM, SAYING, HAVE MERCY ON ME, O "LORD", THOU SON OF DAVID; MY DAUGHTER IS GRIEVOUSLY VEXED WITH A DEVIL.
MATTHEW 15:22

AND, BEHOLD, TWO BLIND MEN SITTING BY THE WAY SIDE, WHEN THEY HEARD THAT JESUS PASSED BY, CRIED OUT, SAYING, HAVE MERCY ON US, O "LORD", THOU SON OF DAVID.
MATTHEW 20:30

They confessed Jesus was LORD. It appears that everyone who publically confessed the Lordship of Jesus Christ received their requests from Him. Do not think that you will receive anything from Jesus Christ unless and until you publically confess that He is LORD! Jesus Christ is Lord of me and of you, Jesus Christ is Lord of North and South America, and of Europe, and of Asia, and of Africa, and of Australia.

Jesus is LORD of heaven and earth, but he will not interject himself on behalf of those who refuse to acknowledge His Lordship. However, once we acknowledge that Jesus is Lord, once we have submitted ourselves to his authority, once we begin relying on His Word, there is no need for us to remain in bondage. Regardless of whether anyone confesses the LORD Jesus, Jesus Christ is LORD over everyone and everything. Jesus said:

ALL POWER (*AUTHORITY*) IS GIVEN UNTO ME IN HEAVEN AND IN EARTH.
GO YE THEREFORE, AND TEACH (MAKE DISCIPLES OF) ALL NATIONS, BAPTIZING THEM IN THE NAME OF THE FATHER, AND OF THE SON, AND OF THE HOLY GHOST:
TEACHING THEM TO OBSERVE ALL THINGS WHATSOEVER I HAVE COMMANDED YOU: AND, LO, I AM WITH YOU ALWAYS, EVEN UNTO THE END OF THE WORLD. AMEN.
MATT. 28:18-19

You might think, "Wait a second, I was taught that Jesus delegated His authority to the Apostle Peter, not to all Christians." Let us read a verse concerning the authority of Jesus Christ:

AND WHAT IS THE EXCEEDING GREATNESS OF HIS POWER TO US-WARD WHO BELIEVE, ACCORDING TO THE WORKING OF HIS MIGHTY POWER,
WHICH HE WROUGHT IN CHRIST, WHEN HE RAISED HIM FROM THE DEAD, AND SET HIM AT HIS OWN RIGHT HAND IN THE HEAVENLY PLACES,
FAR ABOVE ALL PRINCIPALITY, AND POWER, AND MIGHT, AND DOMINION, AND EVERY NAME THAT IS NAMED, NOT ONLY IN THIS WORLD, BUT ALSO IN THAT WHICH IS TO COME:
AND HATH PUT ALL THINGS UNDER HIS FEET, AND GAVE HIM TO BE THE HEAD OVER ALL THINGS TO THE CHURCH,
WHICH IS HIS BODY, THE FULNESS OF HIM THAT FILLETH ALL IN ALL.
EPHESIANS 1:19-23

You might say, "I understand from the Bible that Jesus Christ has all authority, but I am a nobody, I do not have any authority." However, if you go to the next Chapter in Ephesians, you will see that all believers sit with Christ on the right hand of God and share His authority.

**BUT GOD, WHO IS RICH IN MERCY, FOR HIS GREAT LOVE WHEREWITH HE LOVED US, EVEN WHEN WE WERE DEAD IN SINS, HATH QUICKENED US TOGETHER WITH CHRIST, (BY GRACE YE ARE SAVED;)**
**AND HATH RAISED US UP TOGETHER, AND MADE "US" SIT TOGETHER IN HEAVENLY PLACES IN CHRIST JESUS:**
**EPHESIANS 2:4-6**

The Apostle Paul is talking about *all* Christians. Sitting on God's right hand signifies the *authority* of Jesus Christ. We are *in* Jesus Christ.

Do you see that in the spiritual dimension, we have already died, been resurrected and raised up to sit in heavenly places *in* Christ Jesus, on the right hand of God the Father? In the spirit realm, in the kingdom of God, we sit on the right hand of God in Jesus Christ. It is God's good pleasure to give us *authority* in His Son, Jesus Christ. We have *all authority in Jesus Christ*!

Christians have been delegated authority for a specific purpose. That purpose is to manifest the fruits of the Spirit and dominion of Jesus Christ over the whole earth in the name of the Father, the Son and the Holy Ghost. We are made kings and priests, and our primary responsibility is to *command* that the devil let loose of everyone and everything he keeps in bondage that belongs to God.

This is also where it is important to understand the limits of our authority and the limits of the devil's authority. Believe me, the devil also has authority in this world. If somebody is in bondage to Satan, like the children of Israel were under bondage to Pharaoh, they must believe and come out of their bondage willingly. They must confess that Jesus is Lord willingly.

*Nobody can be in bondage to the devil against their will*! God, will not force people to come out of Egypt or out the World. However, if someone or something is under God's authority (*all Christians*), we do not need guns or baseball bats, we simply command and expect to be obeyed. God has the power to ensure that His Word, *spoken* by His servants, who He has delegated his authority, will be obeyed.

**FOR I AM THE LORD: I WILL "SPEAK", AND THE WORD THAT I SHALL "SPEAK" SHALL COME TO PASS; IT SHALL BE NO MORE PROLONGED: FOR IN YOUR DAYS, O REBELLIOUS HOUSE, WILL I "SAY" THE WORD, AND WILL PERFORM IT, SAITH THE LORD GOD.**
**EZEKIEL 12:25**

God is not a finite individual, God is infinite and God is SHAD-DAH'-EE (ALMIGHTY).

**SHAD-DAH'-EE**: from shaw-dad'; a primitive root; to be burly, i.e. powerful; the Almighty.

If God says he will do something, do not doubt his Word, it will be performed. That is why we must diligently search His Word. That is why we must *know* His Word. That is why we must *memorize* His Word. That is why we must *speak* His Word. God's Word is the authority by which we act. Faith cometh by hearing and *hearing* by the Word of God, and we can put our hope and our confidence in God's Word.

Do you see how authority works?

If I were to walk into your house, sit in your favorite chair, and demand that you feed me lunch because I am an employee of the Federal Government, you would quickly show me to the door or call the police. I have no authority over you while you are in your own house. However, if I, or another employee of the Bureau of Indian Affairs, discover somebody is trespassing on an Indian Reservation, as an employee of the Federal Government, and as part of my responsibility over Indian Trust lands, I must tell them to stop trespassing.

Now do you understand why Christians of the present day are not able to do what the Christians in the Book of Acts were able to do?

Because many Christians today simply do not know God's Word, neither do they know or understand their authority in Jesus Christ. Many Christians today do not take authority and *speak* God's Word when the Devil is trespassing on God's property and on God's people. Many Christians today are similar to a policeman who observes crimes being committed all around them and asks, "Why are all these criminals running around lose, why doesn't somebody do something?"

What if I, as an employee of the Bureau of Indian Affairs, was lazy, and ignored some rancher grazing his cattle on Indian land, or did not know the regulations governing trespass? What if I told them to pay me some money and I would look the other way? What if I didn't bother learning the laws and regulations concerning Indian trust property?

Would you say I was doing a good job? Would you recommend I get a promotion? What does God think about people who claim to be Christians, people who claim to be the servants of Jesus Christ, who never bother *learning* God's Word, and never bother *speaking* God's Word?

I think I know.

I KNOW THY WORKS, THAT THOU ART NEITHER COLD NOR HOT: I WOULD THOU WERT COLD OR HOT.
SO THEN BECAUSE THOU ART LUKEWARM, AND NEITHER COLD NOR HOT, I WILL SPUE THEE OUT OF MY MOUTH.
REVELATIONS 3:15-16

Have you ever been to some government office hoping and expecting help from somebody only to find the people are on break, or out to lunch, or just don't seem to know or care about their job? People with responsibility, who do not want to work.

Then you probably know the frustration that God feels when His servants do not *know* and *speak* His Word with authority.

Can you see the huge advantage a believer has, who knows God's Word, over a believer who does not know God's Word?

Nothing is impossible for a believer who *knows* and *speaks* God's Word because nothing is impossible to God. Listen to what Jesus says to the Jews when they are going to stone him after He told them He was the Son of God:

JESUS ANSWERED THEM, IS IT NOT WRITTEN IN YOUR LAW, I SAID, YE ARE GODS? (SEE PSALM 82:6)
IF HE CALLED THEM "GODS", UNTO WHOM THE WORD OF GOD CAME, AND THE SCRIPTURE CANNOT BE BROKEN;
SAY YE OF HIM, WHOM THE FATHER HATH SANCTIFIED, AND SENT INTO THE WORLD, THOU BLASPHMEST; BECAUSE I SAID, I AM THE SON OF GOD?
JOHN 10:34-36

GODS. G 2316. Theh-os: a deity, especially the supreme Divinity; figuratively a magistrate; by Hebraism very: - X exceeding, God, god [-ly, -ward].

I HAVE SAID, YE ARE "GODS"; AND ALL OF YOU ARE CHILDREN OF THE MOST HIGH.
PSALM 82:6

GODS. H430. El-o-heem': plural of 433; gods in the ordinary sense; but specifically used (in the plural thus, especially with the article) of the supreme God; occasionally applied by way of deference to magistrates; and sometimes as a superlative: - angels, X exceeding, God (gods) (-dess, -ly) X (very) great, judges, X mighty.

He called them gods, unto whom the *Word* of God came! We see the word for gods used in this verse (*eloheem*) actually means gods, but it can also mean a magistrate (somebody with delegated governmental authority).

Why does the scripture say "Ye are gods, unto whom the WORD of God came?

Although Jesus Christ was God incarnate, I believe he limited himself to only the capabilities of an ordinary man.

You may ask, "Jesus walked on the water and raised the dead, how can you say he limited himself to the capabilities of an ordinary man?"

Jesus simply spoke the Word of God with authority, the same as any Christian can do. Ordinary Christians can do what Jesus did, when they are spiritually mature, when they have the WORD OF GOD residing in them, and when they *walk in the spirit* because that is what Jesus said:

**VERILY, VERILY, I SAY UNTO YOU. HE THAT BELIEVETH ON ME (*WORD OF GOD*), THE WORKS THAT I DO SHALL HE DO ALSO; AND GREATER WORKS THAN THESE SHALL HE DO; BECAUSE I GO UNTO MY FATHER.**
**JOHN 14:12**

Of course when a person begins to understand their authority in Jesus Christ, and they start *believing* on Jesus Christ (THE WORD OF GOD), and they begin *speaking* God's Word, they cease being like ordinary unbelievers, and start maturing and becoming Sons of God just like Jesus was the Son of God. The Bible says Jesus is our elder brother.

God says: *Ye are gods* to whom the *Word* of God came. Compared to an unbeliever or a carnal Christian, a mature believer is a god. A mature believer takes authority over his or her circumstances. A mature believer becomes healthy and whole in Spirit, in Soul and in Body. God intended everyone to be like Jesus. Look at what the people of Lycaonia said when the crippled man at Lystra was healed by Paul the Apostle.

**AND THERE SAT A CERTAIN MAN AT LYSTRA, IMPOTENT IN HIS FEET, BEING CRIPPLE FROM HIS MOTHER'S WOMB, WHO NEVER HAD WALKED:**
**THE SAME HEARD PAUL SPEAK: WHO STEADFASTLY BEHOLDING HIM, AND PERCEIVING THAT HE HAD FAITH TO BE HEALED,**
**SAID WITH A LOUD VOICE, STAND UPRIGHT ON THY FEET. AND HE LEAPED AND WALKED.**
**AND WHEN THE PEOPLE SAW WHAT PAUL HAD DONE, THEY LIFTED UP THEIR VOICES, SAYING IN THE SPEECH OF LYCAONIA, THE "GODS" ARE COME DOWN TO US IN THE LIKENESS OF MEN.**
**ACTS 14:8-11**

Why did the people of Lycaonia believe that Paul and Barnabus were gods?

It was not because Paul and Barnabus were supermen, it was because all unbelievers are so degraded by *unbelief* in God's Word, and have fallen so far from God's original purpose for mankind. Unbelievers are degraded because they have lost their authority, because of their unbelief in God's Word. Jesus compared the Pharisees and their followers to blind men.

**LET THEM ALONE: THEY BE BLIND LEADERS OF THE BLIND. AND IF THE BLIND LEAD THE BLIND, BOTH SHALL FALL INTO THE DITCH.**
**MATTHEW 15:14**

There is a quote by Desiderius Erasmus, which says:

*"In the land of the blind, the one-eyed man is king."*

Imagine living in a world of blind people, where people are constantly walking into walls and falling into ditches, always fearful because there is danger seemingly around every corner. Also imagine you have perfect vision, and you are able to avoid all the dangers and pitfalls that all the blind people simply cannot avoid. Some blind people can become very adept at maneuvering in the darkness, but they are still blind. Imagine a world of blind people stumbling and crawling. However, you can see everything and are not afraid, you can run and leap over every obstacle.

Wouldn't you be like a god to all those blind people?

When we become mature believers, we are under God's authority and become what God originally intended for us to be when he first created mankind. Compared to an unbeliever, who is in darkness because of unbelief, a mature believer is a god! Also, the Word of God says the children of the Most High are gods.

Do not children mature into the likeness of their Father?

A word of warning; when you start knowing and understanding things that regular people cannot know and understand in their fallen state, you will probably become very frustrated. Strangers may recognize that you have supernatural abilities and knowledge, but when you tell your family and friends about an opportunity or danger that is very obvious to you, often times they will ignore you and proceed on the same dangerous path.

Unbelievers that you know and love will be hurt and will hurt others simply because they will not listen to you. It is a common occurrence. Family and friends who have known you all your life, when you were still a part of the world, are the hardest people to convince that you have changed. You cannot force people to see the light. The best you can do in this situation is to *speak God's Word* to them, intercede and pray for them. You must perform your priestly duties for all the blind people of the world, but especially for the Church and your family. If you want to better understand your authority as a Christian, I suggest you read, *The Authority of the Believer* by J.A. MacMillan.

# CHAPTER 7

## *WALKING BY FAITH = WALKING IN THE SPIRIT.*

I heard a preacher on the radio say that if a Christian is not healed, it was not because they lacked faith. He said that God sometimes has a purpose for Christians to be sick. I am not sure which Bible he gets his doctrine from, but it is not the Bible I own and read. If you are a Christian and you are sick, or crippled, or blind, or paralyzed, or have the plague, it is NOT God's will for your life!

Does God love us? If God wants to teach us a lesson by allowing us to have AIDS or cancer, He has a funny way of showing us His love. I am sure that my earthly Dad would not give me cancer to teach me a lesson.

Why would my heavenly Father give me cancer to teach me a lesson?

If you are a Christian sitting in a wheel chair or confined to a bed, and you are hoping that someday you will finally learn your lesson, and God will send some man or woman of great faith to cure your paralyzed legs, I am afraid you are in for a long wait. Lack of faith in God's Word is the *only* reason a Christian can remain sick!

ACCORDING TO "YOUR" FAITH BE IT UNTO YOU.
MATTHEW 9:29

AND HE COULD THERE DO NO MIGHTY WORK, SAVE THAT HE LAID HIS HANDS UPON A FEW SICK FOLK, AND HEALED THEM.
AND HE MARVELLED BECAUSE OF "THEIR" UNBELIEF.
MARK 6:5-6

If Jesus Christ Himself was prevented from doing a mighty work because of the people's unbelief, how can Billy Graham, or Oral Roberts, or Benny Hinn do a mighty work in spite of a person's unbelief? I am confident nobody will heal you, including God Himself, if you do not *believe* God's Word.

Now people are going to say, "Mike, you are so cruel, you know people can't help being blind, crippled or sickly." But I say, "Oh yes they can!" Guess what, I have some good news for all the sick people in the world. There are two easy steps you can take to be healthy, to be wealthy, to be free, to be happy and to be wise.

First step: Be *converted*!

THEREFORE SPEAK I TO THEM IN PARABLES; BECAUSE THEY SEEING SEE NOT; AND HEARING THEY HEAR NOT, NEITHER DO THEY UNDERSTAND.
AND IN THEM IS FULFILLED THE PROPHECY OF ESAIAS, WHICH SAITH, BY HEARING YE SHALL HEAR, AND SHALL NOT UNDERSTAND; AND SEEING YE SHALL SEE, AND SHALL NOT PERCEIVE:

FOR THIS PEOPLE'S HEART IS WAXED GROSS, AND THEIR EARS ARE DULL OF HEARING, AND THEIR EYES THEY HAVE CLOSED; LEST AT ANY TIME THEY SHOULD SEE WITH THEIR EYES, AND HEAR WITH THEIR EARS, AND SHOULD UNDERSTAND WITH THEIR HEART, AND SHOULD BE "CONVERTED", AND I SHOULD "HEAL" THEM.
MATTHEW 13:13-15

CONVERTED. G1994. Ep-ee-stref'-o: to revert (literally, figuratively or morally): - come (go) again, convert, (re-) turn (about, again).

You have to do the exact opposite of what you have been doing. You have to stop your rebellion against God, *confess* the LORD Jesus Christ, *believe* that God raised Him from the dead and *repent* from your own dead works (abilities, deeds).

Second step: *Speak God's Word to the problem.*

WE HAVING THE SAME SPIRIT OF FAITH, ACCORDING AS IT IS WRITTEN, I BELIEVED, AND THEREFORE HAVE I "SPOKEN"; WE ALSO BELIEVE, AND THEREFORE "SPEAK".
2 CORINTHIANS 4:13

Instead of not believing and listening to God's Word, you have to *believe* and begin *speaking* and *hearing* what God has to say about a situation. Do not listen to anybody who contradicts the Word of God. If you go to a church where the Preacher contradicts God's Word, immediately leave and find a church where the Word of God is preached. If you go to a hospital where the Doctor contradicts God's Word, leave and find a Doctor who believes the Word of God. Instead of doubting God's Word, you have to start *believing* and *speaking* God's Word.

When God was giving me revelation about *memorizing* and *speaking* his Word, one night I had a vivid dream. In my dream, I was in an office with about a dozen people and they were all sitting at desks reading a book and writing in notepads. I also had a book and notepad, but I didn't know what to do. I just sat looking around at everyone as one by one, each person finished writing in their notepads, closed their book and left the room.

Eventually, there was only one man left in the room with me and after he finally finished writing, he stood up and closed his book. Before he left, he said: "Once you learn how to *cipher*, you only have to work two or three hours a day, then you can take the rest of the day off." I was thinking to myself, "I want to work two or three hours a day, I have to go to the library and find a book about ciphering," then I woke up! I thought it was a strange dream and I didn't understand it, but it was one of those vivid dreams that I believe are given by God, which have special meaning, so I prayed for *revelation* and looked up cipher.

**Cipher** means to express in *secret writing* or to solve my arithmetic.

Eventually, when I was talking about my dream to my brother and sister, the revelation came to me.

AND THE DISCIPLES CAME, AND SAID UNTO HIM, WHY SPEAKEST THOU UNTO THEM IN "PARABLES"?
MATTHEW 13:10

PARABLES. G3850. Par-ab-ol-ay': a similitude ("parable"), i.e. (symbolic) fictitious narrative (of common life conveying a moral), adagemor; - comparison, figure, parable, proverb.

HE ANSWERED AND SAID UNTO THEM, BECAUSE IT IS GIVEN UNTO YOU TO KNOW THE MYSTERIES OF THE KINGDOM OF HEAVEN, BUT TO THEM IT IS NOT GIVEN.
FOR WHOSOEVER HATH, TO HIM SHALL BE GIVEN, AND HE SHALL HAVE MORE "ABUNDANCE": BUT WHOSOEVER HATH NOT, FROM HIM SHALL BE TAKEN AWAY EVEN WHAT HE HATH.
THEREFORE SPEAK I TO THEM IN PARABLES: BECAUSE THEY SEEING SEE NOT; AND HEARING THEY HEAR NOT, NEITHER DO THEY UNDERSTAND.
MATTHEW 13:11-13

ABUNDANCE . G4052. Per-is-sooy'-o: to superabound (in quantity or quality) be in excess, be superfluous; also (transitively) to cause to superabound or excel. – (make, more) abound, (have, have more), abundance, (be more) abundant, be the better, enough and to spare, exceed, excel, increase, be left, redound, remain (over and above).

Why did Jesus speak in parables to the crowds, and only explain the parables to his disciples when they were alone?

I believe it was because his disciples put the Kingdom of God before everything else. They left their work, their homes, their families, and everything else important to them in order to follow Jesus. The disciples made following Jesus Christ their primary occupation. That is the kind of person God is looking for, God is looking for the cream of the crop, God demands the very best. God demands His tithe of first fruits. The Apostle Paul explained it like this:

BUT WITHOUT FAITH IT IS IMPOSSIBLE TO PLEASE HIM; FOR HE THAT COMETH TO GOD MUST BELIEVE THAT HE IS, AND THAT HE IS A REWARDER OF THEM THAT "DILIGENTLY" SEEK HIM.
HEBREWS 11:6

DILIGENTLY. G1567. Ek-zay-teh'o: to search out, i.e. (figuratively) investigate, crave, demand, (by Hebraism) worship: - enquire, seek after (carefully, diligently).

God's *chosen* are not people who call themselves Jews or people who call themselves Christians. God's *chosen* people love God with all their heart, and with all their soul, and with all their mind and with all their strength. God wants people who love him as much as he loves them. God wants people who *diligently* seek Him in His Word, like Paul the Apostle:

YEA DOUBTLESS, AND I COUNT ALL THINGS BUT LOSS FOR THE EXCELLENCY OF THE KNOWLEDGE OF CHRIST JESUS MY LORD: FOR WHOM I HAVE SUFFERED THE LOSS OF ALL THINGS, AND DO COUNT THEM BUT DUNG, THAT I MAY WIN CHRIST,

AND BE FOUND IN HIM, NOT HAVING MINE OWN RIGHTEOUSNESS, WHICH IS OF THE LAW, BUT THAT WHICH IS THROUGH THE FAITH OF CHRIST, THE RIGHTEOUSNESS WHICH IS OF GOD BY FAITH:

THAT I MAY KNOW HIM, AND THE POWER OF HIS RESURRECTION, AND THE FELLOWSHIP OF HIS SUFFERINGS, BEING MADE CONFORMABLE UNTO HIS DEATH;

IF BY ANY MEANS I MIGHT ATTAIN UNTO THE RESURRECTION OF THE DEAD.

PHILIPPIANS 3:8-11

The books in the Old and New Testament are similar to books of ciphers. Although the text has a plain and obvious meaning; the text also contains a deep and hidden meaning. You cannot read it once and expect to know all the mysteries of God, and the books of the Bible were never intended to be simple texts. God has made His Word to be like a hidden treasure.

AGAIN, THE KINGDOM OF HEAVEN IS LIKE UNTO TREASURE HID IN A FIELD; THE WHICH WHEN A MAN HATH FOUND, HE HIDETH, AND FOR JOY THEREOF GOETH AND SELLETH ALL THAT HE HATH, AND BUYETH THAT FIELD.

AGAIN, THE KINGDOM OF HEAVEN IS LIKE UNTO A MERCHANT MAN, SEEKING GOODLY PEARLS:

WHO, WHEN HE HAD FOUND ONE PEARL OF GREAT PRICE, WENT AND SOLD ALL THAT HE HAD, AND BOUGHT IT.

MATTHEW 13:44-46

The kingdom of God, the Word of God, is truly a great treasure. God will only give spiritual *revelation* to people who earnestly desire to know Him and His Word. God will show favor to those who *diligently seek Him*! We must set our heart and our desire on spiritual things because we understand that Jesus Christ (*the WORD OF GOD*) is the author(ity) and finisher of our faith.

Without God's Word in our hearts and minds, we are the same as most everyone else, blind men, lost and without hope. We are like ships without an anchor, being cast about every time the winds change direction. However, with God's living Word abiding in us, we are children of the light and children of the Most High. Every obstacle and every opportunity will be made obvious to us. We are God's children and He is our Father. We are under the authority of Jesus Christ, and everything dealing with us and God is under our authority.

IT IS THE GLORY OF GOD TO CONCEAL A THING; BUT THE HONOUR OF KINGS IS TO SEARCH OUT A MATTER.

PROVERBS 23:2

Are you a king? Are you God's chosen? Are you a child of the Most High? Are you a god?

If you are, then you will diligently search and meditate upon and *memorize* God's Word. If you are not, your Bible will probably sit gathering dust, and you will continue being lost, blind and wandering in the wilderness. You will remain sick, poor and foolish. If you do not spend time in God's Word, I doubt that you were ever a Christian to begin with. In which case, I hope somebody is interceding and praying for you!

Why do I say that?

**AS NEWBORN BABES, DESIRE THE SINCERE MILK OF THE WORD, THAT YE MAY GROW THEREBY:**
**I PETER 2:2**

Just as newborn babies naturally desire their mother's milk, a newborn Christian naturally desires the Word of God. We naturally are hungry for the nourishment that will make us grow stronger and help us reach maturity. We did not need anybody to tell us to drink milk when we were babies. A newborn baby naturally desires milk. A person who is truly born again will naturally desire God's Word.

If a person says, "I don't need to read the Bible, me and Jesus got it all worked out." I tend to think they were never saved in the first place. If a person says, I use to read the Bible, but now I don't need to 'cause I've got it all figured out." I tend to think they are either dead or dying in the spirit. You cannot eat for a year and go without eating for a year and survive. You must eat on a regular basis, and if you want your spirit to live and grow, you must imbibe in the Word of God on a regular (daily) basis.

**AND WHEN ABRAM WAS NINETY YEARS OLD AND NINE, AD-O-NOY' APPEARED TO ABRAM, AND SAID UNTO HIM, I *AM* ALMIGHTY GOD *(EL SHAD-DAH'-EE);* WALK BEFORE *(TO FACE)* ME, AND BE THOU PERFECT *(BLAMELESS).***
**GENESIS 17:1**

Abraham is our prime example of faith. Abraham had an intimate relationship with God, but he did not have nearly the revelation available to him, that we have available to us. However, Abraham did know a few very important things about God:

**God *appeared* to Abraham:** God is not some unknowable entity. God wanted and cultivated an intimate relationship with Abraham.
**God is ALMIGHTY (EL SHAD-DAH-EE):** Abraham knew that if God said he was going to do something, God could and would do it. Nothing is impossible to God!
**God wanted Abraham to *walk* before (to face) Him:** God expected something from Abraham. God is not a Genie in a bottle. Abraham did not expect God to serve his every whim and desire. God was not Abraham's servant. Abraham knew and understood that he was God's servant.
**God told Abraham to be *perfect*!** *Uh Oh!*

What was Abraham to do?

Abraham was born in sin just like all the descendents of Adam. Abraham probably felt just as helpless as any one of us when we start comparing our pitiful condition with the perfection of Almighty God. God wants us all to be perfect. God wants us to believe His Word.

# CHAPTER 8

## WHO AND WHAT IS GOD?

IN THE BEGINNING GOD (*EL-O-HEEM*) CREATED THE HEAVEN AND THE EARTH.
GENESIS 1:1

**EL-O-HEEM'**; H430: plural of 433; gods in the ordinary sense; but specifically used (in the plural thus, especially with the article) of the Supreme God; occasionally applied by way of deference to magistrates; and sometimes as a superlative: angels, x exceeding, God (gods)(-dess, -ly), x (very) great, judges, x mighty.

We see in the very beginning of the Bible that God is in The Beginning. In the Beginning...ALMIGHTY! It never ceases to amaze me that somebody can believe that something can come from nothing. As a matter of fact, I believe atheists must be willfully ignorant.

I understand that it is difficult to understand who and what God is because mankind is suffering from massive limitations physically, mentally and spiritually. That is why God must actively seek us out, and give us a revelation of who and what He is in the Bible. However, if somebody claims that the universe and life just sprang into existence out of nothing, it definitely strains their credibility with me.

AND GOD SAID, LET US MAKE MAN IN OUR IMAGE, AFTER OUR LIKENESS; AND LET THEM HAVE DOMINION OVER THE FISH OF THE SEA, AND OVER THE FOWL OF THE AIR, AND OVER THE CATTLE, AND OVER ALL THE EARTH, AND OVER EVERY CREEPING THING THAT CREEPETH UPON THE EARTH.
*So* GOD CREATED MAN IN HIS *OWN* IMAGE, IN THE IMAGE *OF* GOD CREATED HE HIM; MALE AND FEMALE CREATED HE THEM.
GENESIS 1:26-27

When the Bible says that we are made in the image of God, it does not mean God has ten fingers and ten toes. It means that God is a Spirit and we are also spirit. God *breathed* His life into Adam. We have the potential to create just like God creates. We can *speak* physical things into existence with our spoken word just like God speaks physical things into existence with His spoken Word. We can speak life, liberty, light and love into existence because we are the children of the living God.

# CHAPTER 9

## GOD IS A THREE PART BEING = MAN IS A THREE PART BEING

I have heard that a three-part man (body, soul, and spirit) can be likened to a 1) carriage and horses, 2) a driver, and 3) the owner or master riding in the carriage. The carriage and horses represents our body. Our body interacts with, and moves about within the physical world. The driver of the carriage represents our soul. The soul represents our emotions, our thoughts, our intellect, and controls or drives the body, and decides how the body will interact with the physical world. The master of the carriage represents the spirit of man. The spirit of man represents our intuition and conscience.

The spirit of man must have authority over the driver, and thereby over the carriage, because only the spirit knows the final destination of the man. When a man is not a Christian, his spirit is dead and his carriage (body) becomes a hearse. Then, either the soul or the body is in charge. If the soul is in charge, the man's life will appear normal, but he is adrift in the world, and he does not know his purpose or where he is going. The body represents our desires and our passions, and interacts with the world. If the body is in charge, God help the man. If the body is in charge, it is similar to a carriage being dragged about by runaway horses. Everyone will be in serious danger.

God the Father is likened to our spirit. The Father knows everything, the Father is everywhere, the Father is invisible and the Father has final and supreme authority. God the Holy Spirit is likened to our soul. The Holy Spirit leads us, He teaches us, He can be grieved, He fills us, He speaks to us. God the Son interacts with the physical world through His Church. He ate with His disciples, He slept, He wept, He walked, He spoke with authority, He is lead by the Holy Spirit, He is *totally* obedient to the Father. God the Son is the Church's perfect example.

AND THE LORD (*YEH-HO-VAW'*) GOD FORMED MAN *OF* THE DUST OF THE GROUND, AND BREATHED INTO HIS NOSTRILS THE BREATH OF LIFE; AND MAN BECAME A LIVING SOUL.
GENESIS 2:7

YEH-HO-VAH'; from H3068': (The) self-Existent or Eternal; Jehovah, Jewish national name of God: - Jehovah, the Lord.

God has always been and will forever exist, and God is the author and creator of all *life*. At one time I thought I wanted to be a medical doctor. Therefore, I studied biology in college, and eventually I earned a bachelor degree in microbiology. I guess there are still arguments among scientists concerning what is life, and what is not life. Biologists have been studying life for centuries, and they have noticed that living organisms have a few things in common:

1) Living organisms have *organization*, hence the word "organism". Living organisms are separated from their environment by organized cell structures.

2) Living organisms maintain *homeostasis*. Living organisms regulate the internal environment of their cells by regulating when, where, how, and what resources from the external environment are allowed to enter their cells, and they can also eliminate waste products.

3) Living organisms undergo *metabolism*. Living organisms transform external resources into building blocks and energy in order to build and maintain their cellular components.

4) Living organisms respond to *stimuli*. Living organisms interact with the environment. Living organisms have a tendency to be repelled by negative environmental stimuli and tend to be attracted by positive environmental stimuli.

5) Living organisms have the ability to *reproduce* new living organisms.

6) Living organisms possess *coded* information. All living organisms contain coded instructions made up of two types of nucleic acids: deoxyribonucleic acid (DNA) and ribonucleic acid (RNA). All of the cell's properties are determined by its DNA or RNA code.

As you have probably realized, living organisms are *very* complex! Simple viruses possess a complex code of several hundred nucleotides and viruses often need to use another organism's more complicated DNA to reproduce. Nucleotides are the basic subunits of DNA and RNA. The human genome has over three billion (3,000,000,000) nucleotide base pairs! There are many living organisms, some plants for instance, that have even more complex DNA than people!

There have always been some people who believed in what today seem like unreasonable ideas. People once believed the world was flat, and that the sun revolved around the earth. At one time there was a theory called "spontaneous generation" widely accepted by the scientific community for several hundred years. Proponents of spontaneous generation believed that microscopic organisms arose spontaneously from nonliving material. It was only within the last one hundred and fifty years that spontaneous generation was disproved by people like the French chemist, Louis Pasteur and the English physicist, John Tyndall.

However, proponents of evolution still believe in spontaneous generation! They claim spontaneous generation occurred billions of years ago in the "primordial soup", under environmental conditions that are completely different from conditions today. These "scientists" are not exactly sure what the conditions were like billions of years ago. Therefore, they cannot replicate the conditions in a laboratory, neither can they prove exactly how spontaneous generation of living organisms occurred from nonliving material originally.

I am going to make a, not so bold, prediction. "Scientists" will never prove spontaneous generation! Essentially, people believe what they want to believe, whether the belief is reasonable or not. Why am I telling you this? When we attempt to lead somebody to Jesus Christ, he or she cannot be saved by "scientific" arguments and reasoning. The Apostle Paul said it best:

**O TIMOTHY, KEEP THAT WHICH IS COMMITTED TO THY TRUST, AVOID PROFANE AND VAIN BABBLINGS, AND OPPOSITIONS OF SCIENCE FALSELY SO CALLED.**
**I TIMOTHY 6:20**

Needless to say there are plenty of arm chair, brainiac, pseudo scientists, who will try to drag you into arguments about evolution. They will want to talk about dinosaurs and billions of years ago, but don't get dragged into "scientific" arguments because they are mostly only "vain babblings." The *only* hope anybody has is if they *hear* the Word of God!

**IS NOT MY WORD LIKE AS A FIRE? SAITH THE LORD; AND LIKE A HAMMER THAT BREAKETH THE ROCK IN PIECES?**
**JEREMIAH 23:29**

When we enter into stupid verbal sparring matches, we are laying down God's supernatural mighty hammer, and throwing aside the sword of the spirit, which is the Word of God. Don't do it! Many of God's people are being held in bondage. They need to be saved. We cannot save people by our own wit, our own wisdom, or our own strength. People can only be saved and delivered by *hearing* the Word of God! We must *memorize* and *speak* God's Word if we want to deliver people from the darkness into the light, from bondage into liberty.

**AFTER THESE THINGS THE WORD OF THE LORD (YEH-HO-VAW') CAME UNTO ABRAM IN A VISION, SAYING, FEAR NOT, ABRAM: I *AM* THY SHIELD, *AND* THY EXCEEDING GREAT REWARD.**
**AND ABRAM SAID, LORD (AD-O-NOY') GOD (YEH-HO-VEE'), WHAT WILT THOU GIVE ME, SEEING I GO CHILDLESS, AND THE STEWARD OF MY HOUSE *IS* THIS ELIEZER OF DAMASCUS?**
**GENESIS 15:1-2**

AD-O-NOY'. H136: an emphatic form of 113; the Lord (used as a proper name of God only): - (my) Lord.

God is LORD! God is sovereign over everything and everyone. God's eye is on the sparrow. God controls every event from the birth of a baby to the supernova of a dying sun. God is not unapproachable, nor is He unconcerned. God is willing and able to be on intimate terms with everyone, just like he was on intimate terms with Abraham. That is why Abraham is called the father of our faith.

Abraham showed us that a man can be a friend of God. God showed us through Abraham that He wants to be our friend. However, God is not like any other friend, God can and will intervene in *any* circumstance on our behalf. God can part the Red Sea, God can make the sun stand still upon Gibeon and the moon stand still in the valley of Ajalon! All we have to do is *speak* His Word and *believe*. Oh what a friend we have in Jesus!

# PART 2

## EGYPT

*"And You hath he quickened,
Who were dead in trespasses and sins;
Wherein in time past ye walked according to the course of this world,
According to the prince of the power of the air, the spirit that now worketh
in the children of disobedience:"*

*Ephesians 2:1-2*

# CHAPTER 10

## THE LAND OF BONDAGE

*"Jesus is Lord and God has raised Him from the dead!"*

These words are the first step in our *walk in the spirit*. Once you receive the revelation that Jesus Christ has power over all creation, you will no longer be in darkness. The Israelites served as special examples to all believers.

**NOW THESE THINGS WERE OUR EXAMPLES, TO THE INTENT WE SHOULD NOT LUST AFTER EVIL THINGS, AS THEY ALSO LUSTED.**
**I CORINTHIANS 10:6**

The Israelites were in bondage in Egypt and under the authority of Pharaoh. While they remained in Egypt, the Israelites were under Pharaoh's authority. The Israelites in *Egypt* are an example of the unbeliever in bondage to the devil prior to salvation. The unbeliever is in cruel bondage to the world, and to the flesh, and to the devil.

EGYPT. H4714. Mits-rah'-yim: dual of 4693; Mitsrajim, i.e. Upper and Lower Egypt: - Egypt, Egyptians, Mizraim.

BESIEGED. H4693. Maw-tsore': the same as 4692 in the sense of a limit; Egypt (as the border of Palestine): - besieged places, defence, fortified.

BESIEGED. H4692. Maw-tsore': something hemming in, i.e. (objectively) mound (of besiegers), (abstractly) a siege, (figuratively) distress; or (subjectively) a fastness; - besieged, bulwark, defence, fenced, fortress, siege, strong (hold), tower.

We see from its meaning that *Egypt* is a type of spiritual stronghold, or prison, surrounded by besiegers (demons). While we are imprisoned by our flesh, and by our carnal desires, we are in constant distress and limited in our ideas, our circumstances, our hopes, and our dreams. If the carnal unbeliever desires something, he or she strives with all their might to pursue and capture whatever is their heart's desire, whether it is good or evil, only to suffer disappointed hopes continually. Nothing ever seems to work out right for an unbeliever. Even if an unbeliever is seemingly successful, they cannot enjoy their success.

How often have we done or said something, which we regretted afterward? While in bondage, we continue to do the wrong things over and over no matter how hard we attempt to stop, no matter how much we desire to stop?

Pharaoh is an example of Satan, the god of this world. When we are under the world's authority, or Satan's authority, he demands the impossible from us and when we fail, we are punished without mercy.

There is only one reason why everyone does not enjoy all the blessings of God. There is only one reason people do not enjoy health, wealth, wisdom, peace, love and joy! *They do not believe God's Word.*

God's greatest desire is to set our spirits free. He wants our spirit to be one with His Spirit. He wants us to be eternally free. He wants us to let loose of our fleshly desires, and to let ourselves flow with His Holy Spirit. He can then lead us to the destination He has prepared for us. He can take us to the Promised Land. He can take us to our resting place.

People may ask, "Why do I pray for my child, or my sister, or my brother, or my father, or my mother, and they are not saved?"

The answer is simple: because there are so many people who, by their own free will, are in open rebellion against God, and consequently they are in bondage to Satan. If you do not serve God, you serve the Devil. It is that simple. People who are serving the Devil are destroying the earth, they are destroying themselves, and they are destroying the inhabitants of the earth.

They do not consider themselves stewards of God's creation. They are at war with the light, they are at war with life, and they are at war with God. The world is under the law and under the curse. Most people believe they can make it without God. The world believes there can be justice, peace and love apart from God. The world does not believe the Word of God. The world calls God a liar and that is why the world is condemned.

The Book of Hebrews explains why believing God is so important to us and also illustrates why God's *spoken* Word is so special. When God says something, you can *consider it done.* You don't have to wait on God to perform His Word. You can *consider it already performed.* God and His Word are not bound by space or time. By faith, we can hear God's future promises and *know* those *future promises* can be *ours today!*

BY FAITH MOSES, WHEN HE WAS COME TO YEARS, REFUSED TO BE CALLED THE SON OF PHARAOH'S DAUGHTER;
CHOOSING RATHER TO SUFFER AFFLICTION WITH THE PEOPLE OF GOD, THAN TO ENJOY THE PLEASURES OF SIN FOR A SEASON;
ESTEEMING THE REPROACH OF CHRIST GREATER RICHES THAN THE TREASURES IN EGYPT: FOR HE HAD RESPECT UNTO THE "RECOMPENSE" OF THE REWARD.
HEBREWS 11:24-26

*Recompense* is something given or done, to make up for, or compensate for a loss. Moses had everything Egypt had to offer. He was the adopted son of Pharaoh's daughter. However, he understood that what Egypt had to offer could not be compared to what God had to offer. In Egypt, Moses could have indulged in all the pleasures of the flesh, but he would never have attained the greatness God had planned for him.

Somehow, possibly by reading scripture that he had in his possession, possibly by listening to his Hebrew family and very probably by *revelation,* Moses knew that God had something great in store for him. *See* Acts 7:25. Moses knew that God was going to use him to deliver Israel from bondage. He knew that the riches and glory of Egypt paled in comparison to what God had waiting for him in Christ. At first, Moses must have believed God had placed him in the House of Pharaoh to be in a position to deliver Israel. However, that was not the case. It was not Moses' position in the House of Pharaoh that would deliver Israel, but Moses' *belief* in God's Word that would deliver Israel.

Moses had to reject his Egyptian family, and his status as the grandson of Pharaoh, and flee to the *wilderness*. Moses understood that eventually, God would more than compensate him for everything he would leave in Egypt.

We see from chapter 11 in the Book of Hebrews that Moses foresaw the reproach of Christ hundreds of years before Jesus was ever born.
We also understand that King David, and all the prophets in the Bible, knew that one day God would send a savior and a kinsman redeemer. Because it was God who promised a future Messiah, the saints of old knew that God's promises were as good as done. They trusted because God had made a promise to them, they could walk in that promise even before it was fulfilled. They could *walk in the spirit*.

How much more should the saints of our generation *walk in the spirit* when Jesus has already been raised from the dead?

Why do we have to go into the *wilderness* after our salvation? By force of habit, prior to our salvation, we have spent a lifetime relying on our own knowledge, our own strength, our own connections, our own resources. God drives us into the wilderness to put us in a place where we cannot rely on ourselves any longer. God puts us into a place where we must rely on God! Moses fled into the wilderness. King David fled into the wilderness. Jesus Christ was led by the Spirit into the wilderness, and He is our perfect example. Jesus Christ *only relied on the Word of God*!

This is a promise that Jesus made to everyone who will believe God and *Walk in the Spirit*.

**AND JESUS ANSWERED AND SAID, VERILY I SAY UNTO YOU, THERE IS NO MAN THAT HATH LEFT HOUSE, OR BRETHREN, OR SISTERS, OR FATHER, OR MOTHER, OR WIFE, OR CHILDREN, OR LANDS, FOR MY SAKE, AND FOR THE GOSPEL'S,**
**BUT HE SHALL RECEIVE A HUNDREDFOLD NOW "IN THIS TIME", HOUSES, AND BRETHREN, AND SISTERS, AND MOTHERS, AND CHILDREN, AND LANDS, WITH PERSECUTIONS; AND IN THE WORLD TO COME ETERNAL LIFE.**
**MARK 10:29-30**

I believe that Jesus is telling his disciples, and every believer, that most people spend their time and energy pursuing the wrong things. People pursue after money, houses, lands and relationships and they end up not reaching their goals. However, if a person spends their time and energy knowing God, and pursuing after God's plan for his or her life, then God will more than compensate them for anything in the World they might lose. The time you spend *meditating* on God's Word, and seeking God's plan for your life, will pay huge dividends. The end result will be all the things the world promises and more, most importantly it finally results in *eternal life*! God is not a skinflint and God is not Ebenezer Scrooge. God wants us to have houses and lands and relationships, but he wants us to have them the right way... His way. *Trust in God*!

TRUST IN THE LORD, AND DO GOOD; SO SHALT THOU DWELL IN THE LAND, AND VERILY THOU SHALT BE FED.
DELIGHT THYSELF ALSO IN THE LORD; AND HE SHALL GIVE THEE THE DESIRES OF THINE HEART.
COMMIT THY WAY UNTO THE LORD; TRUST ALSO IN HIM; AND HE SHALL BRING IT TO PASS.
AND HE SHALL BRING FORTH THY RIGHTEOUSNESS AS THE LIGHT, AND THY JUDGMENT AS THE NOONDAY.
PSALM 37:3-6

I have heard many people put down the prosperity gospel, and the Word of Faith gospel. Probably because they are either ignorant of the power and promises of God's Word, or they cannot admit that if they are sick and poor, they must be on the wrong path. Therefore, they attack those who preach health, wealth and wisdom for Christians. I understand where they are coming from, it is hard when you are poor, sick and foolish to admit that you might be on the wrong path. Like I said before, I was mostly on the wrong path for twenty years.

When I first heard Kenneth Copeland, Creflo Dollar, or Kenneth Hagan preach the *Word of faith*, I just figured they were trying to con dumb people out of their money, even though they rarely asked for money, which is probably why I continued to watch them. It is easy to be envious of people who are healthy, wealthy and wise, especially when you are sick, poor and foolish. The Gospel means, *Good News*! It does not mean remaining sick, poor and ignorant, which would be *bad news,* as far as I am concerned.

Finally, by the grace of God, I figured out that true prosperity: in health, wealth and wisdom can only come from spiritual maturity. Spiritual maturity can only come from *meditating* on, *memorizing, speaking* and *hearing* the Word of God. Spiritual maturity can only come from having God's Word become a part of your spirit. Spiritual maturity will only come when you are *walking in the spirit*.

THE HEART OF THE WISE TEACHETH HIS MOUTH, AND ADDETH LEARNING TO HIS LIPS.
PROVERBS 16:23

How do wise men and women teach their mouth and add learning to their lips?

They *memorize* and *repeat* wise words. They repeat God's Word over and over and over again! By constant *repetition*, by constantly *speaking* God's living Word, by continual *meditation*, we teach our mouth and add learning to our lips. We become *wise* in the sight of God and in the sight of men!

**HAPPY IS THE MAN THAT FINDETH WISDOM, AND THE MAN THAT GETTETH UNDERSTANDING.**

**FOR THE MERCHANDISE OF IT IS BETTER THAN THE MERCHANDISE OF SILVER, AND THE GAIN THEREOF THAN FINE GOLD.**

**SHE IS MORE PRECIOUS THAN RUBIES; AND ALL THE THINGS THOU CANST DESIRE ARE NOT TO BE COMPARED UNTO HER.**

**LENGTH OF DAYS IS IN HER RIGHT HAND; AND IN HER LEFT HAND RICHES AND HONOUR.**

**PROVERBS 3:13-16**

I have heard some preachers say we are under a different covenant from Abraham, he was under the old covenant, and we are under the new covenant, but I believe we are under the same covenant as Abraham, we are under the covenant of grace, and Abraham was also under the covenant of grace. Abraham is the example for all true believers.

# CHAPTER 11

## KNOWLEDGE OF GOOD AND EVIL = THE LAW AND THE CURSE

There have only been two covenants since the beginning of time. One covenant is the covenant of the law, the law says, "Everything depends on my actions. I can be righteous apart from God. I can be wise apart from God. I can be prosperous apart from God. I can have life apart from God. I can *earn* my own salvation, my own wealth, my own wisdom and my own health. I can keep the law by my own strength. I am self-sufficient!  That is what the serpent promised Eve in the garden if she would eat the forbidden fruit.  The serpent promised Eve that she and Adam would be as gods by disobeying God! The serpent told Eve that God was a liar.

*Everyone who believes that God is a liar will have their part in the lake of fire*!

The more that a person increases in the knowledge of Good and Evil, the more they will experience the curse. That is why so many Christians suffer from sickness, poverty and ignorance because they are trying to keep the law. If you are under the law, you can be prosecuted. It does not matter whether you are ignorant of the law or are knowledgeable about the law. It does not matter if you believe the law is irrational or unjust. If you are under the law, you can be prosecuted to the full extent of the law. Satan is called the *accuser of our brethren*. Satan is a prosecutor and a persecutor of mankind.

**AND THE GREAT DRAGON WAS CAST OUT, THAT OLD SERPENT, CALLED THE DEVIL, AND SATAN, WHICH DECEIVETH THE WHOLE WORLD: HE WAS CAST OUT INTO THE EARTH, AND HIS ANGELS WERE CAST OUT WITH HIM.**
**AND I HEARD A LOUD VOICE SAYING IN HEAVEN, NOW IS COME SALVATION, AND STRENGTH, AND THE KINGDOM OF OUR GOD, AND THE POWER OF HIS CHRIST: FOR THE ACCUSER OF OUR BRETHREN IS CAST DOWN, WHICH ACCUSED THEM BEFORE OUR GOD DAY AND NIGHT.**
**REVELATION 12:9-10**

Satan's job is to accuse, prosecute and persecute mankind. If you are under the law, you open the door to his accusations, his prosecution and his persecution. You cannot be under the law and remain safe. Most of the world is under the law:

On the streets people say, *what comes around goes around*. The Hindu and Buddhist warn of *Bad Karma* when you do evil acts. The Old Testament says *an eye for an eye and a tooth for a tooth*. There are only two types of people in the world: 1) those under grace (*mature Christians*) and 2) those under the law (*everybody else*). If you are trying to keep the law, whether you are a Hindu, a Moslem, a Jew, a Catholic or a Protestant, you are not under *grace*!

*You are either under the law or you are under grace*!

# CHAPTER 12

## KNOWLEDGE OF JESUS CHRIST = GRACE AND THE BLESSING

The second covenant is the *covenant of grace*, the covenant of grace proclaims, "Everything depends on Jesus Christ. All of my righteousness, wisdom, prosperity, love, hope, charity and eternal life are free unmerited gifts from God, I must be totally dependent on God and *believe* His Word. God is my father and God loves me. If God loves me than I know everything he *says* is for my own good. The more that we increase in the knowledge of Jesus Christ and His perfect love, the more we will experience His blessing.

If Christians would spend more time *memorizing* and contemplating all that Jesus has accomplished by His death and resurrection, we would begin experiencing God's blessings with an ever increasing revelation of Jesus Christ. There is a special type of immunity under international law called *"Diplomatic Immunity"*.

Under diplomatic immunity, a diplomat is prohibited from being arrested or criminally prosecuted for *any* violations of local law. If a diplomat is caught while committing a crime, he must be released if he declares his diplomatic immunity. Christians have diplomatic immunity in the world. We can be accused by Satan, but we cannot be prosecuted if we declare our immunity. We must declare our immunity because we are under the covenant of grace, we are NOT under the law.

BLESS THE LORD, O MY SOUL: AND ALL THAT IS WITHIN ME, BLESS HIS HOLY NAME.
BLESS THE LORD, O MY SOUL, AND FORGET NOT ALL HIS BENEFITS:
WHO FORGIVETH ALL THINE INIQUITIES; WHO HEALETH "ALL" THY DISEASES;
WHO REDEEMETH THY LIFE FROM DESTRUCTION; WHO CROWNETH THEE WITH LOVING-KINDNESS AND TENDER MERCIES;
WHO SATISFIETH THY MOUTH WITH GOOD THINGS; SO THAT THY YOUTH IS RENEWED LIKE THE EAGLES.
PSALM 103:1-5

Many Christians are still under the law and tend to think, if I am good, God will be happy with me and bless me, but if I am bad, God will be mad at me and curse me. However, that is not how God works. God does everything the exact opposite of how the world does things. The world rewards effort. If you are athletic, or intelligent, or rich, or have connections, you will do great in the world, but God is looking for just the opposite:

FOR YE SEE YOUR CALLING BRETHREN, HOW THAT NOT MANY WISE MEN AFTER THE FLESH, NOT MANY MIGHTY, NOT MANY NOBLE, ARE CALLED:
BUT GOD HATH CHOSEN THE FOOLISH THINGS OF THE WORLD TO CONFOUND THE WISE; AND GOD HATH CHOSEN THE WEAK THINGS OF THE WORLD TO CONFOUND THE THINGS WHICH ARE MIGHTY;
AND BASE THINGS OF THE WORLD, AND THINGS WHICH ARE DESPISED, HATH GOD CHOSEN, YEA, AND THINGS WHICH ARE NOT, TO BRING TO NOUGHT THINGS THAT ARE:

**THAT NO FLESH SHOULD GLORY IN HIS PRESENCE.**
**BUT OF HIM ARE YE IN CHRIST JESUS, WHO OF GOD IS MADE UNTO US WISDOM, AND RIGHTEOUSNESS, AND SANCTIFICATION, AND REDEMPTION:**
**THAT, ACCORDING AS IT IS WRITTEN, HE THAT GLORIETH, LET HIM GLORY IN THE LORD.**
**I CORINTHIANS 1:26-31**

Rejoice if you are puny and weak. Bless the Lord if you are poor and have no connections with the rich and powerful. Shout if you aren't the smartest person in your school. You are the type of person God is looking for in order to pour out His blessing and reveal His grace to the world. You will rely on God because you know you cannot rely on yourself or anybody else. God wants the whole world to know the following:

**THAT THE RACE IS NOT TO THE SWIFT, NOR THE BATTLE TO THE STRONG, NEITHER YET BREAD TO THE WISE, NOR YET RICHES TO MEN OF UNDERSTANDING, NOR YET FAVOUR TO MEN OF SKILL; BUT TIME AND CHANCE HAPPENETH TO THEM ALL.**
**ECCLESIASTES 9:11**

I compare mature Christians who *walk in the spirit* to rich people's children. Rich kids do not worry about getting into the best colleges or the most lucrative occupations because of their own merit. They are confident that they will get the very best, not because they are anything special, but because of their relationship with their parents.

You might be the dumbest kid in your school, but if your last name is Gates, Buffet, Helu', Ellison, or Kamprad, there is a really, really, really good chance that you will get into the University of your choice. Your parents will be able to pull strings to get you into the best Universities, and later on you will move up the career ladder in an excellent occupation, starting out at the top rung of the ladder!

Don't you think that God can set things up for His children as well?

One difference is that a rich kid's parents cannot make them wise or righteous, but God can and will prepare His children for anyplace He puts them. God can and will make you righteous, wise, healthy and prosperous.

**THE BLESSING OF THE LORD, IT MAKETH RICH, AND HE ADDETH NO SORROW WITH IT.**
**PROVERBS 10:22**

God has made one thing perfectly clear, we must not test God when he says not to do a thing.

**THOU SHALT NOT TEMPT THE LORD THY GOD.**
**MATTHEW 4:7**

However, God asked the Israelites to test him by doing a specific thing. I believe that you do not even have to be a Christian and God will honor this specific promise.

**BRING YE ALL THE TITHES INTO THE STOREHOUSE, THAT THERE MAY BE MEAT IN MINE HOUSE, AND "PROVE" ME NOW HEREWITH, SAITH THE LORD OF HOSTS, IF I WILL NOT OPEN YOU THE WINDOWS OF HEAVEN, AND POUR YOU OUT A BLESSING, THAT THERE SHALL NOT BE ROOM ENOUGH TO RECEIVE IT.**
**MALACHI 3:10**

PROVE. H974. Baw-khan': a primitive root; to test (especially metals); generally and figuratively to investigate; - examine, prove, tempt, try (trial).

People might believe this is putting Christians under the law, and not under grace and faith, but a lot of people do not understand faith and grace. If you wake up in the morning, it is by the grace of God. If you are healthy, it is by the grace of God. If you are wealthy, it is by the grace of God. If you are wise, it is by the grace of God. If you have a revelation, it is by the grace of God. If you have joy, it is by the grace of God. If you are God's chosen, it is by the grace of God. We cannot earn our health, or our wealth, or our wisdom, or our happiness. However, God will do what he pleases with what belongs to Him and *all of creation belongs to God*!

If God says be obedient, give to the poor, and I will pour you out a blessing, then we must have faith that he can and he will pour us out a blessing. He is testing us by allowing us to test him. He is allowing us a chance to believe by experience and by believing His Word. Do we have enough faith to be obedient and prove God? The Book of James explains that faith is not just hearing, but obeying and doing the Word of God.

**BUT BE YE "DOERS" OF THE WORD, AND NOT HEARERS ONLY, DECEIVING YOUR OWN SELVES. FOR IF ANY BE A HEARER OF THE WORD, AND NOT A DOER, HE IS LIKE UNTO A MAN BEHOLDING HIS NATURAL FACE IN A GLASS:**
**FOR HE BEHOLDETH HIMSELF, AND GOETH HIS WAY, AND STRAIGHTWAY FORGETTETH WHAT MANNER OF MAN HE WAS.**
**BUT WHOSO LOOKETH INTO THE PERFECT LAW OF LIBERTY, AND CONTINUETH THEREIN, HE BEING NOT A FORGETFUL HEARER, BUT A DOER OF THE WORK, THIS MAN SHALL BE BLESSED IN HIS DEED.**
**JAMES 1:22-25**

First we need to *know* God's Word, then we must *believe* God's Word, then we must *do/obey* God's Word. Of course if we do not believe, we will not give money to the poor, we will not study to show ourselves approved, and we will continue on as we did before salvation. This does not mean you can blindly give tithes and offerings to your church, pastor, preacher, priest, evangelist, or favorite charity and expect God to pour you out a blessing. In the Old Testament, the priest had specific duties:

1) The priest offers *oblations* to God. *See* Leviticus 2:4. An oblation is merely a present we give God. Something to show our love and affection, just like a present we would give to anybody else we love.
2) The priest examines all offerings. *See* Leviticus 1:10. We are to give God the best we have and not our second hand junk.

3) The priest offers sin offerings. *See* Leviticus 4:3. We know that Jesus, as our High Priest, has made the final and perfect sin offering for ever, and ever, for all believers. *See* Hebrews 10:12

4) The priest intercedes for the people. *See* Numbers 16:47 and Leviticus 16:13. We know that Jesus is our High Priest and intercedes for all believers. *See* Hebrews 7:25

5) The priest examines the sick. *See* Leviticus Ch. 12, 13,14 and 15. We know that by/with his stripes we ARE healed. *See* I Peter 2:24 and Isaiah 53:5.

6) The priest taught the Law and the knowledge of God. *See* II Chronicles 17:9 and 30:22.

7) The priest accepts tithes to care for their needs and to care for the poor. *See* Deuteronomy 26:12. We know that Christians must care for the poor. *See* Matthew 19:21, Luke 14:13, John 12:6, John 13:29, Romans 15:26, Galatians 2:10. We should make sure that when we contribute money or gifts to a church or charity, they are actually helping the needy and the poor with a good portion of our contribution.

The Old Testament Priests served a great many functions: Social Services, Public Health, Law and Education, etc. Giving a tenth or a tithe of what we earn for all these services seems pretty cheap compared to modern times. If you give to good causes and especially to the poor, there are numerous promises by God in the Old and New Testament that you will prosper.

**GIVE, AND IT SHALL BE GIVEN UNTO YOU; GOOD MEASURE, PRESSED DOWN, AND SHAKEN TOGETHER, AND RUNNING OVER, SHALL MEN GIVE UNTO YOUR BOSOM. FOR WITH THE SAME MEASURE THAT YE METE WITHAL IT SHALL BE MEASURED TO YOU AGAIN.**
**LUKE 6:38**

You might say, "I pay 30% or more of everything I earn in taxes to the government and a lot of my taxes are going to help the poor." You are right, many people do pay a large portion of their income to the government. Unfortunately, only a small portion goes to feeding and taking care of the poor. That is why giving to the poor is so important if you really want to prosper. When you specifically give to a church or charity that takes care of the poor, you will get more bang for your buck, so to speak. God has specifically promised in both the Old and New Testament to take care of people who are generous to the poor.

**FOR GOD LOVETH A CHEERFUL GIVER.**
**II CORINTHIANS 9:7 AND SEE DEUTERONOMY 15:7-10**

Now there might be some people who say, "Wait a second, God isn't talking about giving to the poor, He is talking about giving to support the church, or synagogue, or temple. These people are wrong! The Apostle Paul collected offerings for the *poor* saints in Jerusalem, but he supported himself and those with him by working. See Romans 15:26-27.

I HAVE COVETED NO MAN'S SILVER, OR GOLD, OR APPAREL.
YEA, YE YOURSELVES KNOW, THAT THESE HANDS HAVE MINISTERED UNTO MY NECESSITIES, AND TO THEM THAT WERE WITH ME.
I HAVE SHOWN YOU ALL THINGS, HOW THAT SO LABOURING YE OUGHT TO SUPPORT THE WEAK, AND TO REMEMBER THE WORDS OF THE LORD JESUS, HOW HE SAID, IT IS MORE BLESSED TO GIVE THAN TO RECEIVE.
ACTS 20:33-35

We should support missionaries and others who devote their lives to sharing the gospel with the lost, but our main responsibility is to share our blessings with our brothers and sisters in Christ, and with a lost and desperate world. Giving of our time and resources is a manifestation of God's blessing in our own life, and offers us an opportunity to share with the lost world the good news, and the source of our great blessings and abundance.

The source of all God's blessing is *believing* in God's Word (Jesus Christ). We do not give to get. We give because we have access to an inexhaustible supply. We give because we have access to our Father's inexhaustible abundance and riches.

IS NOT THIS THE FAST THAT I HAVE CHOSEN? TO LOOSE THE BANDS OF WICKEDNESS, TO UNDO THE HEAVY BURDENS, AND TO LET THE OPPRESSED GO FREE, AND THAT YE BREAK EVERY YOKE?
IS IT NOT TO DEAL THY BREAD TO THE HUNGRY, AND THAT THOU BRING THE POOR THAT ARE CAST OUT TO THY HOUSE? WHEN THOU SEEST THE NAKED, THAT THOU COVER HIM; AND THAT THOU HIDE NOT THYSELF FROM THINE OWN FLESH?
THEN SHALL THY LIGHT BREAK FORTH AS THE MORNING, AND THINE HEALTH SHALL SPRING FORTH SPEEDILY: AND THY RIGHTEOUSNESS SHALL GO BEFORE THEE; THE GLORY OF THE LORD SHALL BE THY REREWARD.
THEN SHALT THOU CALL, AND THE LORD SHALL ANSWER; THOU SHALT CRY, AND HE SHALL SAY, HERE I AM. IF THOU TAKE AWAY FROM THE MIDST OF THEE THE YOKE, THE PUTTING FORTH OF THE FINGER, AND SPEAKING VANITY.
AND IF THOU DRAW OUT THY SOUL TO THE HUNGRY, AND SATISFY THE AFFLICTED SOUL; THEN SHALL THY LIGHT RISE IN OBSCURITY AND THY DARKNESS BE AS THE NOONDAY.
AND THE LORD SHALL GUIDE THEE CONTINUALLY, AND SATISFY THY SOUL IN DROUGHT, AND MAKE FAT THY BONES: AND THOU SHALT BE LIKE A WATERED GARDEN, AND LIKE A SPRING OF WATER, WHOSE WATERS FAIL NOT.
ISAIAH 58:6-11

I think a lot of rich atheists understand what a lot of poor Christians do not understand. If you really want to prosper you MUST *give* to the poor and feed the hungry! God is not a respecter of persons. God will bless an obedient atheist more than a disobedient Christian.

You might ask, "Then why be a Christian if I can be an atheist and prosper?"

The answer is simple, no matter how happy, healthy and wealthy an atheist is, he is still going to hell, but no matter how pitiful, sick and poor a Christian is, he still has eternal life. I must say however, a pitiful, poor, sickly, immature Christian gives a pretty poor testimony to the world. Remember, we are not talking about salvation, we are talking about *walking in the spirit* and being a mature Christian. God is not saying, "You scratch my back and I'll scratch your back." God does not need anybody to scratch His back!

You cannot out give God. You cannot earn your way into heaven, and giving to the poor is not a business deal with God. God is simply saying in Deuteronomy 15:10 that if you trust His Word, and are obedient to His Word by giving to the poor, He will make sure that you will prosper and be blessed. When you are stingy, when you do not give to the poor, it is a sure sign of unbelief and immaturity in the spirit. God can bless as he sees fit, and if he promises to prosper those who are generous to the poor, I suggest we all start being generous to the poor. Giving to the poor is the one time that God asks us to test Him.

### HE THAT GIVETH UNTO THE POOR SHALL NOT LACK: PROVERBS 28:27

Great wealth without spiritual maturity is a very dangerous thing. Please do not read this book and only start pursuing great wealth. I believe it is not only possible, but assured that a person will become very prosperous if they set aside at least a tenth of their earnings to help the poor; however, great wealth without wisdom is not a blessing, it is a curse. I knew a young man whose father died and left him a large inheritance. He died within a year of a drug overdose. It is more important to leave your children an example of righteousness than great wealth.

A serious danger that rich atheist *and* rich Christians face is the enjoyment of prosperity that is directly linked to their charity to the poor. It is easy to believe we have it all together if we are enjoying the best this world has to offer. We eat the best foods. We live in big, comfortable homes. We travel where we want to go. We have all the gadgets that we need to occupy our abundant free time. It is easy to start believing we are God's special people. We have it all worked out.

However, if people look a little deeper, they will notice that these prosperous people hate their jobs. They disrespect their spouse. They do not exhibit the fruits of the spirit: love, joy, peace, longsuffering, gentleness, goodness, faith and they live pretty miserable lives. Do not think because you are blessed in material things, you are necessarily on the right path. If you are not experiencing joy unspeakable, and the peace of God, which passeth all understanding, you have not reached the destination God has prepared for you.

# CHAPTER 13

## THE DEVIL AND DEMONS ARE REAL

Not only the Old and New Testament, but many ancient texts and writings speak of invisible entities, which every so often cross the paths of ordinary people. Usually, when this happens, the meeting is a precursor to extraordinary events. Ancient peoples, and some not so ancient, have even sought these entities out. However, there is an old saying, "Beware of what you want, because you might get it."

According to ancient literature and legend, almost every culture has some type of dealings with these invisible entities. The ancient Greeks called these entities daimon.

DEVIL. G1142. Dah'ee-mown: from daio (to distribute fortunes); a daemon or supernatural spirit (of a bad nature): - devil.

Arab tradition called these entities *jinn*. These were supernatural beings that could take on human or animal form, and they often sought to influence human affairs. The word *jinn* is probably the root of the word *genius*. It was the Latin belief that a *genius*, or guardian spirit, was assigned to a person at birth. It is also the modern name we give someone who displays a very high intellectual endowment. It was the ancient belief that anyone who displayed some extraordinary ability must have obtained the favor of some powerful invisible entity. Much of ancient mankind's time, energy and resources were spent attempting to obtain the favor of these entities, or at least trying to appease them. This is also where we get the idea of the *familiar spirit*. It was believed that a *familiar spirit* could attach itself to a family and be passed down from generation to generation.

**Familiar** means an intimate; a close companion or formerly, a demon or evil spirit is believed to act as an intimate servant; a familiar spirit.

Much of the practice of *sorcery* was an attempt to appease or control these invisible entities. The *spirit* would then be used to benefit the sorcerer and to cause harm to his or her enemies. The Word of God is adamant; we are not to seek out the friendship of invisible entities. A great deal of Jesus Christ's time was spent delivering people from demonic oppression. Most, if not all, disease and infirmity in the New Testament was directly attributed to demon activity and apparently it can begin in infancy.

AND THEY BROUGHT HIM UNTO HIM: AND WHEN HE SAW HIM, STRAIGHTAWAY THE SPIRIT TARE HIM; AND HE FELL ON THE GROUND, AND WALLOWED FOAMING.
AND HE ASKED HIS FATHER, HOW LONG IS IT AGO SINCE THIS CAME UNTO HIM? AND HE SAID, OF A CHILD.
AND OFTTIMES IT HATH CAST HIM INTO THE FIRE, AND INTO THE WATERS, TO DESTROY HIM: BUT IF THOU CANST DO ANY THING, HAVE COMPASSION ON US, AND HELP US.
JESUS SAID UNTO HIM, IF THOU CANST BELIEVE, ALL THINGS ARE POSSIBLE TO HIM THAT BELIEVETH.

AND STRAIGHTAWAY THE FATHER OF THE CHILD CRIED OUT, AND SAID WITH TEARS, LORD, I BELIEVE; HELP THOU MINE UNBELIEF.

WHEN JESUS SAW THAT THE PEOPLE CAME RUNNING TOGETHER, HE REBUKED THE FOUL SPIRIT, SAYING UNTO HIM. THOU DUMB AND DEAF SPIRIT, I CHARGE THEE, COME OUT OF HIM, AND ENTER NO MORE INTO HIM.

AND THE SPIRIT CRIED, AND RENT HIM SORE, AND CAME OUT OF HIM: AND HE WAS AS ONE DEAD INSOMUCH THAT MANY SAID, HE IS DEAD.

BUT JESUS TOOK HIM BY THE HAND, AND LIFTED HIM UP; AND HE AROSE.

MARK 9:20-27

People like to believe there are invisible entities protecting them (angels), but people do not want to believe there are invisible evil entities (demons) out to get them, and frankly I do not blame them. There was a time when I had my doubts about the reality of angels and demons. I have been reading the Bible fairly regularly since I was about twelve years old, and I thought I believed in angels and demons, but truthfully for a long time, I probably did not. A portion of my family is religious and portion of my family is agnostic/atheistic. However, the agnostic/atheistic portion is getting smaller all the time. Praise God!

Even though I have professed myself a Christian since I was twelve years old, if anybody talked about angels or demons, I tended to take this type of talk with a grain of salt. I was a realist, if I could not see it or touch it, I did not worry about it too much. I liked to think I was opened minded, but I did not want to go off the deep end and have people think I was a nut.

One night I experienced a visit by a shadow entity (a demon). When I was in my early twenties, I woke up one night with a shadow of a man standing next to my bed. When I saw this person in my dark bedroom, it seemed to have substance, but I couldn't make out any details or features. The shadow walked to the foot of my bed and then I asked, "Who are you?"

Immediately, the shadow came to the head of my bed, grabbed my throat and started choking me. I grabbed one of its thumbs with my right hand, but could not pull its hands from around my throat. I couldn't breathe or speak and after a moment, I let loose of its thumb and soon thereafter, it released its hands from around my throat. Then it started walking back to the foot of my bed. I sat up with a shout and grabbed at it, but my hand hit the wall and it disappeared.

I sat in bed with my heart pounding. I turned on the light, looked around and I thought, 'that was the weirdest dream I've ever had.' I had a classic fear reaction, my skin was crawling, my heart was pounding and the hair on the back of my neck was standing up. I went out into the hallway, turned on the light and looked around. The experience was so real! Needless to say, I slept with my light on for awhile after that experience.

I told my older sister about the experience the next day and she told me it was a demon. She then reminded me of something that happened to her when I was attending college at Oregon State University. At the time, she lived in Salem, Oregon, and I had visited her during the weekend. She told me that one night she heard her oldest son gasping for air and thrashing around, but when she went to check on him, he was sleeping peacefully. She said that strange things were happening to him when he slept in his bedroom. When other people would stay with her and sleep in his room, they would also experience breathing problems.

One night, my cousin stayed in the room and she said she woke up with a shadow of a man on top of her, and she could not breath or *speak*. My cousin finally was able to whisper, "Jesus", and the shadow fled. My sister decided to get rid of the thing and had some of our cousins come over, and bind any demons in her house by the authority of Jesus Christ.

My sister said they went through every room of her house binding any spirit in the name of Jesus. She said that when she came to the second floor, she saw the shadow of what looked like a man running from one side of the hall, and then it disappeared through a wall. I remembered when she first told me, I thought, 'Linda's going a little overboard with her religion,' but after my own strange experience, I began to believe her and I thought, 'Why would a demon be attacking me?'

At the time, I was working as a janitor at what was called the "Professional Building" in Richland, Washington. It was where Westinghouse Engineers had their offices at the time. I worked swing shift vacuuming the carpets, washing windows and emptying the waste baskets.

Approximately two weeks after my demon experience, a young man started working with me. He professed to be a Witch. The first night I went to the break room, he was sitting cross legged on the floor pulling little pieces of wood, similar to scrabble pieces, from a satin bag. He was different looking because he had very short hair, at the time most young men I knew grew their hair long. I asked him what he was doing, and he told me the symbols on the little pieces of wood were *runes* (old Norse alphabet). He used them to tell the future. Of course I was intrigued, he was the first professing Witch I had ever met.

He told me all kinds of fantastic stories about his travels. He told me about visiting a town populated with spiritualists, being chased by spirits, astral projecting out of his body and other strange stories. I try to keep an open mind, but he seemed to be pretty far out there. I figured he must have used a lot of mind altering drugs.

Then he asked me if I had ever been to the Yakima Delta. The Yakima Delta is where the Yakima River empties into the Columbia River in Washington State. It is a public park with a lot of willows and cottonwoods, kind of an oasis in the desert. I had been there many times fishing, and I had attended high school beer parties there at night.

After I told him that I had been to the Yakima Delta before, he emphasized to me that he did not drink or take drugs. Obviously, he suspected what I was thinking. Then he told me that he had been attacked by a spirit while he was at the Yakima Delta. He said that he had actually physically wrestled with it.

I was thinking, 'Man this guy has really lost his marbles.' Then I asked him what this spirit looked like and he said, "It's about as tall as you, it's shaped like a man, but it was all black, like a shadow."

My eyes must have been as big as saucers, I said, "Do you believe in coincidence?" He told me that he didn't believe in coincidence. Then I told him what had happened to me when I was sleeping in my bedroom two weeks before. I also told him that I was a Christian, and that I believed that what had attacked us was a demon. I told him that he better stop practicing witchcraft or eventually the demon would probably kill him. He assured me that he had power to fight the spirit, and he showed me a hunting knife with magic runes carved into the blade.

We both quit that job shortly after that, and I have always wondered what happened to him, whether he was dead or alive. After that experience, I have never doubted that demons exist, that they can manifest themselves physically, and that they desire to harm me and others. I have told the story to many people since then, and I am amazed at how many other people have had the same or similar experiences with demons or shadow people.

PUT ON THE WHOLE ARMOUR OF GOD, THAT YE MAY BE ABLE TO STAND AGAINST THE WILES OF THE DEVIL.
FOR WE WRESTLE NOT AGAINST FLESH AND BLOOD, BUT AGAINST PRINCIPALITIES, AGAINST POWERS, AGAINST THE RULERS OF THE DARKNESS OF THIS WORLD, AGAINST SPIRITUAL WICKEDNESS IN HIGH PLACES.
EPHESIANS 6:11-12

There is a radio show on late at night that occasionally talks about the *shadow* people called *Coast to Coast*. Apparently, *shadow* people (demons) are manifesting themselves on a fairly regular basis these days because there seems to be no shortage of people with stories about them in the United States. I would not be surprised if they are common all over the world.

One characteristic that demons seem to share is they take peoples breath away. This is not surprising since the word for breath is interchangeable with the word for spirit in many languages. Also, people are not able to *speak* and are often paralyzed when these demons manifest themselves. Considering that the *spoken* Word of God is also our spiritual sword, it makes sense they would attempt to disarm us by prevent us from *speaking*.

Some ideas and thoughts come to us, ideas and thoughts do not always come from us.

Let me say it again, some ideas and thoughts come to us, ideas and thoughts do not always come from us. Our mind (soul) is similar to a very sophisticated radio. We can tune into different frequencies and wavelengths. We can receive messages from different sources. Sometimes these sources are not looking out for our best interests. The most obvious example of this phenomena occurred after the Lord Jesus told His disciples that He would be killed and raised again on the third day:

**THEN PETER TOOK HIM, AND BEGAN TO REBUKE HIM, SAYING, BE IT FAR FROM THEE, LORD: THIS SHALL NOT BE UNTO THEE.**
**BUT HE TURNED, AND SAID TO PETER, GET THEE BEHIND ME, SATAN: THOU ART AN OFFENCE UNTO ME: FOR THOU SAVOUREST NOT THE THINGS THAT BE OF GOD, BUT THOSE THAT BE OF MEN.**
**MATTHEW 10:22-23**

Do you see that Jesus recognized the source of Peter's rebuke and immediately came against Satan?

Yes, Satan will use those closest to us in order to prevent us from obeying God. Most of the time, however, the devil will attempt to persuade us by giving us his own thoughts, and try to make us believe his ideas are our own ideas.

**ABOVE ALL, TAKING THE SHIELD OF FAITH, WHEREWITH YE SHALL BE ABLE TO QUENCH ALL THE FIERY DARTS OF THE WICKED.**
**EPHESIANS 6:16**

The fiery darts of the wicked are the evil thoughts sent in our direction by devils. The Devil cannot force us to do what he wants us to do, but he can send sinful thoughts in our direction and hope they find a weak spot. We can drink alcohol and tune into a different frequency. We can take drugs and tune into a different frequency. We can listen to music and tune into a different frequency. We can practice different religious and meditation techniques and tune into a different frequency. There are all kinds of ways that we can change our frequency, and receive thoughts and ideas that are not from us.

People often think they are receiving thoughts or inspiration from God, but their inspiration or revelation is coming from a very different place. That is why it is so important to know the Word of God, and that is why it is so important to commit God's inspired Word to memory, otherwise we can easily be led astray. Any inspiration you receive from God must conform perfectly with the written Word of God (the Bible), if it does not, it is not from God.

**KNOWING THIS FIRST, THAT NO PROPHECY OF THE SCRIPTURE IS OF ANY PRIVATE INTERPRETATION.**
**FOR THE PROPHECY CAME NOT IN OLD TIME BY THE WILL OF MAN; BUT HOLY MEN OF GOD SPAKE AS THEY WERE MOVED BY THE HOLY GHOST.**
**2 PETER 1:20-21**

There have been many men and women who have started whole new cults and church movements after they have received a "new" revelation. Sad to say, many of these new revelations were in direct contradiction to the Word of God. All I can say is, they may have been getting a new revelation, but it was not from God.

I was talking with my little sister one day and I asked her, "Are People that smoke pot really funny, or did they just seem funny because I was smoking pot too?"

She said, "No, people who smoke pot are really funny, I've been around a lot of people smoking pot when I wasn't smoking pot and they are really funny."

When I thought about it, I realized a lot of the time I spent smoking pot and drinking alcohol, I would talk with different people, and they had what seemed to be really profound thoughts and ideas. You have to realize that the people I smoked pot with were teenagers and young adults, and they weren't exactly Albert Einstein or Isaac Newton.

It was after I talked with my sister that I began to understand that taking drugs is a means to open doors into the spiritual realm. If you have ever read books by *Carlos Casteneda*, you probably know that shamans have been using mind altering drugs to contact spirit entities for a very long time. I believe God created us to interact with the spirit world because He is a Spirit; however, we have left the path God meant for us and have, often times unknowingly, made contact with spiritual forces beyond our understanding.

**GOD IS A SPIRIT: AND THEY THAT WORSHIP HIM MUST WORSHIP HIM IN SPIRIT AND IN TRUTH.**
**JOHN 4:24**

Just because you hear a radio commercial urging you to buy a car, you should not automatically grab your checkbook and run down to the nearest car dealer. A lot of people believe that every idea that pops into their head is their idea and it leads to many problems. Of course our major problem is *sin*, when a thought comes to us, which indulges the flesh, our natural minds will dwell on it because, prior to spiritual maturity, we are carnally minded and eventually we will act on it, ignoring the warnings from our *intuition* and *conscience*.

Our mind/soul is a great battle field. There are multitudes of evil, seducing spirits in the world. These evil spirits can send us thoughts that will seduce us into indulging our fleshly appetites. Without divine protection, we will fail every time.

Over a period of time, if we continually ignore our *conscience* and *intuition*, we eventually become so disobedient that our *intuition* and *conscience* no longer work. Eventually, because of non-use, our *intuition* will atrophy, and we become spiritual cripples. We tune into the devil's frequency, and all that we can hear is seducing spirits, then we come under complete bondage. A sure sign of demon possession is the lack of control of our own tongue.

**AND THE TONGUE IS A FIRE, A WORLD OF INIQUITY; SO IS THE TONGUE AMONG OUR MEMBERS, THAT IT DEFILETH THE WHOLE BODY, AND SETTETH ON FIRE THE COURSE OF NATURE; AND IT IS SET ON FIRE OF HELL.**
**JAMES 3:6**

The devil will always come using three (3) methods of attack because they are mankind's carnal weak spots:

LOVE NOT THE WORLD, NEITHER THE THINGS *THAT ARE* IN THE WORLD. IF ANY MAN LOVE THE WORLD, THE LOVE OF THE FATHER IS NOT IN HIM.
FOR ALL THAT IS IN THE WORLD, **(1)** THE LUST OF THE FLESH, AND **(2)** THE LUST OF THE EYES, AND **(3)** THE PRIDE OF LIFE, IS NOT OF THE FATHER, BUT IS OF THE WORLD.
I JOHN 2: 15-16

Let us see how the devil seduces Eve, the mother of all mankind:

NOW THE SERPENT WAS MORE SUBTIL *(CUNNING)* THAN ANY BEAST OF THE FIELD WHICH THE LORD GOD HAD MADE. AND HE SAID UNTO THE WOMAN, YEA, HATH GOD SAID, YE SHALL NOT EAT OF EVERY TREE OF THE GARDEN?
AND THE WOMAN SAID UNTO THE SERPENT. WE MAY EAT OF THE FRUIT OF THE TREES OF THE GARDEN:
BUT OF THE FRUIT OF THE TREE WHICH IS IN THE MIDST OF THE GARDEN. GOD HATH SAID, YE SHALL NOT EAT OF IT, NEITHER SHALL YE TOUCH IT, LEST YE DIE.
AND THE SERPENT SAID UNTO THE WOMAN, YE SHALL NOT SURELY DIE.
FOR GOD DOTH KNOW THAT IN THE DAY YE EAT THEREOF, THEN YOUR EYES SHALL BE OPENED, AND YE SHALL BE AS GODS, KNOWING GOOD AND EVIL.
AND WHEN THE WOMAN SAW THAT THE TREE *WAS* GOOD FOR FOOD *(LUST OF THE FLESH)*, AND THAT IT WAS PLEASANT TO THE EYES *(LUST OF THE EYES)*, AND A TREE TO BE DESIRED TO MAKE *ONE* WISE *(PRIDE OF LIFE)*, SHE TOOK OF THE FRUIT THEREOF, AND DID EAT, AND GAVE ALSO UNTO HER HUSBAND WITH HER; AND HE DID EAT.
GENESIS 3:1-6

A seducing spirit will always come questioning God's Word in order to create doubt in the heart (mind). If you want to kill and destroy someone, the first thing you will attempt to do is disarm them. A seducing spirit will always cast doubt on God's Word, and tempt us with the lust of our flesh, the lust of our eyes and the pride of life.

Without God's divine protection, and without knowing how to fight a spiritual battle, we will eventually succumb to sin, and rebel against God's commandments, which is what the devil desires. The devil wants us to doubt God and believe the devil's lies because then we are defenseless. The seducing spirit's chief desire is to capture our spirits (the Temple of God), and take up residence with our spirit, where only God is suppose to dwell, in the Holy of Holies, and finally to become our Lord in place of God. I believe a person can be devil possessed without appearing out of the ordinary. All self-destructive behavior is related to demonic influence or outright possession.

We can also tune into the God frequency. We can become very receptive to God by continually *memorizing* and *meditating* upon His Word. As we fill up our soul and spirit with God's Word, our spirit will begin to grow, mature, and become more and more sensitive to the voice of God's Holy Spirit. *Speaking* the Word of God *tunes out* the devil's frequency and *tunes in* God's frequency!

God always communicates first to our spirit (*intuition* or *conscience*), then to our soul (*revelation*), then to our flesh (*meditation*) and finally to the world (*logos; spoken word*).

Seducing spirits work in the opposite direction, they communicate from the world to our flesh (*lust of the eyes, lust of the flesh, pride of life*), then to our soul (*sinful thoughts*), and eventually to our spirit (*eliminating the conscience and intuition*). When they finally reach a person's spirit, they take the person captive: body, soul and spirit.

The possessed person will eventually be in total subjugation to demonic spirit(s). The unclean spirit(s) will then take up residence within the spirit of a person's body, in the temple of God. The unclean spirit(s) every desire will also become the possessed person's desire. I believe people only start to act strange when they have several demonic spirits residing in their spirit. If you want a detailed understanding of the Spirit, Soul and Body, I recommend reading *The Spiritual Man* by Watchman Nee.

**THE THIEF COMETH NOT, BUT FOR TO "STEAL", AND TO "KILL", AND TO "DESTROY": I AM COME THAT THEY MIGHT HAVE LIFE, AND THAT THEY MIGHT HAVE IT MORE ABUNDANTLY.**
**JOHN 10:10**

The Devil will do everything possible to lead you away from God because as long as you stay close to God, you cannot be harmed. There is a reason many of the mighty men of the Bible were shepherds: Abraham, Joseph, Moses, and David were all shepherds.

They must have had revelation from God that just like the sheep are in greatest danger when they wander away from the shepherd, mankind is in greatest danger and most vulnerable, when they wander away from God. We are only safe when we keep close to God. We stay close to God by *knowing,* and having *faith* in His Word.

**THE LORD IS MY SHEPHERD; I SHALL NOT WANT.**
**HE MAKETH ME TO LIE DOWN IN GREEN PASTURES; HE LEADETH ME BESIDE THE STILL WATERS.**
**HE RESTORETH MY SOUL: HE LEADETH ME IN THE PATHS OF RIGHTEOUSNESS FOR HIS NAME'S SAKE.**
**PSALM 23:1-3**

A person becomes demon possessed after constantly and willfully leaving God's protection, and submitting to the thoughts given to him or her by seducing spirits and ignoring the Word of God.

The seducing spirit wants to lead a person away from God and His protection. The seducing spirit's chief desire is fulfilled, when the unclean spirit can become Lord in place of God and take up residence, where only God is supposed to dwell, with the possessed person's spirit. Then, instead of being priests of God's temple and stewards of God's creation, the evil spirit will use the possessed person's words to steal God's promises, destroy faith in God, and kill God's temple and his creation.

# CHAPTER 14

## DEVILS CAN POSSESS A CHRISTIAN WHO COMMITS FORNICATION

The devil will immediately start presenting various temptations to Christians after salvation. I am not a legalist, but there are a few things a Christian must absolutely avoid. I believe a Christian cannot be demon possessed unless they *invite* the demon(s) into their body. *Yes, I believe a Christian can potentially become demon possessed*!

I know a lot of people are going to say that I do not know what I am talking about, after all doesn't the Bible say:

GREATER IS HE THAT IS IN YOU, THAN HE THAT IS IN THE WORLD.
I JOHN 4:4

I do *not* believe that a demon can possess the body of a Christian who has the Holy Ghost residing in his/her spirit. However, I do believe a Christian can grieve the Holy Spirit and cause Him to leave. In which case, I guess they would no longer be a Christian. The New Testament specifically says that the believer's body is the temple of God:

KNOW YE NOT THAT YE ARE THE TEMPLE OF GOD, AND THAT THE SPIRIT OF GOD DWELLETH IN YOU?
IF ANY MAN "DEFILE" THE TEMPLE OF GOD, HIM SHALL GOD DESTROY; FOR THE TEMPLE OF GOD IS HOLY, WHICH TEMPLE YE ARE.
I CORINTHIANS 3:16-17

DEFILE. G5351. Fthi'-ro: probably strengthened from *phthio* ( to pine or waste); properly, to shrivel or wither, i.e. to spoil (by any process) or (generally) to ruin (especially figuratively by moral influences, to deprave): - corrupt (self), defile, destroy.

We see that God takes action when somebody defiles His temple. If you are a Christian, your body is God's temple. I would like to use the Old Testament as an example again.

Remember that the Old Testament contains stories that are object lessons for believers. First, we see an example of the glory of the Lord filling the Tabernacle when the children of Israel were wandering in the wilderness, and the glory of the Lord also fills the House of the Lord after the dedication of Solomon:

THEN A CLOUD COVERED THE TENT OF THE CONGREGATION, AND THE GLORY OF THE LORD FILLED THE TABERNACLE.
AND MOSES WAS NOT ABLE TO ENTER INTO THE TENT OF THE CONGREGATION, BECAUSE THE CLOUD ABODE THEREON, AND THE GLORY OF THE LORD FILLED THE TABERNACLE.
EXODUS 40:34-35

AND IT CAME TO PASS, WHEN THE PRIESTS WERE COME OUT OF THE HOLY PLACE, THAT THE CLOUD FILLED THE HOUSE OF THE LORD,
SO THAT THE PRIESTS COULD NOT STAND TO MINISTER BECAUSE OF THE CLOUD: FOR THE GLORY OF THE LORD HAD FILLED THE HOUSE OF THE LORD.
I KINGS 8:10-11

When the glory of God fills the tabernacle and temple in the Old Testament, it serves as an example of the infilling by the Holy Ghost of a Christian after salvation. Second, we see an example of the glory of the Lord *leaving* the temple:

THEN THE GLORY OF THE LORD WENT UP FROM THE CHERUB, AND STOOD OVER THE THRESHOLD OF THE HOUSE.
EZEKIEL 10:4
THEN THE GLORY OF THE LORD DEPARTED FROM OFF THE THRESHOLD OF THE HOUSE, AND STOOD OVER THE CHERUBIMS.
EZEKIEL 10:18

AND THE GLORY OF THE LORD WENT UP FROM THE MIDST OF THE CITY, AND STOOD UPON THE MOUNTAIN WHICH IS ON THE EAST SIDE OF THE CITY.
EZEKIEL 11:23

Why did the glory of the Lord leave the temple in Ezekiel's day?

SON OF MAN, SEEST THOU WHAT THEY DO? EVEN THE GREAT ABOMINATIONS THAT THE HOUSE OF ISRAEL COMMITTETH HERE, THAT I SHOULD GO FAR OFF FROM MY SANCTUARY?
EZEKIEL 8:6

AND HE SAID UNTO ME, GO IN, AND BEHOLD THE WICKED ABOMINATIONS THAT THEY DO HERE.
SO I WENT IN AND SAW; AND BEHOLD EVERY FORM OF CREEPING THINGS, AND ABOMINABLE BEASTS, AND ALL THE IDOLS OF THE HOUSE OF ISRAEL, PORTRAYED UPON THE WALL ROUND ABOUT.
EZEKIEL 8:9-10

In the spirit, God leads Ezekiel deeper and deeper into His temple, and shows the prophet that His temple has become a place of idol worship. His people have filled the house of the Lord with idols. The Apostle Paul said that people who worshipped idols are in actuality worshipping devils. *See* 1Corinthians 10:20.

God's people were *defiling* His temple and therefore God would not stay! When God leaves, His protection leaves as well. It was not long after God's departure that the Babylonians destroyed the temple at Jerusalem, and led the people of Israel into bondage. This serves as a terrible warning to Christians who believe God will never leave. I believe God when He says:

**I WILL NEVER LEAVE THEE, NOR FORSAKE THEE.**
**HEBREWS 13:5**

God will never leave or forsake us. However, I do believe, we can leave and forsake God. I have heard some preachers say, "Once saved always saved!" However, I do not agree with that doctrine at all. As a matter of fact, I believe it is a doctrine of devils. Many Christians are led to believe that once they are baptized, they can do any abomination that pops into their heads without any consequences, but throughout the New Testament, the church is warned not to grieve the Holy Spirit. I believe when a Christian invites devils into God's temple ... God *will leave*!

Who can help us then?

Jesus said there was only one reason a man could divorce His wife and that was for the sin of fornication. *See* Matthew 5:32. A husband and wife represent Jesus Christ and the Church. Jesus said a man can leave his wife for the sin of fornication without blame because God will also leave a person for the sin of fornication without blame. When a man or woman commits fornication after marriage, they lose all legal rights to their spouse. When we drink blood, or fornicate, or worship idols after we are saved, we also lose all rights to God's grace.

**FOR IT IS IMPOSSIBLE FOR THOSE WHO WERE ONCE ENLIGHTENED, AND HAVE TASTED OF THE HEAVENLY GIFT, AND WERE MADE PARTAKERS OF THE HOLY GHOST,**
**AND HAVE TASTED THE GOOD WORD OF GOD, AND THE POWERS OF THE WORLD TO COME.**
**IF THEY SHALL FALL AWAY, TO RENEW THEM AGAIN UNTO REPENTENCE; SEEING THEY CRUCIFY TO THEMSELVES THE SON OF GOD AFRESH, AND PUT HIM TO AN OPEN SHAME.**
**HEBREWS 6:4-6**

Why would so many books in the New Testament give us so many warnings, if it is impossible to lose our salvation?

**AND GRIEVE NOT THE HOLY SPIRIT OF GOD, WHEREBY YE ARE SEALED UNTO THE DAY OF REDEMPTION.**
**EPHESIANS 4:30**

**KNOW YE NOT THAT THE UNRIGHTEOUS SHALL NOT INHERIT THE KINGDOM OF GOD? BE NOT DECEIVED: NEITHER FORNICATORS, NOR IDOLATERS, NOR ADULTERERS, NOR EFFEMINATE, NOR ABUSERS OF THEMSELVES WITH MANKIND,**
**NOR THIEVES, NOR COVETOUS, NOR DRUNDARDS, NOR REVILERS, NOR EXTORTIONERS, SHALL INHERIT THE KINGDOM OF GOD.**
**I CORINTHIANS 6:9-10**

"Hold on," you say, "My minister says once saved always saved, you mean to tell me if I continue getting drunk and fornicating, the Holy Ghost might leave, and I will lose my salvation?"

I never said that ... the *Bible says that*! You see, we always have a choice. Throughout all of eternity we will have a choice, whether to serve God or not to serve God. We do not become automatons once we are saved, we still have free choice. I believe the main purpose God has for allowing sin and rebellion to run its course, is to illustrate to all of His creation the final destructive consequences of rebelling against God.

NOW THEREFORE FEAR THE LORD, AND SERVE HIM IN SINCERITY AND IN TRUTH; AND PUT AWAY THE GODS WHICH YOUR FATHERS SERVED ON THE OTHER SIDE OF THE FLOOD, AND IN EGYPT; AND SERVE YE THE LORD.
AND IF IT SEEM EVIL UNTO YOU TO SERVE THE LORD, CHOOSE YOU THIS DAY WHOM YE WILL SERVE, WHETHER THE GODS WHICH YOUR FATHERS SERVED THAT WERE ON THE OTHER SIDE OF THE FLOOD, OR THE GODS OF THE AMORITES, IN WHOSE LAND YE DWELL: BUT AS FOR ME AND MY HOUSE, WE WILL SERVE THE LORD.
JOSHUA 24:14-15

There are four main avenues by which people invite demons into God's temple:

FOR IT SEEMED GOOD TO THE HOLY GHOST, AND TO US, TO LAY UPON YOU NO GREATER BURDEN THAN THESE NECESSARY THINGS;
THAT YE ABSTAIN FROM 1) MEATS OFFERED TO "IDOLS", AND 2) FROM "BLOOD", AND 3) FROM THINGS "STRANGLED", AND 4) FROM "FORNICATION": FROM WHICH IF YE KEEP YOURSELVES, YE SHALL DO WELL. FARE YE WELL.
ACTS 15:28-29

Why do you think the Apostles identified these four things as activities necessary to avoid? I believe these four activities are hotbeds of demonic activity. If you avoid them, *you will do well*!

KNOW YE NOT THAT YOUR BODIES ARE THE MEMBERS OF CHRIST? SHALL I THEN TAKE THE MEMBERS OF CHRIST, AND MAKE THEM THE MEMBERS OF AN HARLOT? GOD FORBID.
WHAT? KNOW YE NOT THAT HE WHICH IS JOINED TO AN HARLOT IS ONE BODY? FOR TWO, SAITH HE, SHALL BE ONE FLESH.
BUT HE THAT IS JOINED UNTO THE LORD IS ONE SPIRIT.
FLEE "FORNICATION". EVERY SIN THAT A MAN DOETH IS WITHOUT THE BODY; BUT HE THAT COMMITTETH FORNICATION SINNETH AGAINST HIS OWN BODY.
WHAT? KNOW YE NOT THAT YOUR BODY IS THE TEMPLE OF THE HOLY GHOST WHICH IS IN YOU, WHICH YE HAVE OF GOD, AND YE ARE NOT YOUR OWN?

FORNICATION. G4202. Por-ni'-ah: harlotry (including adultery and incest); figuratively idolatry: - fornication.

In ancient times many heathen temples were also brothels. Young men and women were dedicated to a specific god (devil) and they had to have sex with the god's worshipers after the worshipers gave an offering at the temple. As you might imagine, this was a very lucrative business, and these ancient temples accumulated a great deal of wealth, power and influence. They also helped demons to possess and control people.

There is a very interesting story in the Old Testament concerning fornication and its consequences. Balaam was a prophet of God, and he apparently was quite renowned, but he came from the line of Esau. It is obvious that God can give revelation to anybody if they are willing and open to Him. Balaam was quite familiar with God. He told Balak, the King of Edom, God would not curse the Israelites and it was useless to ask. However, Balaam knew of a way to cause God's protection to leave Israel.

**AND ISRAEL ABODE IN SHITTIM, AND THE PEOPLE BEGAN TO COMMIT WHOREDOM WITH THE DAUGHTERS OF MOAB.**

**AND THEY CALLED THE PEOPLE UNTO THE SACRIFICES OF THEIR GODS: AND THE PEOPLE DID EAT, AND BOWED DOWN TO THEIR GODS.**

**AND ISRAEL JOINED HIMSELF UNTO BAAL-PEOR: AND THE ANGER OF THE LORD WAS KINDLED AGAINST ISRAEL.**

**NUMBERS 25:1-3**

Idolatry, fornication and devil worship are intimately connected throughout the Old Testament. They appear to be sins that go hand in hand. We only have hints in the Book of Numbers, but apparently Balaam counseled Balak to have the daughters of Moab entice the men of Israel to have sex with them as part of their worship ceremonies.

**THE CUP OF BLESSING WHICH WE BLESS, IS IT NOT THE COMMUNION OF THE BLOOD OF CHRIST? THE BREAD WHICH WE BREAK, IS IT NOT THE COMMUNION OF THE BODY OF CHRIST?**

**FOR WE BEING MANY ARE ONE BREAD, AND ONE BODY; FOR WE ARE ALL PARTAKERS OF THAT ONE BREAD.**

**BEHOLD ISRAEL AFTER THE FLESH: ARE NOT THEY WHICH EAT OF THE SACRIFICES PARTAKERS OF THE ALTAR?**

**WHAT SAY I THEN? THAT THE IDOL IS ANY THING, OR THAT WHICH IS OFFERED IN SACRIFICE TO IDOLS IS ANY THING?**

**BUT I SAY, THAT THE THINGS WHICH THE GENTILES SACRIFICE, THEY SACRIFICE TO DEVILS, AND NOT TO GOD: AND I WOULD NOT THAT YE SHOULD HAVE FELLOWSHIP WITH DEVILS.**

**YE CANNOT DRINK THE CUP OF THE LORD, AND THE CUP OF DEVILS: YE CANNOT BE PARTAKERS OF THE LORD'S TABLE, AND OF THE TABLE OF DEVILS.**

**I CORINTHIANS 10:16-21**

Paul the Apostle is comparing food offered to idols with the Holy Communion. He says they serve the same function. When we partake in Holy Communion, we are identifying with, and partaking in the body and blood of our Lord Jesus Christ. When we partake in food offered to idols, we are identifying with, and partaking in demonic spiritual activity.

There are many Christians these days that believe it is very liberal and open minded to participate with Hindus, or Buddhists, or Moslems, or Shamans, or New Age practitioners in their ceremonies. Live and let live, they say, Hindus, and Buddhists, and New Agers, and Moslems are good people, they are just on different paths to the same God.

Unfortunately, these Christians are placing themselves in very serious spiritual danger. Hindus, and Buddhist, and Moslems, and New Agers may be nice people, but their ceremonies and rituals are not paths to God. These different paths all lead directly to devils, demons, and to hell. Jesus Christ (the Word of God) is the *only* way to God the Father.

**JESUS SAITH UNTO HIM, I AM THE WAY, THE TRUTH, AND THE LIFE: "NO MAN" COMETH UNTO THE FATHER, BUT BY ME.**
**JOHN 14:6**

Drinking blood has long been associated with demonic activity in the Old Testament. Eating things which have been strangled is simply another method of partaking in blood. God said because of these abominable activities, which the Canaanites were participating in, the land literally spewed or vomited them out. Satan understands that if people begin to participate in these activities, sin becomes full. God's protection will leave them and God cannot forbear judgment anymore. The protection of God is lifted, devils are loosed to kill, steal and destroy.

There is a long list of perversions listed in Leviticus 17 and 18, these perversions that the Canaanites participated in are also clear signs that sin is bearing fruit and the judgment of God is eminent.

**AND THEY SHALL NO MORE OFFER THEIR SACRIFICES UNTO DEVILS, AFTER WHOM THEY HAVE GONE AWHORING.**
**LEVITICUS 17:7**

**YE SHALL EAT THE BLOOD OF NO MANNER OF FLESH: FOR THE LIFE OF ALL FLESH IS THE BLOOD THEREOF: WHOSOEVER EATETH IT SHALL BE CUT OFF.**
**LEVITICUS 17:14**

**MOREOVER THOU SHALT NOT LIE CARNALLY WITH THY NEIGHBOUR'S WIFE, TO DEFILE THYSELF WITH HER.**
**LEVITICUS 17:20**

**THOU SHALT NOT LIE WITH MANKIND, AS WITH WOMANKIND: IT IS ABOMINATION.**
**LEVITICUS 17:22**

**DEFILE NOT YE YOURSELVES IN ANY OF THESE THINGS: FOR IN ALL THESE THE NATIONS ARE DEFILED WHICH I CAST OUT BEFORE YOU:**
**AND THE LAND IS DEFILED: THEREFORE I DO VISIT THE INIQUITY THEREOF UPON IT, AND THE LAND ITSELF VOMITETH OUT HER INHABITANTS.**
**LEVITICUS 17:24-25**

Apparently, over time, sin gets progressively worse and worse until even the land cannot take it anymore. *Sin begins to bear fruit!* God told Abraham eventually the sins of the Amorites would be so great He would replace them with Abraham's descendents.

**BUT IN THE FOURTH GENERATION, THEY SHALL COME HITHER AGAIN: FOR THE INIQUITY OF THE AMORITES IS NOT YET FULL.**
**GENESIS 15:16**

What is so troubling is the fact that many of the sins that are specifically mentioned in the Old and New Testament as being abominations to God, and directly related to devils and idol worship are openly practiced by a great many people today, including people who claim to be Christians! I am afraid that the World and many Christians are being set up to welcome the son of perdition spoken of by Paul the Apostle:

**AND THEN SHALL THAT WICKED BE REVEALED, WHOM THE LORD SHALL CONSUME WITH THE SPIRIT OF HIS MOUTH, AND SHALL DESTROY WITH THE BRIGHTNESS OF HIS COMING:**

**EVEN HIM, WHOSE COMING IS AFTER THE WORKING OF SATAN WITH ALL POWER AND SIGNS AND LYING WONDERS.**

**AND WITH ALL DECEIVABLENESS OF UNRIGHTEOUSNESS IN THEM THAT PERISH; BECAUSE THEY RECEIVED NOT THE LOVE OF THE TRUTH, THAT THEY MIGHT BE SAVED.**

**AND FOR THIS CAUSE GOD SHALL SEND THEM STRONG DELUSION, THAT THEY SHOULD BELIEVE A LIE:**

**THAT THEY ALL MIGHT BE DAMNED WHO BELIEVED NOT THE TRUTH, BUT HAD PLEASURE IN UNRIGHTEOUSNESS.**
**2 THESSALONIANS 2:8-12**

# CHAPTER 15

## SATAN'S MASTER PLAN

The Bible reveals Satan's master plan:

(1) Possess a Man and Mankind
(2) Speak blasphemy against God
(3) Overcome the Saints of God
(4) Rule the Earth
(5) Make War on God

AND THEY WORSHIPPED THE DRAGON WHICH GAVE POWER (*AUTHORITY*) UNTO THE BEAST: AND THEY WORSHIPPED THE BEAST, SAYING, WHO IS LIKE UNTO THE BEAST? WHO IS ABLE TO MAKE WAR WITH HIM?
AND THERE WAS GIVEN UNTO HIM A MOUTH SPEAKING GREAT THINGS AND BLASPHEMIES; AND POWER (*AUTHORITY*) WAS GIVEN UNTO HIM TO CONTINUE FORTY *AND* TWO MONTHS (3 AND ½ YEARS).
AND HE OPENED HIS MOUTH IN BLASPHEMY AGAINST GOD, TO BLASPHEME HIS NAME, AND HIS TABERNACLE, AND THEM THAT DWELL IN HEAVEN.
AND IT WAS GIVEN UNTO HIM TO MAKE WAR WITH THE SAINTS, AND TO OVERCOME THEM: AND POWER (*AUTHORITY*) WAS GIVEN HIM OVER ALL KINDREDS (*TRIBES*), AND TONGUES, AND NATIONS.
AND ALL THAT DWELL UPON THE EARTH SHALL WORSHIP HIM, WHOSE NAMES ARE NOT WRITTEN IN THE BOOK OF LIFE OF THE LAMB SLAIN FROM THE FOUNDATION OF THE WORLD.
REVELATION 13:4-8

Eventually the Devil and his angels are cast into the earth. *See* Revelation 12:9. Satan possesses a man and uses that man to *speak* blasphemy. The Devil also uses words as weapons and to accomplish his purposes. The Devil understands better than anyone that words are dangerous weapons. The Devil will give his authority to a man to rule over the earth. We see Satan's plan is successful for forty-two months, but when he decides to gather his demon possessed army, and make war against God, his master plan quickly unravels, and the Saints of God make a big come back.

AND I SAW THE BEAST, AND THE KINGS OF THE EARTH, AND THEIR ARMIES, GATHERED TOGETHER TO MAKE WAR AGAINST HIM THAT SAT ON THE HORSE, AND AGAINST HIS ARMY.
AND THE BEAST WAS TAKEN (*CAPTURED*), AND WITH HIM THE FALSE PROPHET THAT WROUGHT MIRACLES BEFORE HIM, WITH WHICH HE DECEIVED THEM THAT HAD RECEIVED THE MARK OF THE BEAST, AND THEM THAT WORSHIPPED HIS IMAGE. THESE BOTH WERE CAST ALIVE INTO A LAKE OF FIRE BURNING WITH BRIMSTONE.
REVELATION 19:19-20

The question is, "Who will you choose to believe and serve?"

We were created to serve God. Do you want to be the temple of God or a haunt of demons? I know people will say, just because you are not a Christian does not mean you will become demon possessed. Perhaps they are correct now, but in the end of this *age*, I believe our only choice will either be to take the Mark of the Beast and be possessed by devil(s) or to accept Jesus Christ as LORD, and be full of the Holy Ghost. Let me repeat it again, either you will be the temple of the Father, the Son, and the Holy Ghost, or you will take the Mark of the Beast and be possessed by evil spirits.

You have probably figured out that I believe the Great Tribulation is drawing near, and the arrival of the Anti-Christ is at hand. You have also probably figured out that I believe the Church will be delivered through the Great Tribulation and not delivered out of it. I believe the Mark of the Beast is not only for the Beast to identify his followers, but for the Saints of God to identify the followers of the Beast. Remember, accepting the Mark of the Beast is an unforgiveable sin. *See* Revelation 14:9-10. Once someone takes the Mark of the Beast, they cannot be saved, they are forever in the enemies camp.

Therefore, *do not take the mark of the beast*! Also, whether it is your spouse, your child, your mother, or your brother, or your best friend, if they take the Mark *avoid them*. I believe the Mark of the Beast will be very obvious for everybody to recognize, so do not be afraid that you will be taking the Mark of the Beast unawares.

I believe there will be two types of Christians in the last day. We will either be a mature Christian, full of the Word of God, *walking in the spirit*, or a carnal Christian, who does not know the Word of God, carnal Christians walk in the flesh. The mature Christian will be similar to the two witnesses in the Book of Revelation:

**AND IF ANY MAN WILL HURT THEM, FIRE PROCEEDETH OUT OF THEIR "MOUTH", AND DEVOURETH THEIR ENEMIES: AND IF ANY MAN WILL HURT THEM, HE MUST IN THIS MANNER BE KILLED.**
**REVELATION 11:5**

The mature Christian will come and go as they are led by the Spirit of God. The mature Christian will be full of the *Word* of God and will not fear anybody. The Anti-Christ and his followers will be running and hiding from mature Christians.

The carnal Christian will be constantly afraid, running and hiding from the enemy, not knowing where to turn because they do not know the authority and power of God's *Word*. This type of Christians will be weak and afraid because they never knew Jesus Christ (The *Word* of God). The Devil and his followers will slaughter these types of Christians; or else false, so-called Christians, will turn in mass to accept the Mark of the Beast.

You might say, but what about the rapture? Isn't Jesus Christ going to rapture the Church before the Great Tribulation?

There are a lot of people I respect and admire who believe that the Church will be raptured (taken out of the world) before the Great Tribulation. There are also quite a few people who believe the Church will be raptured in the middle of the Great Tribulation. However, there are also a lot of people I respect who believe the Church will go all the way through the Great Tribulation. Even if there is a rapture event, it may only be God's elect, prior to the Anti-Christ being revealed, those who are *walking in the spirit* who God takes out prior to the Great Tribulation.

FOR THE MYSTERY OF INIQUITY DOTH ALREADY WORK: ONLY HE WHO NOW LETTETH WILL LET, UNTIL HE BE TAKEN OUT OF THE WAY.
AND THEN SHALL THAT WICKED BE REVEALED, WHOM THE LORD SHALL CONSUME WITH THE SPIRIT OF HIS MOUTH, AND SHALL DESTROY WITH THE BRIGHTNESS OF HIS COMING.
2 THESSALONIANS 2:7-8

AND ENOCH "WALKED" WITH GOD: AND HE WAS NOT; FOR GOD TOOK HIM.
GENESIS 5:24

What should we do?

We need to *walk with God,* we need to prepare to fight the enemy.

Shouldn't we hope and pray for the best, but prepare for the worst?

If we start getting serious about *speaking* and *memorizing* God's *Word* and preparing for battle. If we are obedient to the great commission, then if we are raptured before the great tribulation, before the Anti-Christ is revealed, all is well and good. When we see Jesus, He will say, "Well done, my good and faithful servant."

However, if we decide to spend all of our time shopping, or watching television, or working, or playing video games, or lounging on the couch, and do not ever take time to read and memorize God's Word, we are going to seriously regret it when the Anti-Christ arrives on the world scene and we are not raptured. What is Jesus going to say to us when we have been so lazy, and we have not filled our lamps with oil by memorizing and speaking God's Word?

AFTERWARD CAME ALSO THE OTHER VIRGINS, SAYING, LORD, LORD, OPEN TO US.
BUT HE ANSWERED AND SAID, VERILY I SAY UNTO YOU, I KNOW YOU NOT.
WATCH THEREFORE, FOR YE KNOW NEITHER THE DAY NOR THE HOUR WHEREIN THE SON OF MAN COMETH.
MATTHEW 25:11-13

What must I do to be saved? The Bible shows us that salvation is easy, it is so easy a lot of people cannot believe it.

BUT WHAT SAITH IT? THE **WORD** IS NIGH THEE, EVEN IN THY MOUTH, AND IN THY HEART; THAT IS, THE WORD OF FAITH, WHICH WE PREACH;

THAT IF THOU SHALL CONFESS WITH THY MOUTH THE LORD JESUS, AND SHALT BELIEVE IN THINE HEART THAT GOD HATH RAISED HIM FROM THE DEAD, THOU **SHALL** BE SAVED.
ROMANS 10:8-9

That is *walking in the spirit* in a nut shell! Have you ever heard the expression, you have to walk the talk? It means doing what you said you were going to do. *Walking in the Spirit* is just the opposite. You have to *talk the walk*. Here is my definition of Hell:

**HELL.** n. Knowing for all eternity that but for my foolish pride and my refusal to publicly confess three simple words, "Jesus is LORD," I should have boldly entered into the gates of heaven, and enjoyed God's blessings forever and ever.

PRIDE GOETH BEFORE DESTRUCTION, AND AN HAUGHTY SPIRIT BEFORE A FALL.
PROVERBS 16:18

Believing and salvation comes after *hearing* the Word of God and publically *confessing* the Lord Jesus Christ. Becoming a mature Christian comes after continually *speaking* and *hearing* the Word of God. That is why Jesus says:

THE WORDS THAT I "SPEAK" UNTO YOU, THEY ARE SPIRIT; AND THEY ARE LIFE.
JOHN 6:63

We see in the Book of Exodus that through a series of miracles, God forced Pharaoh to allow the Israelites to leave Egypt. The Israelites plundered the Egyptians of all their gold and silver and began *walking* to the Promised Land. After our salvation, all born again believers must start *walking in the spirit* to the Promised Land. The Promised Land is a place of spiritual maturity, where God's promises are fulfilled for all believers, if we can get there. However, we see that most of the Israelites never had the faith to enter into the Promised Land.

AND CALEB STILLED THE PEOPLE BEFORE MOSES, AND SAID, LET US GO UP AT ONCE, AND POSSESS IT; FOR WE ARE WELL ABLE TO OVERCOME IT.
BUT THE MEN THAT WENT UP WITH HIM SAID, WE BE NOT ABLE TO GO UP AGAINST THE PEOPLE, FOR THEY ARE STRONGER THAN WE.
NUMBERS 13:30-31

Do you see the main problem of the Israelites?

They were comparing their strength with the strength of the Canaanites. They were relying on their own judgment and their own strength. Of course, they could not have taken the Promised Land by their own strength; however, they discounted the Almighty Word of God.

AND THE LORD SAID UNTO MOSES, HOW LONG WILL THIS PEOPLE PROVOKE ME? AND HOW LONG WILL IT BE ERE THEY "BELIEVE" ME, FOR ALL THE SIGNS WHICH I HAVE SHOWN AMONG THEM?
NUMBERS 14:11

The church is packed full of Christians who have been delivered from the authority of Satan, they have seen miracles of healing, they have seen miracles of finance, yet they are still unbelievers in God's Word, they are carnal Christians. They do not have the faith to enter into the promises of God.

Remember all the people who doubted God's Word died in the wilderness, and only their children were allowed to enter into the Promised Land. I believe that we are in the last generation before the return of Jesus Christ, and it will be this last generation of believers, who are *walking in the spirit,* who God will allow to enter into His Promised Land.

BECAUSE ALL THOSE MEN WHICH HAVE SEEN MY GLORY, AND MY MIRACLES, WHICH I DID IN EGYPT AND IN THE WILDERNESS, AND HAVE TEMPTED ME NOW THESE TEN TIMES, AND "HAVE NOT HARKENED TO MY VOICE".
SURELY THEY SHALL NOT SEE THE LAND WHICH I SWARE UNTO THEIR FATHERS, NEITHER SHALL ANY OF THEM THAT PROVOKED ME SEE IT:
BUT MY SERVANT CALEB, BECAUSE HE HAD ANOTHER SPIRIT WITH HIM, AND HATH FOLLOWED ME FULLY, HIM WILL I BRING INTO THE LAND WHEREINTO HE WENT; AND HIS SEED SHALL POSSESS IT.
NUMBERS 14:22-24

Please do not be like the unbelieving children of Israel who died in the Wilderness. Start *speaking* God's Word, start *believing* God's Word, hearken to God's voice and enter into the Promised Land.

# PART 3

## SINAI

*"They wandered in the wilderness in a solitary way;*
*They found no city to dwell in.*
*Hungry and thirsty, their soul fainted in them.*
*Then they cried unto the Lord in their trouble,*
*And he delivered them out of their distresses.*
*And he led them forth by the right way, that they might go to a city of*
*habitation."*

**Psalm 107:4-7**

# CHAPTER 16

## WANDERING IN THE WILDERNESS

While the Israelites were wandering in the wilderness, God brought them to Mount Sinai and there He gave them the Law. The Law reveals to us God's perfect will, but also reveals our weakness and our desperate need for God's deliverance. No matter how hard we try in the flesh, we are incapable of keeping the law.

The Israelites in the wilderness are an example of carnal Christians who are still relying on their own wisdom and their own strength. They have been rescued from the bondage of sin and Satan. They have crucified the flesh and have been resurrected with Christ, but old habits of the flesh die hard. They begin to try and do what is right and they attempt to please God with their own actions, by their own righteousness. They attempt to obey the law. They have not discovered that no matter what they do, it will never be enough.

Attempting to keep the law by our own strength will only lead us through a wilderness, a barren waste land. Most of the Israelites never reached the Promised Land because they did not believe all of the promises of God. They had enough faith in God's Word to paint the lintels of their doorways with blood and thus escape the angel of death. They had enough faith to cross the Red Sea and thus escape Pharoah's army. However, when they arrived at Mount Sinai, the people received commandments from God that were impossible for them to obey. They did not have enough faith to enter into the Promised Land.

YEA, THEY DESPISED THE PLEASANT LAND, THEY "BELIEVED NOT" HIS WORD:
BUT MURMURED IN THEIR TENTS, AND HEARKENED NOT UNTO THE VOICE OF THE LORD.
PSALM 106:24-25

The Israelites wandering in the wilderness are a perfect example of most of the modern day Church. Many Christians can confess the Lordship of Jesus Christ, believe that God raised Him from the dead and get baptized, but then they fall far short when it comes to believing ALL of God's *promises*!

Many Christians insist on earning the blessings of God, they just cannot believe God desires to give them all the good things He has promised them in His Word. God promised to lead the Israelites to a land flowing with milk and honey, but they refused to enter in, and although they repented, God would not let them enter into the Promised Land.

Are you refusing to believe and enter into God's promises to the Church? Do you believe you must earn God's approval and blessing?

FOLLOW PEACE WITH ALL MEN, AND HOLINESS, WITHOUT WHICH NO MAN SHALL SEE THE LORD:
LOOKING DILIGENTLY LEST ANY MAN FAIL OF THE GRACE OF GOD; LEST ANY ROOT OF BITTERNESS SPRINGING UP TROUBLE YOU, AND THEREBY MANY BE DEFILED;
LEST THERE BE ANY FORNICATOR, OR PROFANE PERSON, AS ESAU, WHO FOR ONE MORSEL OF MEAT SOLD HIS BIRTHRIGHT.
FOR YE KNOW HOW THAT AFTERWARD, WHEN HE WOULD HAVE INHERITED THE BLESSING, HE WAS REJECTED: FOR HE FOUND NO PLACE OF REPENTANCE, THOUGH HE SOUGHT IT CAREFULLY WITH TEARS.
HEBREWS 12:14-17

I always wondered why God was so harsh to Esau and the children of Israel. They repented for their sin, why didn't God forgive them? Both Esau and the children of Israel were going to receive a gift from God. Esau was going to receive his birthright and the children of Israel were going to receive the Promised Land flowing with milk and honey. The Bible says that Esau *despised* his birthright. *See* Genesis 25:34. The children of Israel did not *believe* God's promise. *See* Numbers 14:3-11.

Many people believe that after they die, they will have another chance to repent. Therefore, they continue on in their sin and rebellion against God. They reject the free gift of salvation bought and paid for by Jesus Christ. They believe God will forgive them and welcome them with open arms after they die. These people are sadly mistaken because there is no repentance after death. We have only one chance to enter into God's promises. We can only repent while we are alive on the earth. We can only call on God when we are living on earth. After we die there is only judgment if we do not accept the mercy and grace of God here on earth.

JESUS SAID UNTO HIM, IF THOU CANST BELIEVE, "ALL" THINGS ARE POSSIBLE TO HIM THAT BELIEVETH.
MARK 9:23

Do you perhaps believe that Jesus was some kind of Pollyanna, who just didn't get it? You might say, "He just doesn't know what I'm going through." The Bible says that Jesus does know what we are going through! If we believe in the power and authority of Jesus Christ, we are more than conquerors. We can overcome sickness. We can overcome poverty. We can overcome despair. We can overcome sin. We can overcome devils. We can overcome death and hell. We can overcome any obstacle. However, apart from Jesus Christ, we are forever lost.

FOR VERILY HE TOOK NOT ON HIM THE NATURE OF ANGELS; BUT HE TOOK ON HIM THE SEED OF ABRAHAM.
WHEREFORE IN ALL THINGS IT BEHOOVED HIM TO BE MADE LIKE UNTO HIS BRETHREN, THAT HE MIGHT BE A MERCIFUL AND FAITHFUL HIGH PRIEST IN THINGS PERTAINING TO GOD, TO MAKE RECONCILIATION FOR THE SINS OF THE PEOPLE.
FOR IN THAT HE HIMSELF HATH SUFFERED BEING TEMPTED, HE IS ABLE TO SUCCOUR THEM THAT ARE TEMPTED.
HEBREWS 2:16-18

If you believe the Books of the New Testament, and if you're a Christian you should believe the New Testament, you must believe that Jesus could do what he said he could do. You must also believe that Christians can do what Jesus said we could do. He said: *all things are possible to him who believeth*! What things? *All things*! Then there can be only one reason why we cannot receive God's many promises. *We do not believe God's Word*!

# CHAPTER 17

## RESISTING TEMPTATION

What must we do when doubt comes? What must we do when temptation comes? We must look to our Lord Jesus Christ for an example of the proper response when the devil comes to put us through tribulations, temptations and trials:

THEN WAS JESUS LED UP OF THE SPIRIT INTO THE WILDERNESS TO BE TEMPTED OF THE DEVIL.

AND WHEN HE HAD FASTED FORTY DAYS AND FORTY NIGHTS, HE WAS AFTERWARD A HUNGERED.

AND WHEN THE TEMPTER CAME TO HIM, HE SAID, IF THOU BE THE SON OF GOD, COMMAND THAT THESE STONES BE MADE BREAD *(LUST OF THE FLESH)*.

BUT HE ANSWERED AND SAID, IT IS WRITTEN, **MAN SHALL NOT LIVE BY BREAD ALONE, BUT BY EVERY WORD THAT PROCEEDETH OUT OF THE MOUTH OF GOD.** (*SEE* DEUT. 8:3)

THEN THE DEVIL TAKETH HIM UP INTO THE HOLY CITY, AND SETTETH HIM ON A PINNACLE OF THE TEMPLE,

AND SAID UNTO HIM, IF THOU BE THE SON OF GOD, CAST THYSELF DOWN: FOR IT IS WRITTEN, HE SHALL GIVE HIS ANGELS CHARGE CONCERNING THEE: AND IN THEIR HANDS THEY SHALL BEAR THEE UP, LEST AT ANY TIME THOU DASH THY FOOT AGAINST A STONE *(PRIDE OF LIFE)*.

JESUS SAID UNTO HIM, IT IS WRITTEN AGAIN, **THOU SHALT NOT TEMPT THE LORD THY GOD.** (*SEE* DEUT. 6:16)

AGAIN THE DEVIL TAKETH HIM UP INTO AN EXCEEDING HIGH MOUNTAIN, AND SHEWETH HIM ALL THE KINGDOMS OF THE WORLD, AND THE GLORY OF THEM *(THE LUST OF THE EYES)*;

AND SAITH UNTO HIM, ALL THESE THINGS WILL I GIVE THEE, IF THOU WILT FALL DOWN AND WORSHIP ME.

THEN SAITH JESUS UNTO HIM, GET THEE HENCE, SATAN: FOR IT IS WRITTEN, **THOU SHALT WORSHIP THE LORD THY GOD, AND HIM ONLY SHALT THOU SERVE.** (*SEE* DEUT. 6:13; 10:20)

MATTHEW 4:1-10

Do you see that Jesus refused to rely on His own strength? If Jesus was going to rely on the strength of His flesh, He would have made sure to eat a hearty breakfast before He confronted the devil. Instead He fasted for forty days prior to His battle in the wilderness.

Jesus Christ *only relied on the Word of God!* For years, I wondered what fasting was all about. I fasted because I noticed in the Holy Scriptures that God's people fasted when they really desired something from God, but I did not really understand it. Fasting illustrates that we have come to the end of our physical rope. We no longer have confidence in our own strength and our own wisdom. We finally must turn only to God to deliver us from the problem. We have turned away from our own strength, and we have turned completely to rely on God's almighty power. If God's Word says, *"Man shall not live by bread alone, but by every Word that proceedeth out of the mouth of God,"* then Jesus was not going to rely on eating bread. He was not going to put any confidence in His flesh. Jesus was going to rely completely on God's Word!

**BUT THE HOUR COMETH, AND NOW IS, WHEN THE TRUE WORSHIPPERS SHALL WORSHIP THE FATHER IN SPIRIT AND IN TRUTH: FOR THE FATHER SEEKETH SUCH TO WORSHIP HIM.**
**GOD IS A SPIRIT: AND THEY THAT WORSHIP HIM MUST WORSHIP HIM IN SPIRIT AND IN TRUTH.**
**JOHN 4:23-24**

Do you see how our Lord Jesus Christ responded when the devil tempted him in the wilderness?

He did not grit his teeth and repeat, "I'm not gonna turn the loaves into bread," over and over again. He did not start an exercise program and begin to bulk up on a high protein diet. He did not start practicing Socratic debating techniques.

Jesus simply *spoke* the Word of God. Do you see how He resisted the devil? Jesus *spoke* the Word of God. Do you see how He defeated the devil? Jesus *spoke the Word of God!*

Jesus was able to tune into the God frequency, the same way that we can tune into the God frequency. Jesus did not pull a copy of the Torah out of his back pocket and start reading silently to himself. God's Word was in him. His weapon was the *spoken* Word of God. Jesus is the *spoken* Word of God.

How did Jesus know the Word of God? He *memorized* the Word of God!

**IT IS THE SPIRIT THAT QUICKENETH; THE FLESH PROFITETH NOTHING: THE WORDS THAT I "SPEAK" UNTO YOU, THEY ARE "SPIRIT", AND THEY ARE LIFE.**
**JOHN 6:63**

When John the Baptist sent his disciples to ask Jesus whether He was the Messiah or, "He that should come." Jesus told them:

**GO AND SHOW JOHN AGAIN THOSE THINGS WHICH YE DO HEAR AND SEE:**
**THE BLIND RECEIVE THEIR SIGHT, AND THE LAME WALK, THE LEPERS ARE CLEANSED, AND THE DEAF HEAR, THE DEAD ARE RAISED UP, AND THE POOR HAVE THE GOSPEL PREACHED TO THEM.**
**MATTHEW 11:4-5**

Jesus was giving John the Baptist's disciples a reference out of the Book of Isaiah concerning the coming of God:

**SAY TO THEM THAT ARE OF A FEARFUL HEART, BE STRONG, FEAR NOT: BEHOLD, YOUR GOD WILL COME WITH VENGEANCE, EVEN WITH A RECOMPENCE; HE WILL COME AND SAVE YOU.**
**THEN THE EYES OF THE BLIND SHALL BE OPENED, AND THE EARS OF THE DEAF SHALL BE UNSTOPPED.**
**THEN SHALL THE LAME MAN LEAP AS AN HART, AND THE TONGUE OF THE DUMB SING:**
**ISAIAH 35:4-6**

If you have a reference Bible, you will see that Jesus quoted liberally from the Old Testament. Jesus *knew* the Word of God! Jesus *spoke* the Word of God! Jesus *is* the Word of God incarnate! He also expected John the Baptist to *know* God's Word! God expects *everyone* to *know* and *believe* the Word of God! Ignorance of God's Word is no excuse. When Jesus told the story of Lazarus and the Rich man, the Rich man begs Father Abraham to send Lazarus back to his brethren to warn them about the torments of hell:

**ABRAHAM SAITH UNTO HIM, THEY HAVE MOSES AND THE PROPHETS; LET THEM HEAR THEM. AND HE SAID, NAY, FATHER ABRAHAM: BUT IF ONE WENT UNTO THEM FROM THE DEAD, THEY WILL REPENT.**
**AND HE SAID UNTO HIM, IF THEY "HEAR NOT" MOSES AND THE PROPHETS, NEITHER WILL THEY BE PERSUADED, THOUGH ONE ROSE FROM THE DEAD.**
**LUKE 16:29-31**

Jesus illustrates in this story that God expected the rich man's brothers to *know* the Word of God. Claiming to be ignorant of God's Word will not excuse you from going to hell!

People seem to forget that Jesus was the Son of man as well as the Son of God. He suffered the same limitations as we now suffer. Jesus overcame the world and Satan by *memorizing* and *speaking* the Word of God. Jesus was an expert with the sword of the spirit by the time He was twelve years old.

**AND IT CAME TO PASS, THAT AFTER THREE DAYS, THEY FOUND HIM IN THE TEMPLE, SITTING IN THE MIDST OF THE DOCTORS, BOTH HEARING THEM, AND ASKING THEM QUESTIONS.**
**AND ALL THAT HEARD HIM WERE ASTONISHED AT HIS UNDERSTANDING AND ANSWERS.**
**LUKE 2:46-47**

Christians must also have the Word of God residing in their soul/mind. When the seducing spirits come to seduce you, and *they will come*, you must have the Word of God hidden inside your soul, and you must *speak* the Word of God or you will be continually defeated.

Now do you understand why so many Christians live defeated lives?

They do not have the Word of God abiding in them and they rarely, if ever, s̱
Word of God when they are attacked by seducing spirits. Christians will attempt
the law, but for whatever reason they will not *believe* and *speak* God's Word. Th
growing short and the night is fast approaching. It is time for the saints of God ...
up our *only* offensive spiritual weapon, and begin *speaking and believing the Word of
God.*

**AND TAKE THE HELMET OF SALVATION, AND THE "SWORD" OF THE SPIRIT, WHICH IS
THE WORD OF GOD.
EPHESIANS 6:17**

My dad served in the United States Navy on a ship landing equipment, tanks and
marines on the South Sea Islands during World War II. He told me that the marines
would spend hours sharpening their bayonets before an invasion landing. A sharp
bayonet in a pitched battle could mean the difference between life and death! It is
estimated that between 65 and 75 million people lost their lives during World War II. It
was the greatest conflict that the World has ever seen.

A greater conflict is fast approaching. According to the Book of Revelation, not millions
but billions of lives will be lost. It will be a battle for the souls of billions of people.

Will you be prepared? Will your spiritual sword be sharpened to a razor's edge?

There will only be two types of Christians before the great and dreadful Day of the Lord.
Either you will be running and hiding from the enemy or the enemy will be running and
hiding from you. Either you will be a deliverer or you will need deliverance. Before the
battle starts is the time for preparation, not in the midst of the battle. Start *memorizing*
and *speaking* God's Word now!

Speaking God's Word to oneself is similar to sword practice. If you owned a sword and
your life depended on being able to use it, you would practice every day, you would not
keep it in your attic gathering dust. However, a lot of Christians do just that. Their *spirit
sword* is never used. The Bible sits on the bookshelf gathering dust and the Devil abuses
them like they are the Devil's whipping boy. People see Christians living defeated lives
and people wonder what profit is it to be a Christian. These immature, lazy Christians
give Jesus Christ and His Gospel message a bad name.

Does being able to *speak* the Word of God make a difference?

You bet it does! It makes all the difference in the World. Some people appear to have it
all together, but in fact their lives are a mess. Jesus called these people hypocrites
(actors) because they are pretending to be somebody different from who they really are.

However, a mature Christian is the real deal. A mature Christian has the Word of God
hidden in their heart. When the Devil comes and tries to tempt them to sin, they *speak*
the Word of God. When the Devil tries to make them sick, they *speak* the Word of God.
When the Devil tries to steal God's blessings from them, they *speak* the Word of God.

# CHAPTER 18

## SOWING AND REAPING

Jesus compared speaking the Word of God to planting seeds of wheat. *See* Matthew 13.

When we *speak* God's Word, we are planting a
seed in our spirit and in every spirit that hears us speak God's Word. The Word of God *not spoken* is like a seed not planted. If a seed is not planted, and if God's Word is not spoken, neither the seed nor the Word will produce any fruit. However, if we *speak* and *hear* God's Word, and wait patiently with faith, eventually the Word of God will bear fruit. Each seed bears a specific type of fruit and every Word of God also bears specific fruit.

Therefore, if we want health, we must *speak* God's Word concerning health. If we want joy, we must *speak* God's Word concerning joy. If we want peace, we must *speak* God's Word concerning peace. If we want prosperity, we must *speak* God's Word concerning prosperity. If we want love, we must *speak* God's Word concerning love. If we want salvation for a loved one, we must *speak* God's Word concerning salvation. We may receive a bumper crop by speaking God's Word, but we should not expect it to last forever. I will give you an example in my own life.

When I was a boy, I read my Bible almost every day. However, I did not have the same revelation about God's Word as I do today. I was a baby Christian. One day I suddenly became terribly sick, I started having seizures. My mother took me to several doctors and none of them gave me much hope for a cure. We were told that if I took medicine, I could "manage" the illness. We were told I would probably have to live with the illness the rest of my life because it could not be cured. I very nearly lost my faith in God.

I cried out to God, "Why have you allowed this to happen to me?"

My relationship with God went downhill pretty fast. I definitely did not have the patience of Job. However, when all the doctors told me there was no cure, eventually I had to turn to the only place that gave me some hope, God's Word! I searched through the Bible, and found every scripture verse I could find concerning God's promises to heal and there are many. Then I wrote them in large print on pieces of paper and taped them on my bedroom walls. Every night I would *speak* God's healing Word out loud praying that he would heal me. I did not have a great deal of faith at the time, but I was persistent.

I continued to do this for many years and I don't mean to brag, but I was probably in nearly perfect health by the end of that time. All by speaking the Word of God! I wasn't even living a very righteous or obedient life, but I eventually did believe God's Word concerning healing. I finally went to a new Doctor and I told him that I wanted to stop taking my seizure medication. Surprisingly, after giving me some tests, he said, "Go ahead." I did quit taking medication, and I have never had to take medicine for that particular ailment ever again.

However, I made a mistake. When I was confident that I was healed of that particular ailment, I took all of God's healing scriptures off my bedroom walls and stopped praying God's healing Word every night, then slowly but surely I started losing my health. I began gaining weight. I hurt my back. I had colds every winter and an assortment of other minor ailments.

Then it finally dawned on me. I need to start doing what I was doing when I was so healthy. I need to continually plant the Word of God in my spirit, if I want to continue enjoying good health. I need to *speak* God's *healing* Word just like I did when I was young and sickly! I need to continually sow God's Word to my spirit if I want to continually reap his promises in my life. Our physical reality is only a reflection of our spiritual reality.

The same is true for all of God's promises, we need to continually *memorize* and *speak* God's promises to ourselves and to anybody else who will listen. *Speaking* God's Word is the only way to set the captives free, including ourselves. If you are sick, you want to be healed of course, but do not limit yourself only to God's healing Word, also speak God's Word concerning *love, righteousness, hope, joy, peace* and *prosperity*. You will be amazed at the results. Your spirit is an unlimited field for planting God's Word.

My little sister was also stricken with a chronic illness. I told her how I was healed by praying and speaking God's Word to myself. A few months later, I asked her if she had been speaking God's healing Word to herself. She said, "I tried it, but what you told me doesn't work." I don't know how long she "tried it", maybe a week, maybe a month, maybe a few months, but we cannot *try walking in the spirit*, we must *live walking in the spirit continually*!

My sister made the same mistake that I made. She thought that what I told her was some kind of formula to make God heal her. Speaking God's Word is not a formula, it is not magic. We must speak God's Word as a way of life. If we do not continually *walk in the spirit,* and continually *speak* God's Word, we will eventually lose any progress that we have made. Speaking a promise from God once and expecting to be healed forever is similar to believing we can eat one meal and then expecting that we will be full forever. It is also similar to planting a crop of wheat only one year and then expecting a bumper crop of wheat every year thereafter. The natural world does not work that way and the Holy Spirit does not work that way.

In the Book of Hebrews, the Apostle Paul tells us why most of the Israelites who left Egypt never entered into the Promised Land, but died in the Wilderness. The reason the Israelites failed to reach the Promised Land is the same reason many Christians also do not enjoy the abundance of God's promises. Entering into the Promised Land represents entering into all of God's promises for the Church. Entering into God's rest, which He has prepared for us from the foundation of the world, requires *faith*! God does not want us to wait until we die to enter into His rest, God expects us to enter His rest *right now*!

**LET US THEREFORE FEAR, LEST, A PROMISE BEING LEFT US OF ENTERING INTO HIS REST, ANY OF YOU SHOULD SEEM TO COME SHORT OF IT.**
**FOR UNTO US WAS THE GOSPEL PREACHED, AS WELL AS UNTO THEM: BUT THE WORD PREACHED DID NOT PROFIT THEM, NOT BEING "MIXED" WITH FAITH IN THEM THAT HEARD IT.**
**HEBREWS 4:1-2**

MIXED. G4786. Soong-kat-an'-noo-mee: to commingle, i.e. (figuratively) to combine or assimilate: - mix with, temper together.

The Apostle Paul was telling the saints in the Book of Hebrews not to make the same mistake as the Israelites did by wandering in the wilderness. The ancient Israelites could not enter into the Promised Land because they did not *mix* God's Word with *faith*. They believed God enough to escape Egypt, but their faith was found wanting when it came to appropriating all that God had promised them. They heard the Word preached, but the Word was not *mixed* with faith. Remember that *mixed* means to *assimilate* or to make it a part of our faith.

How do we *mix* God's Word with faith?

*Faith commeth by hearing and hearing by the Word of God.* We must *memorize* God's Word in order to assimilate it with our faith. We have to *speak* God's Word over and over. We must *hear* God's Word over and over. *Once a week is not enough!*

Paul is basically telling us that the Word *preached* to the Israelites went in one ear and out the other. The Word did not get down into their spirits. If Warren Buffet wrote you a check for a billion dollars, you would probably rush down to the bank and try to cash it, but if a beggar on the street wrote you a check for a billion dollars, you would probably toss it in the trash. Then you would walk away and forget it.

Why? Because you see the beggar's circumstances, and you do not believe the beggar possesses the resources to keep his promises.

This was how the ancient Israelites and many Christians today treat God. They treat God like a beggar. They do not believe God is *capable* of healing them or keeping His promises! They really do not believe God can make them prosperous, wise or happy. They really do not believe God has the power to deliver them from sickness, or to deliver them from debt, or to deliver them from sin. They would have more faith in a promise from Warren Buffet than from God.

What is wrong with this picture? The main problem is not that God is unable to perform His promises. The main problem is the believer's lack of faith in God's ability to perform His promises. Therefore, the believer cannot appropriate what God has promised them.

If somebody gave you a ten dollar check, you would probably have faith that there was enough money in the bank to cash it, but if somebody gave you a billion dollar check, you might doubt that the money was really in the bank. It all depends on your belief in the person's ability to keep their promise. People can believe in God's little promises, but they just cannot believe in God's big promises. They can believe God will heal a cold but not AIDS. They are just like Abraham when he heard that he and Sarah was going to have a baby in their old age.

**THEN ABRAHAM FELL UPON HIS FACE, AND LAUGHED, AND SAID IN HIS HEART, SHALL A CHILD BE BORN UNTO HIM THAT IS AN HUNDRED YEARS OLD? AND SHALL SARAH, THAT IS NINETY YEARS OLD BEAR?**
**GENESIS 17:17**

One reason for unbelief is because the average Christian does not know or has not heard the promises of God in the first place. They might go to church every Sunday, but for whatever reason, the Word of healing has never been preached, so they continue suffering from sickness. The Word of prosperity has never been preached, so they continue suffering from poverty. The Word of wisdom has not been preached, so they continue suffering in ignorance.

What should they do?

They should search the Bible and see for themselves what God says about sickness and poverty. They should appropriate God's promises for themselves. They need to *mix* God's Word concerning healing and prosperity into their spirit with faith by *speaking* and *hearing* His Word. They need to *assimilate* God's Word into their spirit with faith. They need to be transformed by the *renewing* of their minds.

**AND BE NOT CONFORMED TO THIS WORLD: BUT BE YE TRANSFORMED BY THE "RENEWING" OF YOUR MIND, THAT YE MAY PROVE WHAT IS THAT GOOD, AND ACCEPTABLE, AND PERFECT, WILL OF GOD.**
**ROMANS 12:2**

RENEWING. G342. An-ak-ah'-ee-no-sis: renovation: - renewing.

You have to picture the unsaved mind as an old house in complete disrepair and falling apart. Also, visualize the old house has been infested with mice, rats and all kinds of vermin, doubt, bad thoughts and ideas, which were never meant to use the house as a residence. God wants to put the flesh to death, but He wants to renovate your mind.

Have you ever seen the before and after pictures of an old house that has been repaired and renovated?

Sometimes you can hardly believe it is the same place. The Holy Spirit is more than able to make your mind a brand new place. The Holy Spirit can replace fear with faith; He can replace selfishness with love; He can replace pride with meekness; He can replace strife with peace; He can replace foolishness with wisdom; He can replace despair with hope.

**LIE NOT ONE TO ANOTHER, SEEING THAT YE HAVE PUT OFF THE OLD MAN WITH HIS DEEDS;**
**AND HAVE PUT ON THE NEW MAN, WHICH IS RENEWED IN KNOWLEDGE AFTER THE IMAGE OF HIM THAT CREATED HIM:**
**COLOSSIANS 3:9-10**

So we see that the new man is renewed in knowledge.

What knowledge? The knowledge of Jesus Christ (the WORD OF GOD) renews our minds.

As we become more and more familiar with the LORD, we are transformed into His image. As we *speak* the Word of God, our mind is renewed. We begin speaking with authority. We begin speaking with wisdom. We begin speaking with faith.

Why do so many people hear the Word of God and continue on as before, in bondage to the world, full of doubt and disbelief, while only a few become mighty warriors of faith and enter into God's rest? Why do so many people remain dead wood, while so few catch on fire for God?

The answer is *unbelief*, their mind is still focused on the world and their circumstances instead of the unbreakable Word of God.

Prior to salvation, the spirit is dead and the soul(mind) is controlled by the flesh(body). A person's spirit, soul, and body look like this:

| SPIRIT | SOUL(MIND) | FLESH(BODY) |
|---|---|---|

LIFE    →         →         →         DEATH

Prior to salvation, the spirit is dead and has no power; therefore, the flesh is in control of the unbeliever and the unbeliever is being led towards death and away from God. After salvation, the spirit is alive, but the soul (mind), by force of habit and lack of knowledge, is still being controlled by the flesh:

| SPIRIT | SOUL(MIND) | FLESH(BODY) |
|---|---|---|

LIFE    ←         →         →         DEATH

The key to becoming a mature Christian is renewing our mind. We need to train our mind to start following after the desires of the spirit instead of following after the desires of the flesh:

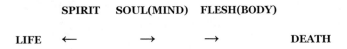

| SPIRIT | SOUL(MIND) | FLESH(BODY) |
|---|---|---|

LIFE    ←         ←         ↓         DEATH

After we become mature Christians, we understand, by the Word of God, that our flesh is dead, but our spirit is alive and our soul (mind) must be renewed and controlled by our spirit, which in turn is led by the Holy Spirit. We begin a journey in the opposite direction. We begin *walking in the spirit* toward eternal life with our eternal companion, the Holy Spirit.

How do you get your soul (mind) to begin following the spirit toward life?

We begin feeding our spirit with the Word of Life. We strengthen our spirit with the Word of God. We *speak* God's Word to our spirit and build up our faith. Eventually, our soul(mind) becomes *congruent* with the spirit and not with the flesh.

CONGRUENT means to be harmonious.

Our mind must begin to agree with the Holy Spirit and God's Word instead of with our dead flesh. Eventually, we will receive an eternal, celestial body.

This is why it is so important for a Christian not to be unequally yoked to a non-Christian?

Imagine trying to run an obstacle course with a dead body strapped to your back. Worse yet, imagine somebody fighting you every step of the way. Many Christians marry non-Christians, enter business deals or partnerships with non-Christians, make close friends with unbelievers, and then they wonder why their circumstances never improve. The unequally yoked Christian wonders why God does not bless them like He blesses other Christians.

If you want to enter into the Promised Land, you must be spiritually mature, and you must not be unequally yoked to an unbeliever. Please listen to me young people. If you marry an unbeliever, you will be stuck until the day one of you dies, or your unbelieving spouse gets saved, or the unbelieving spouse freely leaves you. That is a pretty scary predicament!

Now some people might say, "Hold on, my poor old Grandma is the most saintly person I know and she barely has money for food, she has arthritis, and she is always crying 'cause Grandpa died and left her with a mountain of debt! My poor old Grandma has been faithfully goin' to church every Sunday for the last fifty years!"

If you know somebody like this poor old Grandma, you are not alone. There are plenty of Christians that are in the same boat as poor old Grandma. They are Christians wandering in the wilderness. Many of them will never reach the Promised Land. The Apostle Paul calls these weak believers "carnal." These types of believers continue to be motivated and controlled by their circumstances and not by the Word of God. They continue to rely on their own wisdom and their own strength. They have never matured into spiritual men and women because they do not know the power of God's Word. Mostly, they are trapped because no one has ever explained to them how to grow up and become a spiritually mature Christian.

There are also many Christians who believe God can deliver them from sin, and they truly are saintly, but they do not believe God's Word when He says they are delivered from poverty and sickness.

I put a lot of the blame on the church leadership today. Many church leaders do not have faith. Many church leaders should not be in charge of a lemonade stand, let alone the spiritual health of a congregation. A lot of people are probably not going to like this, but I need to warn Christians about those who they entrust their spiritual health to.

Would you want to drive over a bridge designed by an engineer who has never finished college or have brain surgery from a doctor who attended medical school for a month?

I know everybody has to start somewhere, but nobody should be put in charge of a congregation unless they are spiritually mature.

Nobody should hold any position of authority or any office in the Church unless they are spiritually mature. If I wanted to learn about anything, whether it was being an engineer, or a doctor, or a carpenter, or a spiritually mature Christian, I would look for a teacher who has been doing it for a while, and is acknowledged to be an expert by their peers.

Our spiritual growth is the most important subject in this world and in the world to come. Please do not put yourselves under the authority of a carnal Christian, or even worse, a pretender to the faith. A lot of churches and church leaders are telling their congregations touch not, taste not, handle not, after the commandments and doctrines of men. Many church leaders are wolves preying on the flock.

SET YOUR AFFECTIONS ON THINGS ABOVE, NOT ON THINGS ON THE EARTH.
COLOSSIANS 3:2

Although church leaders are responsible for the immaturity of a lot of Christians, a lot of immature Christians do not want to be mature. They are similar to the grown man who refuses to leave his parent's home. It is comfortable to attend a church once a week and then forget about God.

"Why bother getting intimate with God when the pastor, priest or preacher can do it for me?"

I am afraid there are a lot of Christians who will be in for a big surprise when they stand before the Judgment seat of Christ. The officers of the Church were never meant to be rulers. They were meant to build individual believers into mature Christians and to edify the Church. The Church should be producing mature kings and priests, mature spiritual saints. The Church will be without spot or wrinkle when Jesus comes again. The Church has a mission and Jesus Christ commanded that we attend to our duty.

GO YE INTO ALL THE WORLD, AND PREACH THE GOSPEL TO EVERY CREATURE.
MARK 16:15

The commandment to preach the gospel was to the whole Church, not just the Apostles.

How can a Christian preach the gospel, if they do not know the gospel?

God expects us to become mature and then to be about our Father's business. God expects us to be intimate with Him. God expects us to know his Word and to carry it out. God expects us to be his eyes and ears on the earth. God expects us to be His representatives. God expects us to be kings and priests. God expects us to *preach the Good News*! We are not required to be the student of the same teacher or preacher until we are old and gray. We are not required to sit under the authority of a clergyman or clergywoman until we die.

If you do not want to be like poor old Grandma, just barely hanging on from day to day, you have to set your eyes on Jesus Christ (the Word of God) and *believe the Good News*!

I was in the same boat as poor old Grandma for over twenty years. I would understand that I needed to give up some sin and try as I might, I could not overcome my fleshly desires. I was trying to keep the law by my own strength despite confessing the grace of God. I would get colds every winter, headaches when I didn't get my caffeine fix, and a sore back every time I twisted the wrong way. I would beg and pray to God, "Please heal me." I never knew from day to day if I could pay my rent or pay my utility bills. I knew and confessed Jesus Christ as my personal savior, but I was no different from my unbelieving friends and acquaintances. I just could not believe what God plainly promised in the Old and New Testament.

Why couldn't I believe? Because I did not *mix* God's Word with *faith,* and I did not *speak* God's Word to my circumstances.

I would have hot and cold spells in my spiritual walk. Sometimes I was reading and studying my Bible all the time, attending church regularly, living the straight and narrow. I would talk to people about Jesus, argue and debate about evolution and billions of years ago and never lead anybody to Jesus Christ. Other times, I stopped reading the Bible, slowly stopped attending church, and quickly backslid into old bad habits and sins.

Why was I, and so many Christian like me, so pathetic? I believe we never became mature Christians because we never learned about *walking in the spirit*. We did not have a destination in mind, and we never took the systematic steps required to reach our destination. We did not systematically start *memorizing* and *speaking* God's promises in His Word.

I have attended many churches, some of the pastors were entertaining, some of the teachers were thought provoking, some of the preachers were inspiring, but none of them taught me what I needed to know in order to become a mature Christian. Most of them did not know how to become a mature Christian themselves.

Most of the time I spent at Church was listening to preaching of the law and not grace because the preachers really did not believe the promises of God either. The Apostle Paul gives a brief list of the qualities that a Bishop (overseer) should have. If I was attending a church and the pastor, priest, teacher, preacher, etc., did not possess these basic qualities, I would have to leave and find somebody who did.

A BISHOP THEN MUST BE BLAMELESS, THE HUSBAND OF ONE WIFE, VIGILANT (SELF CONTROLLED), SOBER (DISCIPLINED), OF GOOD BEHAVIOUR, GIVEN TO HOSPITALITY (SHOWING LOVE), APT TO TEACH (QUALIFIED TO TEACH);
NOT GIVEN TO WINE (NOT A DRUNK), NO STRIKER (NOT VIOLENT), NOT GREEDY OF FILTHY LUCRE (NOT WILLING TO GAIN WEALTH BY QUESTIONABLE MEANS); BUT PATIENT, NOT A BRAWLER, NOT COVETOUS;
ONE THAT RULETH WELL HIS OWN HOUSE, HAVING HIS CHILDREN IN SUBJECTION WITH ALL GRAVITY (RESPECTED BY THEIR CHILDREN);
FOR IF A MAN KNOW NOT HOW TO RULE HIS OWN HOUSE, HOW SHALL HE TAKE CARE OF THE CHURCH OF GOD?
NOT A NOVICE (NOT A NEW CONVERT), LEST BEING LIFTED UP WITH PRIDE HE FALL INTO THE CONDEMNATION OF THE DEVIL.
MOREOVER HE MUST HAVE A GOOD REPORT OF THEM WHICH ARE WITHOUT (WELL THOUGHT OF BY PEOPLE OUTSIDE THE CHURCH); LEST HE FALL INTO REPROACH AND THE SNARE OF THE DEVIL.
1 TIMOTHY 3:2-7

A whole book could be written on this passage and probably many have been, but I am going to discuss the parts that are important to the subject at hand. Most pastors, priests, teachers, preachers, bishops, etc., don't spend all their free time at the local bar or bragging about their well stocked liquor cabinet, or their drug habit, or how they chase other people's spouses. *Some do!* Needless to say, if your spiritual mentor is a drunk or a drug addict, or a fornicator, you're in big trouble.

If an unbeliever or outsider approaches your spiritual mentor and asks for help, does he try and help them out and share the gospel of Jesus Christ with them, or does he show the lazy bum to the door? Does he *know* and *speak* the Word of God or does he teach mostly out of *readers digest* and *time magazine* or just about anything but the Bible? Does he say that the Bible is just a book and not the divinely inspired Word of God?

*Flee for your life*!

Has he ever tried to get you or members of your church to put money into questionable investments and money making schemes, or does he demand that you give all your money and all your time to his ministry?

If He does these things, he is not looking out for the Lord's sheep, but he is looking for sheep to shear. Are his young children terrified of him, or disrespectful of him, or do his adult children hate him? They probably know him better than you do.

If preachers, priests, pastors, reverends, etc., do not know and share the *Good News* from the Word of God, they should probably do something else with their lives, like carpentry or farming. They will do the world a whole lot more good and do the Church a lot less harm if they change occupations.

# CHAPTER 19

## BEING FULL OF GOD'S WORD (MIXED WITH FAITH) IS BEING FULL OF THE SPIRIT

Let's see what the apostle Paul had to say about being *Full of the Spirit*.

WHEREFORE BE YE NOT UNWISE, BUT UNDERSTANDING WHAT THE WILL OF THE LORD IS.
AND BE NOT DRUNK WITH WINE, WHEREIN IS EXCESS; BUT BE FILLED WITH THE SPIRIT;
"SPEAKING" TO YOURSELVES IN PSALMS AND HYMNS AND SPIRITUAL SONGS, "SINGING" AND MAKING MELODY IN YOUR HEART (MIND) TO THE LORD;
EPHESIANS 5:17-19

Isn't it clear that the key to *walking in the spirit* and being *full of the Spirit* is *speaking or singing God's Word to yourself?*

The Psalms are God's Word of course and all Hymns and Spiritual songs should be based on God's Word. A word of warning, there are some Hymns and Christian songs these days that actually contradict God's Word. Make sure that you are not singing blasphemy or you may be worse off than if you did not sing at all.

Now days, we are without excuse, there is so much Christian broadcasting on television, the radio, CDs, DVDs, books and on the internet. We should be able to surround ourselves constantly with God's Word. Just make sure it is God's Word! Jesus warned:

TAKE HEED THAT NO MAN DECEIVE YOU.
FOR MANY SHALL COME IN MY NAME, SAYING I AM CHRIST; AND SHALL DECEIVE MANY.
MATTHEW 24:4-5

We need to be so careful when it comes to our spiritual health and growth, just like we need to be careful about our physical health and growth. We would not sit down and stuff ourselves if somebody put a plate of poison plants in front of us. Do not stuff yourself with lies either. It is so important to *know* God's Word. Just going to church does not cut the mustard. If you do not know God's Word, how will you know that what you are listening to at your church is the truth or a lie?

There is a most important reason to take the Apostle Paul seriously.

ALL SCRIPTURE IS GIVEN BY INSPIRATION OF GOD, AND IS PROFITABLE FOR DOCTRINE, FOR REPROOF, FOR CORRECTION, FOR INSTRUCTION IN RIGHTEOUSNESS:
II TIMOTHY 3:16

To me, just silently reading the scripture is similar to seeing a grand feast spread out before us, smelling all the savory dishes, but never getting any nourishment by sitting down to eat. That is why I believe someone can read the scriptures all their lives and still be a hopeless backsliding sinner. That is why we can set people up on a pedestal because of their supposed knowledge of God and they can finally disappoint us. That is why we can read the Bible, go to church and still struggle with sin.

In order to be an over comer, in order to be accounted righteous by God, we need to sit down and eat at the feast God has spread before us. We have to chew (*meditate*) on God's Word and swallow (*memorize*) God's Word, and we have to continue in (*speak, sing*) God's Word *every day*!

FOR IF YE LIVE AFTER THE FLESH, YE SHALL DIE: BUT IF YE THROUGH THE SPIRIT DO MORTIFY (*PUT TO DEATH*) THE DEEDS OF THE BODY, YE SHALL LIVE.
FOR AS MANY AS ARE LED BY THE SPIRIT OF GOD, THEY ARE THE SONS OF GOD.
ROMANS 8:13-14

It is by the Spirit (*the Word of God*) that not only we, but the saints of old were able to put the sinful deeds of their body to death by *speaking and believing God's Word*! The devil, by using our sin infected body, wants us to ignore God's Word, wants us to sin, wants to separate us from GOD by unbelief and wants to kill us. Sin is like a virus, after it takes up residence within us, it will begin to multiply and take over our bodies. Sin will lay you low and eventually it will kill you.

Fortunately, Jesus Christ (*the spoken Word of God*) is our antidote and remedy for sin, the Word of God mortifies our flesh and strengthens our spirit. Our fleshy desires must be put to death in order to release our spirit.

VERILY (TRULY), VERILY (TRULY), I SAY UNTO YOU, EXCEPT A CORN (SEED) OF WHEAT FALL INTO THE GROUND AND DIE, IT ABIDETH ALONE: BUT IF IT DIE, IT BRINGETH FORTH MUCH FRUIT.
HE THAT LOVETH HIS LIFE SHALL LOSE IT; AND HE THAT HATETH HIS LIFE IN THIS WORLD SHALL KEEP IT UNTO LIFE ETERNAL.
JOHN 12:24-25

There is that verily, verily again. Jesus is saying something important! The seed, outer shell or flesh, must die before it can produce fruit. When we *speak* the Word of God, we *mortify*, or put to death our flesh, and the Spirit of God, which dwells with our spirit, is released into the world. Only the Spirit of God can save the lost world, only the Spirit of God can deliver us from sin, sickness, poverty, the devil, death and hell.

We can either believe God or doubt God. God has a simple standard: God says that if we will believe His Word, He will impute Righteousness to us; however, if we disbelieve His Word, He will impute evil to us.

What do I mean by that?

God wants us to be righteous. He wants us to *believe* His Word. He wants us to become one with Him. He wants us to live forever.

You may ask, "If Abraham, Joseph, Moses, and David could become righteous, why did Jesus Christ have to be born, die and be resurrected?"

First we have to understand what God means by *righteousness*.

**WAS NOT ABRAHAM OUR FATHER JUSTIFIED BY WORKS, WHEN HE HAD OFFERED ISAAC HIS SON UPON THE ALTAR?**
**SEEST THOU HOW FAITH WROUGHT WITH HIS WORKS, AND BY WORKS WAS FAITH MADE PERFECT?**
**AND THE SCRIPTURE WAS FULFILLED WHICH SAITH, ABRAHAM BELIEVED GOD, AND IT WAS "IMPUTED" UNTO HIM FOR RIGHTEOUSNESS: AND HE WAS CALLED THE FRIEND OF GOD.**
**JAMES 2:21-23**

IMPUTED – G3049. Log-id'-zom-ahee: to take an inventory, i.e. estimate (literally or figuratively): - conclude, (ac-) count (of), + despise, esteem, impute, lay, number, reason, reckon, suppose, think (on).

We see that a person is *Righteous*, as far as God is concerned, if that person *believes* and is *obedient* to what God has *spoken*. The more you believe God's Word the more righteous you will become. Without faith, it is impossible to please God. Being righteous has nothing to do with doing a lot of good works.

How do we know if someone believes what God has said? That person's life (style) will begin conforming to God's Word.

How will a person begin conforming to God's Word if he does not even know God's Word? How do we know if a person does not believe God's Word? That person's life (style) will NOT conform to God's Word.

**TAKE HEED, BRETHREN, LEST THERE BE IN ANY OF YOU AN "EVIL" HEART OF "UNBELIEF", IN DEPARTING FROM THE LIVING GOD.**
**HEBREWS 3:12**

We see that a person has an *evil* heart, as far as God is concerned, if that person *disbelieves* God's Word and is disobedient to what God has spoken. Everybody who believes God's Word will enter into His rest. Everybody who disbelieves God's Word will not enter into God's rest.
People actually believe they can call God a liar and boldly enter into His presence. They are terribly mistaken. All liars, the children of Satan, the Father of Lies, have their part in the lake that burneth with fire. *See* Revelation 21:8. Only the children of *faith* can enter into the Kingdom and into God's rest. The children of the bondwoman, or the children of the law, are cast out. *See* Galatians Chapter 4.

**BEWARE OF FALSE PROPHETS, WHICH COME TO YOU IN SHEEP'S CLOTHING, BUT INWARDLY THEY ARE RAVENING WOLVES.**

**YE SHALL KNOW THEM BY THEIR FRUITS. DO MEN GATHER GRAPES OF THORNS, OR FIGS OF THISTLES?**

**EVEN SO EVERY GOOD TREE BRINGETH FORTH GOOD FRUIT; BUT A CORRUPT TREE BRINGETH FORTH EVIL FRUIT.**

**A GOOD TREE CANNOT BRING FORTH EVIL FRUIT, NEITHER CAN A CORRUPT TREE BRING FORTH GOOD FRUIT.**

**MATTHEW 7:15-18**

We can memorize God's Word, but if we do not believe it, we will not change. The Devil is familiar with God's Word, but He calls God a liar. We know the difference between false prophets and the children of God by their fruits. The children of God *believe* His Word and they begin manifesting their belief by their actions and the fruit of the Spirit.

Once we start filling ourselves with God's perfect word and begin building up our faith, we will begin to change. We *cannot* remain the same carnal person that we were before salvation. The change will not happen overnight, but with patience and perseverance, continually *speaking* God's Word to ourselves every day, we will begin changing.

I believe the change is exponential. At first it will not be noticeable to you or anybody else, but eventually, as the Word of God begins to bear fruit in your life, it will be obvious to you and to everybody. It will be like seeing a child when they are three years old and then seeing the child again when they are twenty years old. The change will be radical and everyone will notice it. If you get the Word inside you and believe, you will change! Your worth is determined by what is inside you.

Which would you choose, a container full of clay, gravel and sand, or a container full of silver, gold and precious jewels? Which container do you think God will choose? Are you God's Chosen? Are to full of the most precious thing in the universe? Are you full of the Word of God?

Every carnal Christian has some problem with sin. One person may have a problem with pride, another with lust, another with greed and another with all three. Mature Christians cannot expect an immature Christian to be a model of virtue any more than an adult would expect a three year old child to hold down a steady job. However, once somebody accepts Jesus Christ as their personal savior, the mature Christian should disciple the newborn Christian in the Word of God.

**CONFESS YOUR FAULTS ONE TO ANOTHER, AND PRAY ONE FOR ANOTHER, THAT YE MAY BE HEALED. THE EFFECTUAL FERVENT PPAYER OF A RIGHTEOUS MAN AVAILETH MUCH.**

**ELIAS WAS A MAN SUBJECT TO LIKE PASSIONS AS WE ARE, AND HE PRAYED EARNESTLY THAT IT MIGHT NOT RAIN: AND IT RAINED NOT ON THE EARTH BY THE SPACE OF THREE YEARS AND SIX MONTHS.**

**AND HE PRAYED AGAIN, AND THE HEAVEN GAVE RAIN, AND THE EARTH BROUGHT FORTH HER FRUIT.**

**JAMES 5:16-18**

We see in the Book of James that our faults are compared to sickness. Both sickness and our faults are the result of sin. An unsaved person cannot help being a sinner any more than a paralyzed person can help being a cripple. Both sickness and sinful acts are the end result of sin, and it is beyond our power to make ourselves whole. You might say, "I can heal myself, I just take some cold medicine or antibiotics." There are ways to relieve symptoms of sickness, but there is no way to be permanently cured from all sickness. However, there is a permanent answer to all sickness and all sin: *Prayer, according to the Word of God*!

If somebody asks us to pray for them because they are sick, what do we say? If somebody asks us to pray for them because they have sin in their lives, what do we say?

"YUK! Get away from me you pitiful and cursed wretch!" Hopefully we don't treat sick people like that, and hopefully we don't treat lost sinners like that because that is how the Pharisees treated people. If we are a mature Christian, we take authority over the disease and/or the sin and cast it out of them in the name of Jesus Christ. If we do not have the faith to cast it out, we should turn to the Word of God, and also direct the sufferer to the Word of God. Jesus also draws a correlation between sin and sickness after he healed a crippled man.

**AFTERWARD JESUS FINDETH HIM IN THE TEMPLE, AND SAID UNTO HIM, BEHOLD, THOU ART MADE WHOLE: SIN NO MORE, LEST A WORSE THING COME UNTO THEE.**
**JOHN 5:14**

Sin and sickness share the same root cause, *unbelief in God's Word*!

**BUT HE WAS WOUNDED FOR OUR TRANSGRESSIONS, HE WAS BRUISED FOR OUR INIQUITIES: THE CHASTISEMENT OF OUR PEACE WAS UPON HIM; AND WITH HIS STRIPES WE "ARE" HEALED!**
**ISAIAH 53:5**

Will you believe the Word of God or will you disbelieve God's Word?

Memorize verses related to healing and encourage the sick person to memorize the healing verses. Repeat the Word of God over and over until the Holy Ghost builds up faith in your spirit. Building up faith in your spirit is similar to building up muscle in your body.

If a body builder has a weakness in his body, he isolates the muscle he wants to make stronger and then he repeatedly lifts a weight until it is built up. We can strengthen our spirit in a similar fashion, we simply identify the weakness in our spirit and then by repeatedly speaking the appropriate Word of God, we strengthen the weakness in our spirit. All our circumstances in life are directly related to our spiritual maturity.

The same remedy that applies to sickness also applies to sin. If a brother or sister in Christ comes to us and confesses a sin, we should direct them to the cure ... Jesus Christ (the *Word of God*)! We do not condemn them and go around gossiping about it to others. We are all sinners saved by grace, but all born again Christians are the righteousness of God in Jesus Christ if they will only apprehend it!

**FOR HE HATH MADE HIM TO BE SIN FOR US, WHO KNEW NO SIN; THAT WE MIGHT BE MADE THE RIGHTEOUSNESS OF GOD IN HIM.**
**II Corinthians 5:21**

Many Christians fail to realize we are not required to "build" character. We are required to recognize, believe and apprehend the character that we already possess in Jesus Christ. There is only one way to do that, and that way is to study to show ourselves approved. We must become knowledgeable about the death and resurrection of Jesus Christ and all that He means to us and all of creation.

We must enter into the Promised Land, the land flowing with milk and honey. We must sail into our safe harbor. We must enter into God's promises for us. Before we enter into the blessings of God, we must *hear* God's Word, and *believe* the blessings that God has prepared for us. We must enter into God's blessing and His rest by *believing* His Word. We must *speak* God's Words of blessing to ourselves and to those around us. We must *walk in the spirit*. It does not matter if we claim to believe God's Word if there is no evidence in our life.

When King David fled from Saul into the wilderness his whole family followed him.

**DAVID THEREFORE DEPARTED THENCE, AND ESCAPED TO THE CAVE ADULLAM: AND WHEN HIS BRETHREN AND ALL HIS FATHER'S HOUSE HEARD IT, THEY WENT DOWN THITHER TO HIM.**
**AND EVERY ONE THAT WAS IN DISTRESS, AND EVERY ONE THAT WAS IN DEBT, AND EVERY ONE THAT WAS DISCONTENTED, GATHERED THEMSELVES UNTO HIM; AND HE BECAME A CAPTAIN OVER THEM; AND THERE WERE WITH HIM ABOUT FOUR HUNDRED MEN.**
**I SAMUEL 22:1-2**

You think you have problems. Try and be responsible for four hundred men, not counting women and children, out in the middle of a desert wilderness. King David had to learn about trusting God. All Christians enter the wilderness after salvation.

Why is entering the wilderness necessary? The Wilderness is the place where we learn to trust God and His Word completely. Until we learn how to be totally dependent on God, we will never be able to leave the Wilderness and enter the Promised Land. David trusted in God's Word to him, while he was in the desert. God told David he would be King of Israel and David believed God. This brings us to the reason for the Wilderness experience. The Wilderness experience serves two purposes:

First, the Wilderness experience helps us to recognize that we cannot trust in our own abilities and strength. Second, the Wilderness experience helps us to realize we can trust totally upon God and His Word. Every Wilderness experience helps us recognize that there are circumstances and problems we just cannot solve by ourselves. We need to learn how to completely rely on God's Word and trust in Him to supply our every need.

# CHAPTER 20

## WHY DO BAD THINGS HAPPEN TO GOOD PEOPLE?

Bad things happen to many people, not because they are necessarily more wicked than any other people, but because God's hedge of protection has been lifted and they are not protected from the enemy.

If you have some chronic problem in your life, whether it is a health problem, a financial problem or a sin problem, you have not reached the Promised Land yet. God will only allow the devil to plague you if you are trusting in yourself and you are not trusting in God.

**THERE WAS A MAN IN THE LAND OF UZ, WHOSE NAME WAS JOB; AND THAT MAN WAS PERFECT AND UPRIGHT, AND ONE THAT FEARED GOD, AND ESCHEWED EVIL.**
**JOB 1:1**

Most people know the story of Job. According to the Bible, Job was perfect and upright. Why did God allow Satan to bring so much misery down upon Job? I think I know ... Job was a legalist, he was one of those blessed people who had everything going for him, he was rich, he had good health, he had a loving family and good friends, but there was one thing he lacked. He did not completely trust God. He believed that God's nature was mercurial.

Job believed that if he was good, God would bless him, but Job believed that if he was bad, God would bring down all kinds of trouble on him. That, by the way, was what Job's three friends believed too. Job was never sure that his good relationship with God would last. Job was afraid that someday he would mess up and God would come down on him with both feet.

Job was continually anxious, even in the midst of his prosperity and health, because he did not really trust God. Job was a legalist and he believed he was successful and prosperous because of his own good works. However, he was never sure that he would not accidently offend God and be punished.

**FOR THE THING WHICH I GREATLY FEARED IS COME UPON ME, AND THAT WHICH I WAS AFRAID OF IS COME UNTO ME.**
**I WAS NOT IN SAFETY, NEITHER HAD I REST, NEITHER WAS I QUIET; YET TROUBLE CAME.**
**JOB 3:25-26**

Job had the same mistaken notion that all legalist have: If I scratch God's back, God will scratch my back.

God gives His longest speech in the Bible to Job and his friends, basically God says: I do not need you, or anybody else, to scratch my back!

The only person God did not reprimand in the Book of Job was Job's youngest friend Elihu. I believe God did not reprimand him because Elihu understood where God was coming from.

**IF THOU SINNEST, WHAT DOEST THOU AGAINST HIM? OR IF THY TRANSGRESSIONS BE MULTIPLIED, WHAT DOEST THOU UNTO HIM?**
**IF THOU BE RIGHTEOUS, WHAT GIVEST THOU HIM? OR WHAT RECEIVETH HE OF THINE HAND?**
**JOB 35:6-7**

If you can understand this simple truism, you are well on our way to receiving all that God has prepared for you. *We cannot do anything for God, but He loves us anyway*!

If a child does not listen to their mother's warning and touches a hot stove, the child suffers the pain, the mother does not suffer pain, but she suffers distress. The same principal applies to sinful mankind. When we sin, we hurt ourselves and other people, but we do not hurt God. We do cause God distress because *God loves everyone*!

Why does a new born baby's mother and father love their child? A new born child cannot do anything for his or her parents. Similarly, we cannot do anything for God. Job was receiving all his blessings from God, simply because God loved him. Unfortunately, Job had to go through a desperate wilderness experience before he realized that his good works did not impact God one way or another. Job had to learn that His good works were as filthy rags to God. How much more should Christian saints trust in the provision and blessing of God today?

**HE SHALL COVER THEE WITH HIS FEATHERS, AND UNDER HIS WINGS SHALT THOU TRUST: HIS "TRUTH" SHALL BE THY SHIELD AND BUCKLER.**
**THOU SHALT NOT BE AFRAID FOR THE TERROR BY NIGHT; NOR FOR THE ARROW THAT FLIETH BY DAY;**
**NOR FOR THE PESTILENCE THAT WALKETH IN DARKNESS; NOR FOR THE DESTRUCTION THAT WASTETH AT NOONDAY.**
**A THOUSAND SHALL FALL AT THY SIDE, AND TEN THOUSAND AT THY RIGHT HAND; BUT IT SHALL NOT COME NIGH THEE.**
**PSALM 91:4-7**

God's *truth* is our shield and buckler. God's Word is the *sword* of the spirit. I am not saying that once you become mature spiritually, you will not encounter any problems ever again. As long as we are on this earth, in our mortal bodies, we will encounter problems. God will allow Satan to test us in order to reveal our legalism and our self-reliance.

God only allows the curse of the law in order to turn us back to God and His Word for help. When sickness comes, when financial setbacks come, when temptation comes, we have a sword and we have a shield. We do not have to remain sick. We do not have to remain poor. We do not have to remain sinners. We must stop relying on our own strength and wisdom, turn to God's Word of Truth, the sword of the spirit, and then we must boldly go to war against all the giants in the land. We, who have the New Testament and knowledge of the perfect work of Jesus Christ, for and on our behalf, should have much more faith in God then the children of Israel. Our Wilderness journey does not have to last forty years. We can enter into the Promised Land right now!

# PART 4

## THE LAND OF CANAAN

*"O Lord, truly I am thy servant;*
*I am thy servant, and the son of thine handmaid;*
*Thou has loosed my bonds.*
*I will offer to thee the sacrifice of thanksgiving,*
*And will call upon the name of the Lord."*

**Psalm 116:16-17**

# CHAPTER 21

## THE PROMISED LAND

BUT THIS SHALL BE THE COVENANT THAT I WILL MAKE WITH THE HOUSE OF ISRAEL; AFTER THOSE DAYS, SAITH THE LORD, I WILL PUT MY LAW IN THEIR INWARD PARTS AND WRITE IT IN THEIR HEARTS, AND WILL BE THEIR GOD, AND THEY SHALL BE MY PEOPLE.
AND THEY SHALL TEACH NO MORE EVERY MAN HIS NEIGHBOUR, AND EVERY MAN HIS BROTHER, SAYING, KNOW THE LORD: FOR THEY SHALL ALL KNOW ME, FROM THE LEAST OF THEM UNTO THE GREATEST OF THEM, SAITH THE LORD: FOR I WILL FORGIVE THEIR INIQUITY, AND I WILL REMEMBER THEIR SIN NO MORE.
JEREMIAH 31:33-34

I believe that during the millennial reign of Jesus Christ, all peoples will be memorizing, speaking and singing the scriptures from the day they are able to talk. Mothers and fathers will be singing scripture verses to their babies in their cribs. Grandmothers and Grandfathers will be reading scripture verses to their grandchildren. God's people will live as long as trees. *See* Isaiah 65:22.

Visions and dreams will be common place. Angels and celestial human beings will be interacting with mankind on a regular basis. Everyone will have an intimate relationship with God. Everyone will be *walking in the spirit*. However, we don't have to wait until the millennial reign to experience a close walk with Jesus Christ. We can start walking with Jesus right now.

If you *walk in the spirit* for any length of time, you cannot help but experience the *blessing* of God, any more than you can jump in a lake and not experience being wet. When you completely trust in God's Word, when you *walk in the spirit*, you will be completely surrounded by God, and His *blessing,* just like you are completely surrounded by water when you dive into a lake.

I WILL DWELL IN THEM, AND WALK IN THEM; AND I WILL BE THEIR GOD, AND THEY SHALL BE MY PEOPLE.
2 CORINTHIANS 6:16

I believe the Apostle Paul was attempting to explain to the Corinthians that the promises God made to the prophets of Israel were available to them immediately. They did not have to wait for some future far away millennial reign of Jesus Christ. If Jesus Christ reigns in our hearts, we can have God's blessing right away.

God has always wanted intimacy with mankind; however, because of sin there has been a great gulf between God and mankind. Before Adam ate from the tree of the knowledge of good and evil, he was perfectly intimate with God. Adam understood and trusted in God's love just as surely as any child understands and trusts in their parents love.

I remember the struggles I went through after I became a Christian. If I sinned, I would stop praying and stop reading my Bible. My fellowship with God would suffer because my sins made me afraid to approach God. However, that is a terrible mistake.

When we sin, we need to do exactly the opposite and spend more time with God. We need to understand that the sacrifice of Jesus Christ on the cross was perfectly sufficient. We can boldly approach our Father in heaven whether we sin or not.

# CHAPTER 22

## SERENDIPITY = THE BLESSING OF GOD

After sin and the fall, the fear of judgment took the place of the perfect confidence Adam had in God before he sinned. When Jesus Christ forsook the glory of heaven to become a man, and then meekly took the place of man on the cross for the sins of the world, there could be no mistake or doubt, God loved mankind despite our sins. God still desired to be intimate with mankind. God did not just love us when we were perfectly obedient. God loved us even when we were disobedient.

God will always love us and He will always want the best for us. However, the *blessing* is not available to those who walk in disobedience and do not believe God's Word. Walking in obedience, and trusting in God's Word, is the same as *walking in the spirit.*

**Serendipity** means an aptitude for making fortunate discoveries accidently.

Some of the most famous and fortuitous discoveries ever made were made by sheer dumb luck, as even the discoverers will admit. Many of these types of discoveries made the discoverer rich and famous. Alexander Fleming discovered Penicillin after he failed to disinfect cultures of bacteria when leaving on his vacation. When he returned from vacation he found the cultures contaminated with *Penicillium* molds, which had killed the bacteria. Charles Goodyear accidently left a piece of rubber and some sulfur on a hot plate and discovered vulcanization of rubber. Art Fry wanted a way to keep his bookmarks in his hymn book at his church, he attended a college seminar on a new adhesive and invented Post-It Notes. Perhaps Art Fry knew something most other people don't!

O LET THE NATIONS BE GLAD AND SING FOR JOY; FOR THOU SHALT JUDGE THE PEOPLE RIGHTEOUSLY, AND GOVERN THE NATIONS UPON EARTH, SELAH.
LET THE PEOPLE PRAISE THEE, O GOD; LET ALL THE PEOPLE PRAISE THEE.
THEN SHALL THE EARTH YIELD HER INCREASE; AND GOD, EVEN OUR OWN GOD, SHALL BLESS US.
GOD SHALL BLESS US; AND ALL THE ENDS OF THE EARTH SHALL FEAR HIM.
PSALM 67:4-7

A whole book could be written about serendipity, and I believe all these accidents were not accidents at all. I believe God can and does make people and events come together according to His good purposes. I believe serendipity is just another word for the *blessing* of God. *See* James 2:23. One of God's great pleasures is to bless the righteous.

FOR THOU, LORD, WILT BLESS THE RIGHTEOUS; WITH FAVOUR WILT THOU COMPASS HIM AS WITH A SHIELD.
PSALMS 5:12

Remember, being righteous to God simply means *believing* His Word!

BLESSING – H1293. Ber-aw-kaw': benediction; by implication prosperity: - blessing, liberal, pool, present.

The *blessing* of God comes from being intimate with God. When you *walk in the spirit* good things will begin to happen. Good things will start to happen to you, and to everyone and everything around you. Joseph is a good example of how God blesses those with whom He is intimate. If you know the story of Joseph, you probably noticed how he always ended up being in charge no matter what his circumstances.

AND THE LORD WAS WITH JOSEPH, AND HE WAS A "PROSPEROUS" MAN; AND HE WAS IN THE HOUSE OF HIS MASTER THE EGYPTIAN.
AND HIS MASTER SAW THAT THE LORD WAS WITH HIM, AND THAT THE LORD MADE ALL THAT HE DID TO "PROSPER" IN HIS HAND.
AND JOSEPH FOUND GRACE IN HIS SIGHT, AND HE SERVED HIM: AND HE MADE HIM OVERSEER OVER HIS HOUSE, AND ALL THAT HE HAD HE PUT INTO HIS HAND.
AND IT CAME TO PASS FROM THE TIME THAT HE HAD MADE HIM OVERSEER IN HIS HOUSE, AND OVER ALL THAT HE HAD, THAT THE LORD "BLESSED" THE EGYPTIAN'S HOUSE FOR JOSEPH'S SAKE; AND THE "BLESSING" OF THE LORD WAS UPON ALL THAT HE HAD IN THE HOUSE, AND IN THE FIELD.
GENESIS 39:2-5

It was obvious to Potiphar, that whenever he made Joseph responsible for something, it prospered. What did Abraham, Joseph, Moses and King David have in common? They were all intimate with God and believed His Word!

For some reason, some Christians read about the Old Testament saints and say, "They were under the Old Covenant, long life, great riches, and wisdom ain't for us. Christians are supposed to be sickly, poor, and stupid because it builds character."

If that is the case, maybe we should forget the new covenant and get back under the old covenant. How come the Old Testament saints seem to be a lot better off than many modern day Christians? People quote the Book of James out of context:

GO TO NOW; YE RICH MEN, WEEP AND HOWL FOR YOUR MISERIES THAT SHALL COME UPON YOU.
YOUR RICHES ARE CORRUPTED, AND YOUR GARMENTS ARE MOTHEATEN.
YOUR GOLD AND SILVER IS CANKERED; AND THE RUST OF THEM SHALL BE A WITNESS AGAINST YOU, AND SHALL EAT YOUR FLESH AS IT WERE FIRE. YE HAVE HEAPED TREASURE TOGETHER FOR THE LAST DAYS.
JAMES 5:1-3

Wow! Who would want to be rich after hearing this condemnation? However, let's read some more verses from the Book of James:

**BEHOLD, THE HIRE OF THE LABOURERES WHO HAVE REAPED DOWN YOUR FIELDS, WHICH IS OF YOU KEPT BACK BY "FRAUD", CRIETH: AND THE CRIES OF THEM WHICH HAVE REAPED ARE ENTERED INTO THE EARS OF THE LORD OF SABAOTH.**

**YE HAVE LIVED IN PLEASURE ON THE EARTH, AND BEEN "WANTON"; YE HAVE NOURISHED YOUR HEARTS, AS IN A DAY OF SLAUGHTER.**

**YE HAVE CONDEMNED AND "KILLED" THE JUST; AND HE DOTH NOT RESIST YOU.**

**JAMES 5:4-6**

There is more than one way to become prosperous, or to skin a cat, so to speak. You can become prosperous God's way, by *walking in the spirit*. You can also become rich and prosperous the world's way. The world's way to riches is to scratch and claw your way to the top. It is the survival of the fittest model of prosperity. You take advantage of people whenever you can and you step on whoever gets in your way. You lie, cheat, steal, kill and destroy, and it doesn't matter if it's your mother, your brother, or your best friend.

The world's method is surely a road to wealth and/or prison, but you probably understand why God has problems with that particular method to prosperity. God's road to riches is simply to *believe* His Word. All riches belong to God and come from God, so you either have to receive wealth directly from God, or you have to receive wealth from somebody who has received riches from God, or you have to steal riches from somebody who has received wealth from God.

Why do you think God condemns stealing? Thieves are trying to accumulate wealth apart from God's correct way, which is intimacy with God.

Many Christians fail to realize that might does not make right. Just because somebody is rich and famous does not mean they are a good person. Just because somebody is the mayor, or congressman, or minister of the biggest church in town does not mean they are automatically a good Christian. Conversely, just because somebody is well off, does not automatically make them a bad person. There is a right way to attain spiritual, mental and physical prosperity.

We are required to comprehend and apprehend the character of Jesus Christ. We must *memorize* and *speak* God's Word both to ourselves and to those around us. We must become intimate with God! Learning and speaking God's Word is not meant only for ministers, preachers and priests. Learning and speaking God's Word is a requirement for all true believers.

**THIS I SAY THEN, WALK IN THE SPIRIT, AND YE SHALL NOT FULFIL THE LUST OF THE FLESH.**

**FOR THE FLESH LUSTETH AGAINST THE SPIRIT, AND THE SPIRIT AGAINST THE FLESH: AND THESE ARE CONTRARY THE ONE TO THE OTHER: SO THAT YE CANNOT DO THE THINGS THAT YE WOULD.**

**BUT IF YE BE LED OF THE SPIRIT, YE ARE NOT UNDER THE LAW.**

**GALATIANS 5:16-18**

Paul is trying to explain that the carnal man, the old man, desires to fulfill the desires of the flesh. The desires of the flesh always lead to death and destruction. The old man wants to trust in his own strength and his own wisdom. The old man *wants to be under the law* and receive all the glory. The old man likes to say, "I picked myself up by my own bootstraps." The old man likes to say, "I did it all myself, I deserve all the credit." Christians are required to repent from dead works, whether they appear bad or good.

The mature Christian is exactly the opposite. The mature Christian realizes that under the law, he is condemned and cursed. The mature Christian is totally reliant on God and totally trusts God's promises. The mature Christian realizes that he only has dominion over his flesh as long as he *walks in the spirit*. The mature Christian gives God all the glory. The mature Christian will not have to struggle to read and memorize God's Word. Reading and memorizing God's Word will be the chief joy of his/her life.

# CHAPTER 23

## WALKING IN THE SPIRIT = THE FRUIT OF THE SPIRIT

When you *walk in the spirit,* you do not have to worry about breaking the law, because that is the last thing that will enter your mind. Your chief and only desire will be to please God. You will probably walk around with a stupid grin on your face. How could you not? Everything will be going right for you. Everything you set your hand to will prosper. You will be surrounded by God's blessing.

When the devil comes, you will swat him away like a fly. The devil will stop being a terror and simply become an annoyance. After a while, the devil may even stop bugging you. You will have to start getting involved with other people's problems if you don't want to actually lose your spiritual fighting skills. Like Joseph, Moses, Gideon and King David, you will become a Deliverer!

BUT THE FRUIT OF THE SPIRIT IS LOVE, JOY, PEACE, LONGSUFFERING, GENTLENESS, GOODNESS, FAITH,
MEEKNESS, TEMPERANCE: AGAINST SUCH THERE IS NO LAW.
AND THEY THAT ARE CHRIST'S HAVE CRUCIFIED THE FLESH WITH THE AFFECTIONS AND LUSTS.
IF WE LIVE IN THE SPIRIT, LET US ALSO WALK IN THE SPIRIT.
LET US NOT BE DESIROUS OF VAIN GLORY, PROVOKING ONE ANOTHER, ENVYING ONE ANOTHER.
GALATIANS 5:22-26

Jesus said, "By their fruit you will know them." *See* Matthew 12:33. When you become a mature Christian, people will not have to ask, they will know that you are the real deal. Either they will be repelled by you, or they will be drawn to you. You should know that the Holy Spirit will draw people to you just like He drew people to King David, just like He drew people to Jesus Christ.

People are drawn to a fruit tree by its fruit, and people are drawn to a mature Christian by the fruits of the Spirit. Many people will love you, and probably many more will hate and envy you. Jesus said, "If they persecuted me, they will persecute you." *See* John 16:20. However, your reaction to them will be different than before you became a mature Christian.

They may annoy you, but you will also feel pity for them. You will pray that God will open their eyes. You will speak the Word of God to them, and have the honor of leading them to Jesus Christ. You will disciple them and watch them grow into mature Christians. These same people who hated you will end up being the people who will love you the most.

**Testament** means to testify, make a will, or in the Bible, a covenant.

Mature Christians are not under the Old Covenant. The Old Covenant was similar to a two-party contract. God said, "Obey me and I will bless you." God said, "Disobey me and I will allow the blessing to depart and the curse to come upon you." The Old Covenant was based on the actions of two parties, God and mankind. Mankind could never fulfill their side of the bargain.

The New Covenant is similar to a Last Will and Testament with a Trustee. The New Covenant has four parties, God the Father, God the Son, God the Holy Spirit and the Church. God the Father says, "My Son has fulfilled the Old Covenant and I give Him *all of creation*."

God the Son says, "I have died and fulfilled the Old Covenant, I have eliminated the curse, I am resurrected, and I have inherited all God the Father's creation and I freely *give* all my Father's blessings and all His creation to the Church ... forever."

God the Holy Spirit as trustee says, "I will give the Church all the Son's blessing, which Christ has passed on to her, when she is mature enough to handle the blessings. I will grant the Church the blessings from God the Father when she has reached maturity and is *walking in the spirit*."

**WHETHER PAUL, OR APOLLOS, OR CEPHAS, OR THE WORLD, OR LIFE, OR DEATH, OR THINGS PRESENT, OR THINGS TO COME; ALL ARE YOURS;
AND YE ARE CHRIST'S; AND CHRIST IS GOD'S.
I CORINTHIANS 3:22-23**

The New Testament saints could never keep the Old Covenant any more than the Old Testament saints can keep the Old Covenant. All the promises and blessings that the Old Testament saints received were under the New Covenant. They had *faith* in the promised Savior Messiah, and his perfect atonement for the sins of the world before Jesus ever arrived on earth. They had faith because they knew and believed God's Word, and therefore they received the blessing from God before Jesus Christ was ever born, before He ever died, before He ever rose from the dead and before He ever sat on the right hand of God the Father.  The Old Testament saints believed God's Word just like we must believe God's Word!

# CHAPTER 24

## WALKING IN THE SPIRIT

Before we can reach a certain destination, we must decide where we want to go, how we are going to get there and then we have to go there. I guess now days, we can take a car, or a train, or a plane, but in the spirit dimension, there is only one way to reach the spiritual Promised Land. "We must *walk in the spirit*!

*THERE IS* THEREFORE NOW NO CONDEMNATION TO THEM WHICH ARE IN CHRIST JESUS, WHO "WALK" NOT AFTER THE FLESH, BUT AFTER THE SPIRIT.
ROMANS 8:1

WALK - G4043. per-ee-pat-eh'-o: to tread all around, i.e. walk at large (especially as proof of ability); figuratively to live, deport oneself, follow (as a companion or votary): - go, be occupied with, walk (about).

Salvation is easy, as a matter of fact we have nothing to do with our salvation other than hearing the gospel and accepting it; however, growing up into a spiritually mature Christian, and *walking in the spirit* takes some work on our part. The word *walk* in the Greek means to be occupied with someone or something. It means spending intimate time with them. It means: to spend time with them, to follow them, to *talk* with them, to be their companion or votary (a devoted and ardent supporter).

How do we show our devotion to somebody? How do we know we love a person? Don't we want to spend our time with them? Don't we spend our resources, our minds and our strength, trying to please and know them? Don't we want to pattern our lives around them? Don't we *talk* with them? Don't we pursue them? Isn't that how we recognize that we love someone?

FOR THEY THAT ARE AFTER THE FLESH DO MIND *(SET THEIR MINDS ON)* THE THINGS OF THE FLESH; BUT THEY THAT ARE AFTER THE SPIRIT THE THINGS OF THE SPIRIT.
FOR TO BE CARNALLY MINDED *IS* DEATH; BUT TO BE SPIRITUALLY MINDED *IS* LIFE AND PEACE.
ROMANS 8:5-6

Our *mind* is a great spiritual battle ground. If our mind dwells on desires of the flesh, we will eventually set about to apprehend those fleshy desires. If our mind dwells on desires of the spirit, we will eventually set our minds and our goals to apprehend spiritual things. So what are the things of the Spirit? Jesus makes everything perfectly clear:

IT IS THE SPIRIT THAT QUICKENETH (GIVES LIFE); THE FLESH PROFITETH NOTHING: THE "WORDS" THAT I "SPEAK" UNTO YOU, *THEY* ARE "SPIRIT", AND *THEY* ARE LIFE.
JOHN 6:63

We understand that the Words Jesus *spoke,* they are spirit and life. We also understand that we need to get Jesus' Words into our spirit, into our mind and into our mouth. We have to eat and drink the Words that Jesus spoke. We have to write them on the tables of our hearts. We have to *meditate* on them. We have to *memorize* them.

When we have the Word of God in us, *we* become the Word in the *flesh, we* become the Word *incarnate* just like Jesus Christ. We become the walking, talking, *living* Word of GOD on earth. We become God's *anointed.* We become the body of Christ. The more of God's Word we have in us, the more like the Word we will become and the less like the world we will be.

Jesus Christ will increase, while you and your fleshly desires will decrease. If you want to *walk in the spirit,* you must set your mind on spiritual things. You must begin *memorizing* God's Word. You must replace your previous earthly and fleshy desires with heavenly and spiritual desires. You must begin *speaking* and *hearing* God's Word every day.

SO THEN FAITH COMETH BY HEARING, AND HEARING BY THE WORD OF GOD.
ROMANS 10:17

Hearing God's Word is the mechanism whereby our spirit and faith is built up over time. You have probably heard that somebody is weak in faith because they cannot believe for something. The reason everybody is not commanding mountains to be cast into the sea is because they have not *heard* God's Word, and they have not *believed* God's Word.

If you do not hear the Word, how can you believe it? If you hear the Word, how can you believe it if you forget it? That is why we must continually sow God's Word to our spirit. Our spirit is an unlimited field. We do not have to plant a Word of *hope* one year and wait for another year to plant a Word of *love.* We can plant all the promises of God immediately, and receive a bumper crop continually in every area of life.

The Lord Jesus called a newly saved Christian *born again.*

JESUS ANSWERED AND SAID UNTO HIM, VERILY, VERILY, I SAY UNTO THEE, EXCEPT A MAN BE "BORN AGAIN" [ANEW], HE CANNOT SEE THE KINGDOM OF GOD.
JOHN 3:3

When we first hear the Word of God and we believe it, we are born again into a new kingdom, into the spirit kingdom of God. In the spirit, we are spiritual babies. We are weak, we are vulnerable, and there is a grave danger we will remain that way. We will remain spiritual babies unless we grow up and mature in the spirit.

There is only one way we can strengthen our spirits, and that is by nourishing our spirit with Spirit food. Spirit food is the *spoken* Word of God. We *must* take it in, we must *meditate* upon it, we must *speak* it, we must *hear* it, we must *believe* it, and we must make it a part of our spirit just like we make food a part of our bodies.

When you eat, you have to chew the food before it can be swallowed. In order to make the Word of God part of our spirit, we must chew it spiritually. We must *meditate* upon it. We must *speak* God's Word over and over to ourselves until we have it memorized, and then the Word of God becomes a part of our spirit. A clear sign that a person is born again is their sincere desire to *read, hear* and *speak* the Word of God.

BEING BORN AGAIN, NOT OF CORRUPTIBLE SEED, BUT OF INCORRUPTIBLE, BY THE **WORD OF GOD,** WHICH LIVETH AND ABIDETH FOR EVER.
FOR ALL FLESH IS AS GRASS, AND ALL THE GLORY OF MAN AS THE FLOWER OF GRASS. THE GRASS WITHERETH AND THE FLOWER THEREOF FALLETH AWAY;
BUT THE **WORD** OF THE LORD ENDURETH FOR EVER. AND THIS IS THE **WORD,** WHICH BY THE GOSPEL IS PREACHED UNTO YOU.
WHEREFORE LAYING ASIDE ALL MALICE, AND ALL GUILE, AND HYPOCRISIES, AND ENVIES, AND ALL EVIL SPEAKINGS,
AS NEWBORN BABES, DESIRE THE SINCERE "MILK" OF THE **WORD,** THAT YE MAY "GROW" THEREBY;
I PETER 1:23-2:2

All the unlimited resources of God are available to them who will *walk in the spirit,* to them who will feed on God's Word. If you read the autobiographies of many rich and famous people, you will find out quite a lot of them had a parent, or grandparent, or someone very close to them who was familiar with the Word of God and *spoke* the Word of God to them.

Often times, their parents were ministers or missionaries. These types of rich and famous people in the world are often enjoying the blessings and prosperity associated with somebody else's spiritual maturity. Just like the child of a rich parent will enjoy the benefits of their parent's hard work. However, they believe all their prosperity is because they are special. They refuse to give credit where credit is due.

Often times priests, pastors, or church leaders do not understand why their congregations have a problem with sin. Often times priests, pastors, or church leaders do not understand why they have a problem with sin! If a person only hears the Word of God once a week, they will never be spiritually mature. It is like expecting a baby to grow up physically strong and mature on one meal a week. In order for a person to grow up spiritually, they must *hear* and *feed* on the Word of God daily, at least three times a day, preferably continually, every day. Let us Hear the King and Prophet David:

EVENING, AND MORNING, AND AT NOON, WILL I "PRAY", AND "CRY ALOUD"; AND HE SHALL "HEAR" MY VOICE.
PSALM 55:17

The Book of Psalms is full of God's Word as uttered by the Prophet King of Israel, David son of Jesse of the Tribe of Judah. The first psalm is the key to all the psalms and well worth memorizing:

**BLESSED IS THE MAN THAT WALKETH NOT IN THE COUNSEL OF THE UNGODLY, NOR STANDETH IN THE WAY OF SINNERS, NOR SITTETH IN THE SEAT OF THE SCORNFUL.**

**BUT HIS DELIGHT IS IN THE LAW OF THE LORD; AND IN HIS LAW DOTH HE "MEDITATE" DAY AND NIGHT.**

**AND HE SHALL BE LIKE A TREE PLANTED BY THE RIVERS OF WATER, THAT BRINGETH FORTH HIS FRUIT IN HIS SEASON; HIS LEAF ALSO SHALL NOT WITHER; AND WHATSOEVER HE DOETH SHALL PROSPER.**

**THE UNGODLY ARE NOT SO: BUT ARE LIKE THE CHAFF WHICH THE WIND DRIVETH AWAY.**

**THEREFORE THE UNGODLY SHALL NOT STAND IN THE JUDGMENT, NOR SINNERS IN THE CONGREGATION OF THE RIGHTEOUS.**

**FOR THE LORD KNOWETH THE WAY OF THE RIGHTEOUS: BUT THE WAY OF THE UNGODLY SHALL PERISH.**

**PSALM 1:1-6**

MEDITATE - H1897. daw-gaw': a primitive root; to "murmur" (in pleasure or anger); by implication to ponder: - imagine, meditate, mourn, "mutter", roar, X sore, "speak", study, "talk", utter.

When I talk about chewing on the Word, I mean to *meditate* on it. You must *speak* the Word of God over and over to yourself. You will be amazed at the revelation you will receive after *meditating/speaking* a verse (*speaking a verse over and over out loud*) for a day, or a week, or a year.

Have you ever seen a video on television of orthodox Jews studying the torah? A prayer shawl covers their head, they move their bodies up and down at the waist, they *speak* the Word of God out loud, over, and over, they speak God's Word to themselves in order to memorize God's Word.

I can imagine King David with the Torah opened in front of him late at night, a covering over his head, symbolizing God's authority over him, moving his body up and down at the waist, *speaking* the Word of God over, and over, to himself until he knew it backwards and forwards, *memorizing* the Word of God until it became a part of him.

When most people think of King David, the first thing that may come to mind is the great warrior and king, or perhaps his adulterous affair with Bathsheba, and his conspiracy to murder Uriah the Hittite. We understand from the Bible that God did not overlook his sin. King David would pay a terrible price for his sin.

When I think of King David, I think of a shepherd boy guarding his father's sheep from the lion and the bear. I think of a boy who was not highly esteemed by anyone. I think about what God told Samuel when he was sent to anoint David as King, and Samuel was about to anoint David's oldest brother Eliab.

**BUT THE LORD SAID UNTO SAMUEL, LOOK NOT ON HIS COUNTENANCE, OR ON THE HEIGHT OF HIS STATURE; BECAUSE I HAVE REFUSED HIM: FOR THE LORD SEETH NOT**

AS MAN SEETH; FOR MAN LOOKETH ON THE OUTWARD APPEARANCE, BUT THE LORD LOOKETH ON THE "HEART".
I SAMUEL 16:7

HEART – H3824. Lay-bawb': the heart (as the most interior organ); used also like 3820: - + bethink themselves, breast, comfortably, courage, ((faint), (tender) heart (-ed)), midst, mind, x unawares, understanding.

HEART – G2588. Kar-dee-ah': prolonged from a primary *kar* (Latin cor, "heart"); the heart, i.e., (figuratively) the thoughts or feelings (mind); also (by analogy) the middle: - (+ broken) heart (-ed).

The word interpreted in the King James Bible as *heart* in both *HEBREW* and *GREEK*, simply means the mind or thoughts of a man. The *mind* is the great battle field between the spirit and the flesh. Therefore, we see that God is keenly interested in a person's thought life. We can hide our thought life from people, but we cannot hide our thoughts from God. He wants us to be perfect in thought and deed. Jesus made it plain what God expects from everybody:

YE HAVE HEARD THAT IT WAS SAID BY THEM OF OLD TIME, THOU SHALT NOT COMMIT ADULTERY:
BUT I SAY UNTO YOU, THAT WHOSOEVER LOOKETH ON A WOMAN TO LUST AFTER HER HATH COMMITTED ADULTERY WITH HER ALREADY IN HIS HEART.
MATTHEW 5:27-28

God's standard is much higher than man's standard. God not only expects us not to sin, he expects us to not even think about sinning. God expects us to think on spiritual things.

FOR THOUGH WE WALK IN THE FLESH, WE DO NOT WAR AFTER THE FLESH:
(FOR THE WEAPONS OF OUR WARFARE ARE NOT CARNAL, BUT MIGHTY THROUGH GOD TO THE PULLING DOWN OF STRONG HOLDS;)
CASTING DOWN IMAGINATIONS, AND EVERY HIGH THING THAT EXALTETH ITSELF AGAINST THE KNOWLEDGE OF GOD, AND BRINGING INTO CAPTIVITY EVERY" THOUGHT" TO THE OBEDIENCE OF CHRIST;
II CORINTHIANS 10:3-5

You may ask along with the apostles:

## WHO THAN CAN BE SAVED?
MATTHEW 19:25

However, bringing our thoughts into captivity has nothing to do with our salvation. Salvation can occur in a moment, but becoming a mature Christian, maturing into the image of Jesus Christ, is a long journey of many years. I will show you that not only can Christians do what seems impossible to most people, but King David was able to mature spiritually prior to the death and resurrection of Jesus Christ.

# CHAPTER 25

## THE SECRET OF KING DAVID'S SUCCESS

David was not strong in the flesh, as a matter of fact he was probably a puny adolescent when he was chosen by God to be king, but he was spiritually head and shoulders above every man in Israel, aside from perhaps the Prophet Samuel.

What did God see in David's heart that he did not see in the hearts of his brothers, or in the hearts of any other boy or man in Israel?

I believe David was *singing* God's Word, in order to *memorize* it, even when he was a boy. I believe *singing* God's Word was an old tradition long before King David was born, but David was singing songs using God's Word when he was still a boy as a memorization technique. David spent his days following his father's sheep, playing his lyre and *singing* God's Word to himself. Why do I believe that?

AND IT CAME TO PASS, WHEN THE EVIL SPIRIT FROM GOD WAS UPON SAUL, THAT DAVID TOOK AN HARP, AND PLAYED WITH HIS HAND: SO SAUL WAS REFRESHED AND WAS WELL, AND THE EVIL SPIRIT DEPARTED FROM HIM.
I SAMUEL 16:23

Why would an evil spirit flee from Saul just because David played a harp? I am pretty sure the evil spirit would not have fled if David was playing *the boogey woogey blues*. I believe David had set God's Word to music. David was *singing* God's Word! David was full of God's Word, and he was a mighty spiritual warrior when he was still a boy. Later David would write and sing about his relationship with God in the Psalms:

THY "STATUTES" HAVE BEEN MY SONGS IN THE HOUSE OF MY PILGRIMAGE.
PSALM 119:54
THY WORD HAVE I HID IN MINE HEART, THAT I MIGHT NOT SIN AGAINST THEE.
PSALM 119:11

David *sang* and memorized God's word because he had a revelation that it would help him mature spiritually and help him not to sin against God. *Hiding* God's Word in our hearts will also help us not sin against God. David knew that *memorizing* God's Word would strengthen his spirit.

David knew the story of Joseph. He understood that Joseph would rather suffer wrong than sin against God, and in the end Joseph was the deliverance of Israel. When David was a boy, Israel was being dominated by the Philistines living on the coasts of Israel, and David also wanted to be the deliverer of Israel.
Do you want to deliver your family, friends and acquaintances from sickness, from poverty, from oppression of all kinds? *Start memorizing and speaking the Word of God!*

**THE LAW OF THY MOUTH IS BETTER UNTO ME THAN THOUSANDS OF GOLD AND SILVER.**
**PSALM 119:72**

Why was the law of God's mouth better to David than thousands of gold and silver? I believe it was because David knew that faith in God's Word was the source of all his blessings. David realized that knowing God's Word was the source of all his fame and fortune. I am sure that King David knew the Book of Joshua very well:

**THIS BOOK OF THE LAW (TORAH) SHALL NOT DEPART OUT OF THY MOUTH; BUT THOU SHALT "MEDITATE" THEREIN DAY AND NIGHT, THAT THOU MAYEST OBSERVE TO DO ACCORDING TO ALL THAT IS WRITTEN THEREIN: FOR THEN THOU SHALT MAKE THY WAY PROSPEROUS, AND THEN SHALT THOU HAVE GOOD SUCCESS.**
**JOSHUA 1:8**

MEDITATE - H1897. daw-gaw': a primitive root; to murmur (in pleasure or anger); by implication to ponder: - imagine, meditate, mourn, mutter, roar, X sore, speak, study, talk, utter.

*Meditate* is the exact same word that David uses in Psalm 1:2. David understood that hiding the Law of God in his heart (*memorizing* God's Word) would pay dividends that were both temporal and eternal. He understood that God is the creator, and that God is the author of all good things.

There would not have been a Solomon without a David. If you have a reference Bible, you may notice that much of the wisdom of Proverbs comes directly from Psalms. Where do you think the great wisdom and the great riches of Solomon came from?

**BOTH RICHES AND HONOUR COME OF THEE, AND THOU REIGNEST OVER ALL; AND IN THINE HAND IS POWER AND MIGHT; AND IN THINE HAND IT IS TO MAKE GREAT, AND TO GIVE STRENGTH UNTO "ALL".**
**I CHRONICLES 29:12**

This verse from 1 Chronicles, and is part of the speech that King David made after he anointed Solomon as king over Israel. David understood that it was God who gave him riches, strength and honor, it was God who made David great, and it was God who made David King over Israel. David understood, and he greatly desired for Solomon to understand, that God could and would give riches, honor, greatness and strength to ALL if they could only understand why God had chosen him over all his brethren.

God wants to bless everyone who will hear, memorize, believe, obey and speak His Word with authority. Speaking and believing God's Word is the ordained avenue of success in the kingdom of the spirit and in the physical world. Speaking and believing God's Word is *walking in the spirit*. Listen to the wisdom of King David, the Sweet Psalmist of Israel.

**THY WORD HAVE I HID IN MINE HEART (MIND), THAT I MIGHT NOT SIN AGAINST THEE.**
**PSALM 119:11**

WITH MY LIPS HAVE I "DECLARED" ALL THE JUDGMENTS OF THY MOUTH.
PSALM 119:13
I WILL DELIGHT MYSELF IN THY STATUTES; I WILL **NOT FORGET THY WORD.**
PSALM 119:16
O HOW LOVE I THY LAW! IT IS MY MEDITATION **ALL THE DAY.**
I HAVE MORE UNDERSTANDING THAN ALL MY TEACHERS: FOR THY TESTIMONIES ARE MY MEDITATION.
PSALM 119:99
I UNDERSTAND MORE THAN THE ANCIENTS, BECAUSE I KEEP THY PRECEPTS.
PSALM 119:100
THY WORD IS A LAMP UNTO MY FEET, AND A LIGHT UNTO MY PATH.
PSALM 119:105
THE ENTRANCE OF THY WORDS GIVETH LIGHT; IT GIVETH UNDERSTANDING UNTO THE SIMPLE.
PSALM 119:130
I REJOICE AT THY WORD, AS ONE THAT FINDETH GREAT SPOIL.
PSALM 119:162
MY TONGUE SHALL SPEAK OF THY WORD: FOR ALL THEY COMMANDMENTS ARE RIGHTEOUS.
PSALM 119:172

I have more understanding than ALL my teachers? I understand more than the ancients? If we did not know King David's story, we might think he was awfully full of himself, but because we do know how David started out, as a simple shepherd boy, and how he ended up as the king of one of the greatest empires of the ancient world, and that he was greatly beloved by God, we know King David was not full of himself, he was full of God's Word!

# PART 5

## THE BASICS

*"Whom shall he teach knowledge?*
*And whom shall he make to understand doctrine?*
*Them that are weaned from the milk, and drawn from the breast."*

**Isaiah 28:9**

# CHAPTER 26

## BABY STEPS
## (THE FIRST YEAR)

IF YE "ABIDE" IN ME, AND MY WORDS ABIDE IN YOU, YE SHALL ASK WHAT YE WILL, AND IT SHALL BE DONE UNTO YOU.
JOHN 15:7

ABIDE. G3306. Men'-o: a primary verb; to stay (in a given place, state, relation or expectancy): - abide, continue, dwell, endure, be present, remain, stand, tarry (for), X thine own.

We see that Jesus is juxtaposing and comparing two actions. Jesus is stating a basic principal of the kingdom of God. If His Word *abides* in us, we will *abide* in Him. We remain in Jesus Christ only as long as His Word remains in us. This is the main reason we must *memorize* the Word of God, and determine in our hearts that we will diligently absorb God's Word as our continuous daily responsibility.

You may miss a meal, or you may go without food entirely (fasting), but you should never miss *speaking* God's Word to yourself, each and every day.

### PARABLE OF THE SOWER

Having the Words of God abiding in our heart is the very foundation of our assurance that God will answer our prayers and petitions. Jesus Christ is the Word of God.

HEARKEN; BEHOLD, THERE WENT OUT A SOWER TO SOW:
AND IT CAME TO PASS, AS HE SOWED, SOME FELL BY THE WAY SIDE, AND THE FOWLS OF THE AIR CAME AND DEVOURED IT UP.
AND SOME FELL ON STONY GROUND, WHERE IT HAD NOT MUCH EARTH; AND IMMEDIATELY IT SPRANG UP, BECAUSE IT HAD NO DEPTH OF EARTH:
BUT WHEN THE SUN WAS UP, IT WAS SCORCHED; AND BECAUSE IT HAD NO ROOT, IT WITHERED AWAY.
AND SOME FELL AMONG THORNS, AND THE THORNS GREW UP, AND CHOKED IT, AND IT YIELDED NO FRUIT.
AND OTHER FELL ON GOOD GROUND, AND DID YIELD FRUIT THAT SPRANG UP AND INCREASED; AND BROUGHT FORTH, SOME THIRTY, AND SOME SIXTY, AND SOME AN HUNDRED.
MARK 4:3-8

Jesus in the following verses explains the most basic foundational spiritual law to His disciples: *The spiritual law of sowing and reaping.* First, you must sow before you can reap. Second, you most sow on good ground if you want a good harvest. Third, and most important, you must sow the right kind of seed. How do we know this is the most basic spiritual law? When the disciples asked Jesus what the above parable meant, His reply was:

**KNOW YE NOT HIS PARABLE? AND HOW THEN WILL YE KNOW "ALL" PARABLES?**
**MARK 4:14**

This parable is the key to *all* the other parables, this parable is the *key* to every Book in the Bible. This parable is the key to our spiritual growth, maturity and ministry. It is the key to success, prosperity, good health, long life, wealth, love and perfect peace. You cannot minister to others without the Word of God growing, working and ministering in your own life. How can you help the sick if you are sick? How can you help the poor if you are poor? How can you help the lost if you are wandering in the wilderness?

**THE SOWER SOWETH THE "WORD".**
**AND THESE ARE THEY BY THE WAY SIDE, WHERE THE WORD IS SOWN; BUT WHEN THEY HAVE HEARD, SATAN COMETH IMMEDIATELY, AND TAKETH AWAY THE WORD THAT WAS SOWN IN THEIR HEARTS.**
**MARK 4:14-15**

The *wayside* people hear the Word of God, but it never gets down into their spirit because the Devil steals the Word before it can take root. The wayside people might occasionally go to Church on Sunday, or they may not attend Church at all. Their lives do not conform to God's Word. They live their lives the same as everybody else in the world.

The Word either is not heard or it is forgotten and the Word is never applied to their lives and their circumstances; therefore, they get no benefit from hearing the Word of God. They are never delivered from their sins, or poverty, or sickness, or other bad circumstances in life because the Word of God is not mixed with faith. They are constantly seeking knowledge but never coming to the knowledge of the Truth.

**AND THESE ARE THEY LIKEWISE WHICH ARE SOWN ON STONY GROUND; WHO, WHEN THEY HAVE HEARD THE WORD, IMMEDIATELY RECEIVE IT WITH GLADNESS;**
**AND HAVE NO ROOT IN THEMSELVES, AND SO ENDURE BUT FOR A TIME: AFTERWARD, WHEN AFFLICTION OR PERSECUTION ARISETH FOR THE WORD'S SAKE, IMMEDIATELY THEY ARE OFFENDED.**
**MARK 4:16-17**

Once again, the *stony ground* people *hear* the Word, and they do a little better than those whose seed is sown by the wayside. Maybe they hear the Word from an acquaintance or an evangelist. The stony ground people get excited. They might even get on the straight and narrow for awhile. They might read the Bible for a short while. They may even talk to friends and co-workers about Jesus for awhile, but when their circumstances do not change immediately, or they suffer derision and persecution, they fall right back into their old sins and bad habits.

The stony ground people are wandering in the wilderness. They never get to experience the blessings of God because they lack patience, endurance, faith, and most of all they lack direction.

**AND THESE ARE THEY WHICH ARE SOWN AMONG THORNS, SUCH AS HEAR THE WORD. AND THE CARES OF THE WORLD, AND THE DECEITFULNESS OF RICHES, AND THE LUSTS OF OTHER THINGS ENTERING IN, CHOKE THE WORD, AND IT BECOMETH UNFRUITFUL. MARK 4:18-19**

The *thorny* people do even better than the stony ground people. They begin to apply the Word of God in their lives. The blessings of God begin to manifest abundance in their lives. The thorny people begin to bear spiritual fruit. They start enjoying the finer things in life. They may have a nice home, a good occupation and nice income, loving friends and family. However, all the good things in their life start to crowd out their time with God and His Word. They forget their first love. They are the end time Laodicean Church in the third chapter of the Book of Revelation.

The thorny people start spending more and more time enjoying the blessings and spend less and less time with the Author of their blessings. They begin to believe their success is because of their own hard work, so they begin to work harder. They begin to believe their success is because of their friends, family and connections, so they spend more and more time schmoozing with people. They say to themselves, "I have worked so hard, I deserve to relax and enjoy myself." They begin travelling and socializing, and they squander all the blessings of God on enjoying the things of the world.

Eventually, after a time, they stop spending any time with God, their fruitfulness and blessings evaporate. These thorny people believe their salvation is the end all and be all of God's eternal plan. They do not realize that God's primary purpose for individual Christians and the Church is to be fruitful and to *multiply*!

**AND THESE ARE THEY WHICH ARE SOWN ON GOOD GROUND; SUCH AS HEAR THE WORD, AND "RECEIVE" IT, AND BRING FORTH FRUIT, SOME THIRTYFOLD, SOME SIXTY, AND SOME AN HUNDRED. MARK 4:20**

See the action verbs. The fruitful people *hear* the Word, and *receive* it!

# CHAPTER 27

## SPEAK GOD'S WORD

How can you receive God's Word if you do not hear it, and how can you hear God's word if you do not speak it? This is why I say you must *speak* the Word to yourself *every day*! You must *memorize* the Word of God!

RECEIVE. G3858. Par-ad-ekh'-om-ahee: to accept near, i.e. admit or (by implication) delight in: - receive.

DELIGHT THYSELF ALSO IN THE LORD; AND HE SHALL GIVE THEE THE DESIRES OF THINE HEART.
COMMIT THY WAY UNTO THE LORD; TRUST ALSO IN HIM; AND HE SHALL BRING IT TO PASS.
PSALM 37:4-5

We need to *delight* ourselves in God and His Word. Why shouldn't we delight in God's excellent promises to His Church and *speak* God's Word to His People? God's Word promises us good health, wealth, good favor, long life, peace, love, joy, fruitfulness, and a host of other blessings. We need to *speak* God's Word to our friends and to our neighbors, to our families, and most of all to *ourselves*!

THEN THEY THAT FEARED THE LORD "SPAKE" OFTEN ONE TO ANOTHER: AND THE LORD HEARKENED, AND HEARD IT, AND A BOOK OF REMEMBERANCE WAS WRITTEN BEFORE HIM FOR THEM THAT FEARED THE LORD, AND THAT THOUGHT UPON HIS NAME.
AND THEY SHALL BE MINE, SAITH THE LORD OF HOSTS, IN THAT DAY WHEN I MAKE UP MY JEWELS; AND I WILL SPARE THEM, AS A MAN SPARETH HIS OWN SON THAT SERVETH HIM.
MALACHI 3:16-17

The end of our walk is not simply verifying the assurance of our own salvation. The end of our walk is to rest from our own work and to start being a laborer in the fields of the Lord. God wants a great end time harvest of souls for His kingdom. Believe me, when you start filling yourself up with God's Holy Word, you will have no problem witnessing to others. You will not be able to contain God's Word!

FOR SINCE I SPAKE, I CRIED OUT, I CRIED VIOLENCE AND SPOIL; BECAUSE THE WORD OF THE LORD WAS MADE A REPROACH UNTO ME, AND A DERISION, DAILY.
THEN I SAID, I WILL NOT MAKE MENTION OF HIM, NOR SPEAK ANY MORE IN HIS NAME. BUT HIS WORD WAS IN MINE HEART AS A BURNING FIRE SHUT UP IN MY BONES, AND I WAS WEARY WITH FORBEARING, AND I COULD NOT STAY.
JEREMIAH 20:8-9

We see that the prophet Jeremiah was determined NOT to *speak* God's Word because of the derision and the persecution he was suffering, but eventually he could not stop himself from speaking God's Word, and he had to warn Jerusalem of its coming judgment at the hands of the Babylonians.

God does not promise that everybody will welcome you with open arms when you speak His Word, but many will. More than likely, you will suffer persecution, especially from people blinded by legalism, worldly authority and pride. Persecution has always been the experience of those who preach the gospel.

**REMEMBER THE WORD THAT I SAID UNTO YOU. THE SERVANT IS NOT GREATER THAN HIS LORD. IF THEY HAVE PERSECUTED ME, THEY WILL ALSO PERSECUTE YOU; IF THEY HAVE KEPT MY SAYING, THEY WILL KEEP YOURS ALSO.**
**JOHN 15:20**

Now I want to explain the nuts and bolts of *walking in the spirit* and some of the common pitfalls of beginning your *walk*. It is common for people to get excited about memorizing and *speaking* God's Word, or *walking in the spirit,* in the beginning of their walk and they attempt to do too much. Beginning to *walk in the spirit* is very similar to beginning a fitness regimen. You must take baby steps at first. Remember that you are a baby in the spiritual realm when you are first born in the spirit. It is not unusual for people to set unrealistic goals when they begin a physical fitness regimen, and it is also not unusual for people to set unrealistic goals when they begin *walking in the spirit*.

I suggest you keep it simple at first. I began by memorizing God's *Word* for only fifteen (15) minutes a day at first and only one (1) verse per week. I know that a lot of people may say, "I can memorize more of God's *Word* than one verse a week, I'm going to memorize and meditate on scripture verses for at least an hour a day, maybe even two hours!" However, the more you attempt to do at first, the more likely you will end up quitting *walking in the spirit*.

Beginning *speaking* and *memorizing* Bible verses is very similar to beginning lifting weights at a gymnasium, if you try and do too much at first, it is very likely that you will quit altogether. The analogy is very similar to when you begin *walking in the spirit*. If you try to do too much you may fail. You will end up saying, "memorizing Bible verses is just too hard, I can't do this every day." Remember *slow and steady wins the race!*

**WHOM SHALL HE TEACH KNOWLEDGE? AND WHOM SHALL HE MAKE TO UNDERSTAND DOCTRINE? THEM THAT ARE WEANED FROM THE MILK, AND DRAWN FROM THE BREASTS.**
**FOR PRECEPT MUST BE UPON PRECEPT, PRECEPT UPON PRECEPT; LINE UPON LINE, LINE UPON LINE; HERE A LITTLE, AND THERE A LITTLE.**
**FOR WITH STAMMERING LIPS AND ANOTHER TONGUE WILL HE "SPEAK" TO THIS PEOPLE.**
**ISAIAH 28:9-11**

My *walking in the spirit* regimen begins with *speaking* only one (1) Bible verse seven (7) times in the morning when I wake up, seven (7) times in the afternoon, either during my lunch break or when I get home from work, and finally seven (7) times before I go to sleep. I speak one verse for seven days and then I begin a new verse on the seventh day. I only memorize one (1) verse per week the first year.

I *speak* the verse at least seven times during each memorization session. At first, I will look at the verse when I am speaking it and then I will try to *speak* it while not looking at the verse. By about the middle of the week, I am comfortable not looking at the verse when I speak. I also memorize each verse *Word for Word*!

I do not try to get close enough, remember this is the *Word* of God, we must know it perfectly. I promise, memorizing one verse in a week will take less than fifteen minutes a day. I know you are going to say fifteen minutes a day is too easy, but trust me, memorizing God's Word may be the hardest thing you've ever started in your life.

**FOR THE FLESH "LUSTETH" AGAINST THE SPIRIT, AND THE SPIRIT AGAINST THE FLESH: AND THESE ARE CONTRARY THE ONE TO THE OTHER: SO THAT YE CANNOT DO THE THINGS THAT YE WOULD.**
**GALATIONS 5:17**

LUSTETH. G1937. Ep-ee-thoo-meh'-o: to set the heart upon, i.e. long for (rightfully or otherwise): - covet, desire, would fain, lust (after).

When you begin *walking in the spirit,* your spirit is entering into a battle with your flesh, and with the powers of spiritual darkness. Your spirit wants your mind to dwell on spiritual things, but your flesh wants your mind to dwell on worldly things. Your born again spirit desires the exact opposite of what your flesh desires.

Your *flesh* wants everything the world has to offer: expensive foods, designer clothes, big houses, adventure, excitement, fast cars, money, violence, sex, drugs, more money, rock & roll, gangster rap, *death,* etc. (I think you get the picture). The *spirit* wants everything the world cannot offer: love, joy, peace, longsuffering, gentleness, goodness, faith, meekness, temperance, *eternal life,* etc. The spirit and flesh want exactly the opposite things, and will pull your thoughts and desires in exactly opposite directions. The flesh is leading you towards eternal death, and the spirit is leading you towards eternal life. You are beginning the epic battle and journey of your life. You *cannot* fight the flesh with the flesh! If you truly desire spiritual fruit, you must start applying spiritual methods, and begin fighting with spiritual weapons.

Spiritual fruit will draw people to Jesus Christ, just like apples draw people to an apple tree. Unless you are called by God to become an evangelist, you do not need to stand on the street corner handing out religious tracts, and you do not have to go door to door trying to win people to Jesus Christ. These types of activities are mostly works of the flesh.

Often times, newly born again believers want to proclaim the gospel to everybody; however, much of the time they do not know the gospel, and they tend to turn people away from Jesus because they lack what is truly needed to draw people to Jesus Christ. They lack *knowledge* of the Word of God and they lack the *fruits* of the spirit.

**BUT SANCTIFY THE LORD GOD IN YOUR HEARTS: AND BE READY ALWAYS TO GIVE AN ANSWER TO EVERY MAN THAT "ASKETH YOU" A REASON OF THE HOPE THAT IS IN YOU WITH MEEKNESS AND FEAR:**
**I PETER 3:15**

As you grow in spiritual maturity, the Holy Spirit will begin producing spiritual fruit and people will be naturally drawn to you. We do not determine who to bring into the kingdom of God. God decides who to bring into His Kingdom. You will have ample opportunity to share the gospel with many people and you will be prepared to share the correct gospel because you will have God's Word dwelling within you.

If you are called by God to be an evangelist, it will only be after years of preparation and studying God's Word. Apparently, the Apostle Paul did not become an evangelist to the Gentiles until at least three years after his conversion to the faith. *See* Galatians 1:18 and Galatians 2:1.

**GIVE NOT THAT WHICH IS HOLY UNTO THE DOGS, NEITHER CAST YE YOUR PEARLS BEFORE SWINE, LEST THEY TRAMPLE THEM UNDER THEIR FEET, AND TURN AGAIN AND REND YOU.**
**MATTHEW 7:6**

After you begin maturing in the spirit, you will begin to lose a lot of worldly friends and family. Conversely, you will also begin to discover a lot of spiritual friends and family. Remember, birds of a feather flock together.

**IRON SHARPENETH IRON; SO A MAN SHARPENETH THE COUNTENANCE OF HIS FRIEND.**
**PROVERBS 27:17**

I am not saying to dump all your unsaved friends and family. I am just saying that as you grow in the spirit, you will have less and less in common with worldly people. You will naturally gravitate toward spiritual people and spiritual activities. Your desires will change dramatically, and your pursuits will be in a different direction.

Remember what Jesus said:

**IT IS THE SPIRIT THAT QUICKENETH; THE FLESH PROFITETH NOTHING: THE WORDS THAT I "SPEAK" UNTO YOU, "THEY ARE SPIRIT", AND THEY ARE LIFE.**
**JOHN 6:63**

The Words that Jesus *spoke* are spirit, and they are life! Jesus did not *speak* just any old words, Jesus *spoke* the Words of Life. Jesus *spoke* the Word of God.

**THEN JESUS SAID UNTO THEM, WHEN YE HAVE LIFTED UP THE SON OF MAN, THEN SHALL YE KNOW THAT I AM HE, AND THAT I DO NOTHING OF MYSELF; BUT AS MY FATHER HATH TAUGHT ME, I SPEAK THESE THINGS.**
**JOHN 8:28**

Jesus only *spoke* what His Father had taught him. Jesus Christ did not rely on His flesh, He *spoke* the Word of God! Remember, do not just read a Bible verse silently to yourself, *speak* the verse *out loud*!

# CHAPTER 28

## REPETITION = VICTORY

Why do I say *speak* the verse seven times, three times a day, for seven days? Seven is a special number to God. Seven represents completeness. God rested on the seventh day. *See* Genesis 2:2. There are seven days of unleavened bread. *See* Exodus 12:15. Seven times seven years is the year of Jubilee! *See* Leviticus 25:8. Jubilee is a Sabbath of Sabbaths ... a type of God's perfect rest. There are seven lamps of fire burning before the throne of God, which are the seven Spirits of God. *See* Revelation 4:5. Anyway, you get the picture, seven (7) is a special number to God.

There is an interesting story in the Book of 2 Kings of when the Prophet Elisha was dying. Joash, the King of Israel, came to Elisha's bedside and began crying because Israel was being oppressed by the King of Syria. Elisha told Joash that the Lord would deliver Israel from Syria, but Elisha told Joash he had to do something first:

AND HE SAID, TAKE THE ARROWS. AND HE TOOK THEM, AND HE SAID UNTO THE KING OF ISRAEL, SMITE UPON THE GROUND. AND HE SMOTE THRICE, AND STAYED.
AND THE MAN OF GOD WAS WROTH WITH HIM, AND SAID, THOU SHOULDEST HAVE SMITTEN FIVE OR SIX TIMES; THEN HADST THOU SMITTEN SYRIA TILL THOU HADST CONSUMNED IT: WHEREAS NOW THOU SHALT SMITE SYRIA BUT THRICE.
2 KINGS 13:18-19

Why was Elisha angry at King Joash? The King of Israel should have known a basic principle. Any child in Israel would have known that seven signified completeness. I imagine if Joash would have smote the floor seven times, Syria would have ceased being an enemy all together, and probably would have become Israel's strongest ally. We learn from this story that a country's success, just like an individual's success, depends mainly on a person's intimate knowledge of God and His Word.

FOR THE LEADERS OF THIS PEOPLE CAUSE THEM TO ERR, AND THEY THAT ARE LED OF THEM ARE DESTROYED.
ISAIAH 9:16

Why *speak* God's Word three times a day? Remember what the Apostle Peter said about the Word of God being our spiritual milk. A baby does not nurse only once a week, we should *speak* God's Word at least three times a day just like we eat at least three times a day.

EVENING, AND MORNING, AND AT NOON, WILL I PRAY, AND CRY ALOUD: AND HE SHALL HEAR MY VOICE.
PSALM 55:17

Do not let slothfulness steal God's blessing from you. *Speaking* a verse seven times, three times a day, for a total of 21 times a day, will take less than fifteen minutes out of your day. Do you really love Jesus? If you do you will memorize His Words.

**IF A MAN LOVE ME, HE WILL "KEEP" MY WORDS: AND MY FATHER WILL LOVE HIM, AND WE WILL COME UNTO HIM, AND MAKE OUR ABODE WITH HIM.**
**HE THAT LOVETH ME NOT KEEPETH NOT MY SAYINGS: AND THE WORD WHICH YE HEAR IS NOT MINE, BUT THE FATHER'S WHICH SENT ME.**
**JOHN 14:23-24**

KEEP. G5083. Tay-reh'-o: from *teros* (a watch; perhaps akin to 2334); to guard (from loss or injury, properly by keeping the eye upon; and thus differing from 5442, which is properly to prevent escaping; and from 2892, which implies a fortress or full military lines of apparatus), i.e. to note (a prophecy); figuratively to fulfill a command); by implication to detain (in custody; figuratively to maintain); by extension to withhold (for personal ends; figuratively to keep unmarried): - hold fast, keep (-er), (ob-, pre-, re-) serve, watch.

Frankly, if a Christian cannot spend less than fifteen minutes a day, in order to *speak* and *memorize* one verse a week, I question their love for Jesus Christ. It appears from John 14:23-24 that Jesus also questions their commitment. However, if we will dedicate ourselves to *keeping* His Words, Jesus promises that both He and the Father will manifest themselves to us. This is the greatest benefit we receive from memorizing the Word of God. God will become more and more real to us. Our doubt flees away, and it is replaced by our ever increasing faith in God and His provision for our lives.

Remember, you are in a battle with your flesh and the rulers of darkness. Your flesh is infected with sin, and is more than happy for you to remain in bondage to sickness, poverty, fear, despair and death. That is also the place where the Devil wants you. Your only chance for vibrant health, overflowing prosperity, perfect peace and eternal life in this world, as well as the new world to come, is to have perfect trust in God's Word.

# CHAPTER 29

## YOUR BIBLE IS YOUR WORKBOOK

If your first language is English, I recommend that you memorize verses from the King James Bible. Why the King James Version (KJV)? First of all, I believe it is the inspired English translation of God's Word. Most of the King James Bible is based on the William Tyndale (pronounced tindəl) translation. He is the first person to translate the Books of the Bible from the original Hebrew and Greek texts. During William Tyndale's lifetime it was difficult for most common people to learn the Scripture because they did not know ancient Greek, Latin, or Hebrew.

Most people in England could not even read and write English. William Tyndale believed that the way to God was through His Word, and he believed that God's Word should be available to everyone. The Catholic Church believed just the opposite. The Catholic Church believed the way to God was only through obedience to the Catholic Church, and that reading of the Word of God tends to create heretics. When Tyndale requested permission from the Church ecclesiastic authorities to translate the Bible into English, he was flatly denied permission.

Tyndale ignored the Catholic Church leadership and began translating the Bible into English under threat of death.

Within a short time after his death English Bibles using Tyndale's translation were being published in England. Tyndale became a martyr in order to translate the Bible into English, and I believe he was God's anointed vessel to translate the Books of the Bible into English from the original Greek and Hebrew texts.

Tyndale's English translation of the Bible was a major catalyst for the protestant reformation in England and the creation of the Church of England. I also believe the revivals that swept England subsequent to the Word becoming available to the people of England are the main reason the English Empire eventually dominated the world. Where the Word of God is unleashed, prosperity and success will always follow. Where the Word of God is suppressed, poverty and failure will always follow. This applies to individuals as well as to peoples and to nations and to the world.

The King James Bible is a word for word translation of the ancient Greek and Hebrew texts. Any word added for better understanding is *italicized*.

Second, I would use a King James *reference* Bible. Often times, the Books of the Old and New Testament reference other Books in the Bible. Remember that much of Proverbs is taken directly from the Book of Psalms. Most of the Books in the New Testament reference scripture from the Old Testament. It is much easier to understand a verse if you know the original context of the verse.

Often times, false teachers will use verses out of context to confuse you, and lead you away from the simple truth of the gospel. Some false teachers even take another step and actually change the Word of God. I suspect there is an especially deep, hot, black place in hell reserved for these types of false teachers. Some people say that the King James Version is difficult to understand, but the Word of God is always difficult for a person to properly understand unless they have the Holy Spirit giving them revelation.

Third, get a Strong's Concordance of the Bible. The Strong's Concordance is an exhaustive cross-reference of every word in the KJV back to the word in the original Greek and Hebrew text. Each word is given as a number in the Greek and Hebrew dictionaries in the back of the concordance. This will help you find the original Hebrew or Greek word, and you can see how the word is used in context in the other books of the Bible. This will allow you get an even deeper understanding of the original texts.

If you have a computer, I recommend downloading *e-sword*. *E-sword* is a free software program, which gives a Strong Concordance reference number next to every word. It will help you to search the Old and New Testament, and then you can easily find verses in different books of the Bible dealing with the same subject *word* that you are memorizing.

Do not be afraid to write in your Bible. If your Bible is too fancy or expensive to write in, you need to get another Bible. My Grandmother Adeline left her Bible to my dad when she passed away. She had written notes all over in her Bible. She marked every time she read a verse. She had her favorite verses highlighted, and every believer should do the same thing.

If you wanted to be an engineer, or a doctor, or an expert in any field, you would begin a systematic course of study. You would not skim through the learning material, or read the school book once and decide you are an expert.

I still have school books that I use for reference in my work. If you begin to be weary of *speaking* and *memorizing* Bible verses, remember the goal and the benefits. Your goal is to be a king and priest of the Most High God, your goal is to enter into God's perfect rest, your goal is to be fruitful and to multiply. Only by knowing and *speaking* God's Word will you become intimate with God and enjoy all the benefits, which intimacy with the LORD of Lords entails: health, prosperity, joy, peace, everlasting life and salvation for the lost.

BLESS THE LORD, O MY SOUL, AND FORGET NOT ALL HIS 'BENEFITS":
WHO FORGIVETH ALL THINE INIQUITIES; WHO HEALETH "ALL" THY DISEASES;
WHO REDEEMETH THY LIFE FROM DESTRUCTION; WHO CROWNETH THEE WITH LOVING KINDNESS AND TENDER MERCIES;
WHO SATISFIES THY MOUTH WITH GOOD THINGS; SO THAT THY YOUTH IS RENEWED LIKE THE EAGLE'S.
PSALM 103:2-5

My greatest desire is to be a mature spiritual Christian. I would rather be a mature spiritual Christian then the richest man in the world. I promise you, mature Christians are a lot happier! I cannot control whether I will ever be the richest man in the world, but I can control whether I will become a spiritually mature Christian. All Christians should determine in their hearts that they will become spiritually mature. A mature Christian must determine in their heart that they will edify the Church, glorify Jesus Christ, save lost souls (multiply), and serve God.

I encourage you to also use this book as a workbook. If an idea or revelation comes to you while reading this book, write it down in the margins. Use this book while memorizing your one-hundred-and-one (101) foundational Bible verses outlined later in chapters 32-36. Meditate on each verse, and after it is memorized highlight it with a yellow marker or pencil. Practice speaking these Bible verses to yourself three times a day. I promise you in a few short years there will be a radical transformation in your spirit, soul and body.

# CHAPTER 30

## MEDITATION = MEMORIZATION

At the end of each week, I highlight the verse I have memorized either with a colored highlighter or with a pencil or pen. Then I turn to the front of my Bible and write the verse down on the blank pages in the front of my Bible. Then I start memorizing the next verse using the same technique. Each week, look at the verse(s) you have written down at the front of your Bible, and then try to speak them out loud from memory. If you forget a verse, turn to the verse in your Bible and read it out loud again. Over time, you will be amazed at how many verses you will have memorized.

All memorization is simply repetition, repetition, and more repetition! If you follow these instructions, you will gradually build up a large repertoire of Bible verses in your memory bank. I call it a memory bank because the Word of God you have memorized is more valuable than silver and gold. The Word of God you have memorized is better than money in the bank! Go for walks and speak the Word of God to yourself.

MEDITATE - H1897. daw-gaw': a primitive root; to murmur (in pleasure or anger); by implication to ponder: - imagine, meditate, mourn, mutter, roar, X sore, speak, study, talk, utter.

As you meditate on each verse, emphasize *speaking* different words as you memorize the verse. Think about each word and what it means. Look in your Strong's Concordance and find the word in different verses of the Bible and see how it was used. Meditation has been compared to looking at a precious stone from different angles, and seeing how the light reflects and shines off of each facet.

I assure you, if you are faithful in your memorization, meditation and *speaking* of Holy Scripture, you will receive great revelation from the Holy Spirit. Eventually, you *shall be like a tree planted by the rivers of water, that bringeth forth his fruit in his season, his leaf also shall not wither; and whatsoever he doeth shall prosper. See* Psalms 1:3. I believe if you even study, meditate, and *speak* the Word of God on an irregular basis it will pay huge dividends, but if you study on a daily basis, I believe miraculous events and blessings will shower down upon you from heaven.

# CHAPTER 31

## METHODS OF ATTACK AND DEFENSE

You have been warned that a spiritual battle will begin when you seriously determine in your heart to keep (*memorize*) God's Word. The Devil knows that once you become a mature Christian ... *nothing is impossible to you.* Many people will be drawn to Jesus Christ, and lost souls will be delivered out of the Devil's hand. The Devil commonly uses several methods of attack against immature Christians. You must be prepared to meet each method of attack with the appropriate Word of God.

I believe it is better for a Christian to know one-hundred and one (101) foundational verses than to memorize the entire Book of Joel or the entire Book of Galatians. I am not saying you should not memorize an entire Book of the Bible, but I advise you to first memorize some specific foundational verses before you attempt such a task. Wait until you are a mature Christian.

I believe most people can consider themselves mature spiritually after approximately three years of daily memorization and meditation of God's Word. Why three years? Jesus spent three and one-half years ministering to and teaching his disciples. Paul the Apostle waited three years before he began to evangelize the gentiles. A healthy fruit tree should begin to bear a crop of fruit between three and five years.

**AND WHEN HE SAW A FIG TREE IN THE WAY, HE CAME TO IT, AND FOUND NOTHING THEREON, BUT LEAVES ONLY, AND SAID UNTO IT, LET NO FRUIT GROW ON THEE HENCEFORWARD FOR EVER. AND PRESENTLY THE FIG TREE WHITHERED AWAY. MATTHEW 21:19**

When Jesus did not find fruit on what appeared to be a healthy fig tree, He cursed the tree and it died. God expects us to be fruitful. We should not just appear healthy. What would you do if you planted a fruit tree, and after many years it never produced any fruit?

Wouldn't you cut it down and plant another one? I dare say that a lot of Christians are just like the fig tree in the Bible story, a lot of leaves, but no fruit. Determine right now that you will bear fruit for the kingdom of God. As you mature in the spirit, you will become more sensitive to the Holy Spirit. You will have discernment in your life, and you will be more easily led by God. Then you will be able to more easily discern between danger and opportunity. An unsaved person has no such discernment.

# CHAPTER 32

## TOP TEN METHODS OF ATTACK WITH FOUNDATIONAL VERSES

#1 METHOD OF ATTACK: *THERE IS NO GOD.*

1)    THE "FOOL" HATH SAID IN HIS HEART, THERE IS NO GOD.
**PSALMS 14:1**

FOOL. H5036. Naw-bawl'; stupid: wicked (especially impious): - fool (-ish, -ish man, -ish woman), vile person.

2)    FOR THE INVISIBLE THINGS OF HIM FROM THE CREATION OF THE WORLD ARE CLEARLY SEEN, BEING UNDERSTOOD BY THE THINGS THAT ARE MADE, EVEN HIS ETERNAL POWER AND GODHEAD; SO THAT THEY ARE WITHOUT EXCUSE:
3)    BECAUSE THAT, WHEN THEY KNEW GOD, THEY GLORIFIED HIM NOT AS GOD, NEITHER WERE THANKFUL; BUT BECAME VAIN IN THEIR IMAGINATIONS, AND THEIR FOOLISH HEART WAS DARKENED.
4)    PROFESSING THEMSELVES TO BE WISE, THEY BECAME "FOOLS".
**ROMANS 1:20-22**

FOOLS. G3471. Mo-rah'ee-no: to become insipid; figuratively to make (passively act) as a simpleton; - become fool, make foolish, lose savour.

The Word of God is unequivocal:

5)    THE HEAVENS DECLARE THE GLORY OF GOD; AND THE FIRMAMENT SHOWETH HIS HANDIWORK.
**PSALMS 19:1**

Any person who has lived many years, who has experienced and seen all of creation: the sun, the moon and the stars in the firmament, a child in its mother's arms, the birds in the sky, the bees pollinating flowers, the dew upon the grass, the trees shaken by the wind, the oceans teeming with life, and can still say that there is no God, is a fool according to scripture.

It is doubtful that answering such a person or entertaining such a foolish idea will do them or you any good. The person who claims there is no God is spiritually blind, deaf and dumb. They are only fooling themselves. Their only hope is a miracle on the order of causing a blind man to receive their site, or a dead man to rise from the grave.

**BUT IF OUR GOSPEL BE HID, IT IS HID TO THEM THAT ARE LOST:**

IN WHOM THE GOD OF THIS WORLD HATH BLINDED THE MINDS OF THEM WHICH BELIEVE NOT, LEST THE LIGHT OF THE GLORIOUS GOSPEL OF CHRIST, WHO IS THE IMAGE OF GOD, SHOULD SHINE UNTO THEM.
2 CORINTHIANS 4:3-4

I would not waste my time debating an atheist. All you can really do is intercede and pray that God will be merciful and open their ears to the gospel, that they will see the light before it is too late, and that they will believe and confess the Lord Jesus Christ before they die. Speak the Word of God to them when you have an opportunity. Remember, they have been blinded by the God of this world (Satan). When you begin such a task, you are entering into battle with the rulers of darkness.

6)    THE ENTRANCE OF THY WORDS GIVETH LIGHT; IT GIVETH UNDERSTANDING UNTO THE SIMPLE.
PSALM 119:130

Where there is life, there is hope. Do not give up on your unsaved relatives, friends and acquaintances. *Speaking* the Word of God gives light to those in darkness. Our Lord can make the blind to see, and He is still searching for His lost sheep.

#2 METHOD OF ATTACK: *GOD DOES NOT CARE ABOUT YOU.*

7)    FOR GOD SO LOVED THE WORLD, THAT HE GAVE HIS ONLY BEGOTTEN SON, THAT WHOSOEVER BELIEVETH IN HIM SHOULD NOT PERISH, BUT HAVE EVERLASTING LIFE.
JOHN 3:16

If there is one thing that is un-mistakenly clear in the Bible, it is God's love for all of mankind. Nobody who names themselves a Christian should take advantage of anybody else, whether that person is a Christian or not. A Hindu might take advantage of a non-Hindu, a Muslim might take advantage of a non-Muslim, a Jew might take advantage of a non-Jew, but a Christian has no such advantage. Anybody who claims to be a Christian and takes advantage of any other people is either very, very immature in the spirit, or they are a pretender to the faith.

8)    THOU SHALT LOVE THY NEIGHBOUR AS THYSELF.
MATTHEW 19:19

9)    BELOVED, LET US LOVE ONE ANOTHER: FOR LOVE IS OF GOD; AND EVERY ONE THAT LOVETH IS BORN OF GOD, AND KNOWETH GOD.
10)   HE THAT LOVETH NOT KNOWTH NOT GOD; FOR GOD IS LOVE.
I JOHN 4:7-8

All spiritually mature Christians will manifest the love of God because it is the first and main fruit of the spirit. Love is the exact opposite of selfishness.

Selfishness says, "I am first and I will be served."

Love says, "I am last and I will serve."

11) **THE LORD IS MY SHEPHERD; I SHALL NOT WANT.**
12) **HE MAKETH ME TO LIE DOWN IN GREEN PASTURES: HE LEADETH ME BESIDE THE STILL WATERS.**
13) **HE RESTORETH MY SOUL: HE LEADETH ME IN THE PATHS OF RIGHTEOUSNESS FOR HIS NAME'S SAKE.**
14) **YEA, THOUGH I WALK THROUGH THE VALLEY OF THE SHADOW OF DEATH, I WILL FEAR NO EVIL: FOR THOU ART WITH ME; THY ROD AND THY STAFF THEY COMFORT ME.**
15) **THOU PREPAREST A TABLE BEFORE ME IN THE PRESENCE OF MINE ENEMIES: THOU ANOINTEST MY HEAD WITH OIL; MY CUP RUNNETH OVER.**
16) **SURELY GOODNESS AND MERCY SHALL FOLLOW ME ALL THE DAYS OF MY LIFE: AND I WILL DWELL IN THE HOUSE OF THE LORD FOREVER.**

**PSALM 23:1-6**

I do not believe that there are any verses in the Bible, which have comforted more people in the history of the world. The 23rd Psalm is truly full of foundational verses, and it perfectly illustrates God's love and care for each of us for all of our lives. I highly encourage you to memorize the 23rd Psalm as soon as possible after your salvation. Six verses may seem daunting at first, but if you memorize just one verse each week, you will quickly understand just how easily a large amount of scripture can be memorized over time. It is one of the most beautiful and comforting scriptures in all the Books of the Bible.

I have heard people say, "What about all those Canaanites God ordered the Israelites to kill in the Old Testament? God didn't love them very much!"

People need to understand something very important. Despite God's great love for *all* of mankind, He simply cannot allow sin to multiply forever. Eventually, after much patience, God must step in and put a stop to sin. It is called God's perfect justice!

When God allows a person to make the choice whether he or she will eat from the tree of the knowledge of good and evil (or allow them to know and attempt to keep the law), God's greatest desire is for that person to recognize their own inadequacy, and then to turn back to God's perfect supply and inexhaustible resources. Unfortunately, many people do realize their own lack, but instead of turning back to God, they turn to other supernatural resources. They turn to devils. Eventually, as is the case of the Canaanites, after many generations of entertaining devilish relationships, sin bears its deadly fruit.

**NOW THE WORKS OF THE FLESH ARE MANIFEST, WHICH ARE THESE; ADULTERY, FORNICATION, UNCLEANESS, LASCIVIOUSNESS,**
**IDOLATRY, WITCHCRAFT, HATRED, VARIANCE, EMULATIONS, WRATH, STRIFE, SEDITIONS, HERESIES.**

ENVYINGS, MURDERS, DRUNKENESS, REVEILINGS, AND SUCH LIKE: OF THE WHICH I TELL YOU BEFORE, AS I HAVE ALSO TOLD YOU IN TIME PAST, THAT THEY WHICH DO SUCH THINGS SHALL NOT INHERIT THE KINGDOM OF GOD.
GALATIONS 5:19-21

Eventually individual people, individual cities, individual countries, and the entire world can cross the line of no return and destruction swiftly follows. It has happened over and over again, and there are many examples in the various Books of the Bible:

The whole world was destroyed by a flood because of wickedness and violence. The cities of Sodom and Gomorrah were destroyed by fire from heaven. The Canaanites were destroyed by the children of Israel. The Israelites, during the time of Jeremiah the Prophet, were destroyed and taken captive by the Babylonians. It is time for Christians to wake up, look around, and begin to compare their communities with those judged and destroyed in the Bible. We all must start praying for deliverance from the judgment that is surely coming upon the world.

#3 METHOD OF ATTACK: *YOU MUST EARN YOUR OWN SALVATION AND YOU MUST KEEP THE LAW.*

17)  FOR BY GRACE ARE YE SAVED THROUGH FAITH; AND THAT NOT OF YOURSELVES; IT IS THE GIFT OF GOD:
18)  NOT OF WORKS, LEST ANY MAN SHOULD BOAST.
EPHESIANS 2:8-9

19)  FOR WHOSOEVER SHALL KEEP THE WHOLE LAW, AND YET OFFEND IN ONE POINT, HE IS GUILTY OF ALL.
JAMES 2:10

The Books of the New Testament deal mainly with differentiating between the free grace and salvation provided by the death and resurrection of Jesus Christ, and the impossibility of earning our own salvation by keeping the law. Jesus encompassed all the law and the prophets in two simple commandments:

20)  THOU SHALT LOVE THE LORD THY GOD WITH ALL THY HEART, AND WITH ALL THY SOUL, AND WITH ALL THEY MIND. (*SEE* DEUTERONOMY 6:5)
THIS IS THE FIRST AND GREAT COMMANDMENT.
21)  AND THE SECOND IS LIKE UNTO IT, THOU SHALT LOVE THY NEIGHBOUR AS THYSELF. (*SEE* LEVITICUS 19:18)
ON THESE TWO COMMANDMENTS HANG ALL THE LAW AND THE PROPHETS.
MATTHEW 22:37-40

The Book of James calls the second of these commandments given to us by Jesus, the royal law. If you can love your neighbor as yourself, you are truly a king and a priest of God. How well you keep the royal law is also a reflection of how much you love God, and how well you are keeping the first and great commandment. The beloved Apostle John makes the connection between the great commandment and the royal commandment perfectly plain:

**22)** **IF A MAN SAY. I LOVE GOD, AND HATETH HIS BROTHER, HE IS A LIAR: FOR HE THAT LOVETH NOT HIS BROTHER WHOM HE HATH SEEN, HOW CAN HE LOVE GOD WHOM HE HATH NOT SEEN?**
**I JOHN 4:40**

Attempting to earn our own salvation is the greatest stumbling block preventing people from entering into God's perfect rest. When Jesus said, "broad is the way, that leadeth to destruction," and "narrow is the way, which leadeth unto life," *See* Matthew 7:13-14. He was not saying that the broad way was easy and the narrow way was difficult, Jesus was saying there are many avenues leading to destruction and only one way to eternal life.

The Bible says: "So then faith comes by hearing and hearing by the Word of God." *See* Romans 10:17. However, we do not increase our own faith... God increases our faith. Like the Apostle Paul said again: "I have planted. Apollos watered; but God gave the increase. *See* I Corinthians 3:6.

We can plant and water all day long, but if God does not bless us, our crops will fail. Similarly, if we do not plant and water or namely, we do not read, *memorize,* and *speak* God's Word, believing that God will bless us, and mature our spirit, our faith will eventually wither on the vine. I am sure there are Bible scholars in hell because their motives for learning God's Word were not pure and they studied in disbelief.

**23)** **FOR MY YOKE IS EASY, AND MY BURDEN IS LIGHT.**
**MATTHEW 11:30**

Jesus said, He is the *only* way to life, and He does not expect us to be constantly working, and worrying about our own salvation or our own circumstances in this life. He has taken care of everything. Most of the world religions and cults expect us to be constantly working in order to earn our way into heaven.

**24)** **FOR THEY BIND HEAVY BURDENS AND GRIEVOUS TO BE BORNE, AND LAY THEM ON MEN'S SHOULDERS; BUT THEY THEMSELVES WILL NOT MOVE THEM WITH ONE OF THEIR FINGERS.**
**MATTHEW 23:4**

In actuality the narrow way (*Jesus Christ is the narrow way)* is the easiest way of all. The broad way (*ALL the world's other religions*) are beset with tremendous difficulties and they lead to hell. The narrow way, the easiest way, the only way to eternal life, is to believe in God's Word (Jesus Christ) and His perfect grace. The broad way, the difficult way, ALL the other ways lead to destruction!

#4 METHOD OF ATTACK: *JESUS CHRIST WAS A GREAT MAN, BUT HE IS NOT GOD.*

**25)** IN THE BEGINNING WAS THE WORD, AND THE WORD WAS WITH GOD, AND THE WORD WAS GOD.

JOHN 1:1

**26)** AND THE WORD WAS MADE FLESH, AND DWELT AMONG US, (AND WE BEHELD HIS GLORY, THE GLORY AS OF THE ONLY BEGOTTEN OF THE FATHER,) FULL OF GRACE AND TRUTH.

JOHN 1:14

John, the beloved disciple and apostle, makes it clear in the first fourteen verses of the Book of John that Jesus is not an ordinary man. Jesus Christ is God incarnate. God himself came and lived among us, the Word (Jesus Christ) made ALL things, the Word (Jesus Christ) is *life*, the Word (Jesus Christ) is *light*. The Word (Jesus Christ) is God!

**27)** BUT UNTO THE SON, HE SAITH, THY THRONE, "O GOD", IS FOR EVER AND EVER; A SCEPTRE OF RIGHTEOUSNESS IS THE SCEPTRE OF THY KINGDOM.

HEBREWS 1:8

The Apostle Paul also makes it perfectly clear in the first chapter of the Book of Hebrews that Jesus Christ is the Son of God, Jesus Christ is the Messiah, Jesus Christ is God! All the prophecies concerning the Messiah in the Old Testament make clear that God Himself was coming to save mankind, and He did. God was born a man, and He called Himself Jesus (Saviour).

**28)** FOR UNTO US A CHILD IS BORN, UNTO US A SON IS GIVEN: AND THE GOVERNMENT SHALL BE UPON HIS SHOULDER: AND HIS NAME SHALL BE CALLED WONDERFUL, COUNSELLOR, THE MIGHTY "GOD", THE EVERLASTING "FATHER", THE PRINCE OF PEACE.

ISAIAH 9:6

It does not get any clearer than this: Isaiah prophecied in the last days, the mighty *God,* and the everlasting *Father* would be born on earth. Just like man is flesh, soul and spirit in one person, God the Son, God the Holy Ghost, and God the Father is one person. Jesus also makes plain to His disciples that they have been intimate with God the Father because they have been intimate with Him. JESUS IS GOD! JESUS IS THE HOLY GHOST! JESUS IS THE FATHER!

If you want to know what God is really like simply read the four (4) epistles in the New Testament, and learn about Jesus because He and the Father are the same person. When the Holy Ghost comes and dwells with us, He is also Jesus and the Father dwelling within us.

**29)** I AND MY FATHER ARE ONE.

JOHN 10:30

If anybody comes to your door claiming to tell you the truth about Jesus and says that Jesus is not God, please do not invite them into your house unless you are a *mature* Christian, and you are well grounded in the Word of God. You might want to quote the above scripture verses to them, but they will probably have a different Bible than the King James Version, and the literature they hand out will not quote the Bible accurately, or it quotes Bible verses out of context.

People only believe what they want to believe. What separates Christianity from all the world's religions is this: Every other religion claims you can attain salvation on your own. This includes every denomination or cult that claims to be Christian, but is not! Christianity proclaims that belief in the resurrection of Jesus Christ, public confession of His Lordship, and repentance of our own dead works is the one and only way to salvation and eternal life.

#5 METHOD OF ATTACK: *JESUS IS NOT THE ONLY WAY TO GOD.*

30)  JESUS SAITH UNTO HIM, I AM THE WAY, THE TRUTH, AND THE LIFE: NO MAN COMETH UNTO THE FATHER, BUT BY ME.
JOHN 14:6

Just before this verse, Jesus had told His disciples that He is going away. He also explains that He is going to go to His Father's house, and that He is going to prepare a place for them there. Thomas, poor doubting Thomas, asks Jesus how they will be able to find Him, since they do not know the way. Jesus explains that He is the way to His Father's house, the *only* way! We cannot find God by ourselves. We can only find God if we follow His instructions (the Bible/Jesus Christ/God's Word), and do what we need to do, and go where we need to go.

Just like the cloud by day and the fire by night, which led the Israelites in the wilderness, the Word of God (Jesus Christ) leads us through the wilderness and to the Promised Land. There are many people who claim they know the way to the Promised Land, but only God can really show us the way, and we must follow Him and trust in Him.

Every other religion on earth was started by some man, who claimed they had found the way to God. Only Christianity was started by God showing the lost world the proper way back to God.

31)  BE IT KNOWN UNTO YOU ALL, AND TO ALL THE PEOPLE OF ISRAEL, THAT BY THE NAME OF JESUS CHRIST OF NAZARETH, WHOM YE CRUCIFIED, WHOM GOD RAISED FROM THE DEAD, EVEN BY HIM DOTH THIS MAN STAND HERE BEFORE YOU WHOLE.
32)  THIS IS THE STONE WHICH WAS SET AT NOUGHT OF YOU BUILDERS, WHICH IS BECOME THE HEAD OF THE CORNER.
33)  NEITHER IS THERE SALVATION IN ANY OTHER: FOR THERE IS NONE OTHER NAME UNDER HEAVEN GIVEN AMONG MEN, WHEREBY WE MUST BE SAVED.
ACTS 4:10-12

Peter miraculously heals a man lame from birth in the name of Jesus Christ. The priests arrest Peter and John and ask them by what power they had been able to heal the crippled man. The Bible says that Peter, *filled with the Holy Ghost*, tells the priests that the man was healed by the name of Jesus Christ of Nazareth.

We find out in these verses that salvation from sickness, as well as from hell, comes by the name of Jesus Christ, and no other name can save us. This reflects the authority that Christians have in the name of Jesus Christ. Jesus Christ has *all authority* in heaven and in earth! *See* Matthew 28:18.

This was a miraculous event on behalf of an unbeliever. Will not God do even greater miracles on behalf of a believer? If Jesus Christ is not the *only* way to salvation, many Christians throughout history have suffered a lot of persecution and martyrdom for nothing.

#6 METHOD OF ATTACK: *THE BIBLE IS NOT TRUE.*

34)   **ALL SCRIPTURE IS GIVEN BY INSPIRATION OF GOD, AND IS PROFITABLE FOR DOCTRINE, FOR REPROOF, FOR CORRECTION, FOR INSTRUCTION IN RIGHTEOUSNESS:**

35)   **THAT THE MAN OF GOD MAY BE PERFECT, THOROUGHLY FURNISHED UNTO ALL GOOD WORKS.**

**2 TIMOTHY 3:16-17**

*All scripture is inspired by God*! There will be some people, inspired by devils, who will attempt to degrade the Bible by comparing it to other ancient texts. They can only fool the spiritually ignorant. Once you have applied the Word of God to your life, and experienced God's blessings in your life, you will not question the Bible's unique place in all of the World's literature.

INSPIRATION. G2315. Theh-op'-nyoo-stos: divinely breathed in: - given by inspiration of God.

The Word of God was divinely breathed into Holy men of old, and then *spoken* by them, and written down for posterity's sake. The Word of God cannot lead you astray. The Word of God leads you directly to its Author. *You must believe that God's Word is truth*!

#7 METHOD OF ATTACK: *THE BIBLE CAN MEAN DIFFERENT THINGS TO DIFFERENT PEOPLE.*

36)   **KNOWING THIS FIRST, THAT NO PROPHECY OF THE SCRIPTURE IS OF ANY PRIVATE INTERPRETATION.**

37)   **FOR THE PROPHECY CAME NOT IN OLD TIME BY THE WILL OF MAN: BUT HOLY MEN OF GOD SPAKE AS THEY WERE MOVED BY THE HOLY GHOST.**

**2 PETER 1:20-21**

There are many deceivers in the world, who will attempt to explain away the Word of God. However, you must take God at His Word. God is not trying to hide the ball. God will give us greater revelation as we draw closer to Him, but He will never give us a revelation that directly contradicts the plain meaning of His Word.

Only those inspired by the Devil will attempt to contradict God's Word. Remember, the Devil is the Father of lies! He will come adding or subtracting from God's Word. That is why it is important to memorize God's Word exactly. The Devil will always come questioning: *Hath God said? See* Genesis 3:1. Remember the trouble Eve got herself and us into because she did not know God's Word exactly!

#7 METHOD OF ATTACK: *THE DEVIL IS NOT REAL.*

**38)** **H**OW **G**OD ANOINTED **J**ESUS OF **N**AZARETH WITH THE **H**OLY **G**HOST AND WITH POWER: WHO WENT ABOUT DOING GOOD, AND HEALING ALL THAT WERE OPPRESSED OF THE DEVIL; FOR **G**OD WAS WITH HIM.
**A**CTS **10:38**

There is little doubt from the scriptures that our Lord Jesus Christ believed in the devil. The major part of His ministry was casting devils out of people who were oppressed with different maladies. It appears from the Bible that ALL sickness is a direct result of attacks by devils.

Christians can be attacked and made sick just like anybody else, the difference is, no Christian has to remain sick. We have access to the Great Physician, our Lord Jesus Christ. We have access to God's promises to us in His Word. There is so much illness in the church today because many Christians, including the clergy, really do not believe in the Devil, and do not resist him with the Word of God.

**39)** **F**OR WE WRESTLE NOT AGAINST FLESH AND BLOOD, BUT AGAINST PRINCIPALITIES, AGAINST POWERS, AGAINST THE RULERS OF THE DARKNESS OF THIS WORLD, AGAINST SPIRITUAL WICKEDNESS IN HIGH PLACES.
**E**PHESIANS **6:11-12**

I always wondered why there were so few mighty miracles in the Church like those commonly performed by Jesus and the Apostles. Now I understand it is because there is so little faith left in the Church. Today the first thing a Christian will do when they get sick is make an appointment with a doctor. It does not even cross a Christian's mind to resist the Devil.

Why? Modern Christians do not *know* the Word of God. Modern Christians do not *believe* the Word of God. Modern Christians do not believe in devils that can afflict them. Modern Christians are too sophisticated for their own good. I am not saying, "Do not go to doctors when you get sick." If you do not have the sword of the spirit ready to do battle, if you do not have the armor of God, if you do not have faith in God's Word, you had better get help from where ever you can find it.

You MUST have a mature faith before you can stop going to doctors. *Charles Capps* asked, "Why do people think they have faith to cure cancer, if they do not have faith to cure a headache?" We need to build up our faith by *speaking, hearing* and *believing* the Word of God. Faith is not hoping God's Word is true, faith is *knowing* that God's Word is true.

I am also not saying, "Do not take medicine." Often times God wants us to do something prior to being healed, probably to teach us obedience. Jesus anointed the eyes of the blind man with clay. *See* John 9:6. Jesus laid his hands on people. *See* John 13:13. Jesus told the ten lepers to show themselves to the priests. *See* John 17:14. Above all things, we must be sensitive to the Holy Spirit and be obedient to His instructions. However, a mature Christian should not remain sickly for years on end.

If you are sickly all the time, there is obviously a breach in your spiritual defenses. You need to start repairing the breach by *memorizing* and *speaking* healing verses from the Bible. *See* Isaiah 53:5, 1 Peter 2:24, Proverbs 4:20-22, Psalm 107:20, 3 John 1:2. Eventually, your faith will be built up and your health will recover.

**40)** SUBMIT YOURSELVES THEREFORE TO GOD. RESIST THE DEVIL, AND HE WILL FLEE FROM YOU.
JAMES 4:7

How can we resist the devil if we do not believe in the devil? The devil's greatest weapon is deception. He wants to convince the Church, and the world, that only the ignorant and backward believe in devils and demons. Do not be fooled, your enemy is not going to attack you out in the open, and he is not going to reveal his identity if he can help it. The Holy Scriptures teach plainly that we have enemies of spiritual wickedness, the rulers of darkness, who are constantly plotting our destruction.

#8 METHOD OF ATTACK: *GOOD PEOPLE GO TO HEAVEN AND BAD PEOPLE GO TO HELL.*

**41)** THE LORD LOOKED DOWN FROM HEAVEN UPON THE CHILDREN OF MEN, TO SEE IF THERE WERE ANY THAT DID UNDERSTAND, AND SEEK GOD.
**42)** THEY ARE ALL GONE ASIDE, THEY ARE ALL TOGETHER BECOME FILTHY: THERE IS NONE THAT DOETH GOOD, NO, NOT ONE.
PSALM 14:2-3

The Apostle Paul references this verse in the third Chapter of the Book of Romans, where he explains the need for all people, both Jew and Gentile, to be justified by grace and not by works. When we compare people with people, there are obviously some people who are better physically, mentally and morally than some other people, but when we compare all people with God, there is a gulf so vast that all hope is lost.

FOR ALL HAVE SINNED, AND COME SHORT OF THE GLORY OF GOD.
ROMANS 3:23

However, God is greater than our sin, and He has provided a bridge over the gulf between the glory of God and mankind's fallen nature. God has provided His grace, and faith in His Son Jesus Christ bridges the gulf.

43) **NOW THEREFORE WHY TEMPT YE GOD, TO PUT A YOKE UPON THE NECK OF THE DISCIPLES, WHICH NEITHER OUR FATHERS NOR WE WERE ABLE TO BEAR?**

44) **BUT WE BELIEVE THAT THROUGH THE GRACE OF THE LORD JESUS CHRIST WE SHALL BE SAVED, EVEN AS THEY.**
ACTS 15:10-11

In the early days of the Church, there were people who insisted that Christians had to be obedient to the laws of Moses, just like many people today insist Christians have to obey the laws of Moses. Christianity is not based on "touch not, taste not", Christianity is based on *knowing* Jesus Christ (the Word of God).

We are confident that we can boldly approach the throne of God because of our relationship with Him who sits on the throne, not because of our own power or holiness. We do not fear the Day of Judgment because we love God and we know that God loves us. Jesus died for our sins and we share His righteousness.

#9 METHOD OF ATTACK: *GOD ONLY DOES MIRACLES FOR ESPECIALLY GOOD AND HOLY PEOPLE.*

45) **YE MEN OF ISRAEL, WHY MARVEL YE AT THIS? OR WHY LOOK YE SO EARNESTLY ON US, AS THOUGH BY OUR OWN POWER OR HOLINESS WE HAD MADE THIS MAN TO WALK?**

46) **THE GOD OF ABRAHAM, AND OF ISAAC, AND OF JACOB, THE GOD OF OUR FATHERS, HATH GLORIFIED HIS SON JESUS; WHOM YE DELIVERED UP, AND DENIED HIM IN THE PRESENCE OF PILATE, WHEN HE WAS DETERMINED TO LET HIM GO.**
ACTS 3:12-13

47) **AND HIS NAME THROUGH FAITH IN HIS NAME HATH MADE THIS MAN STRONG, WHOM YE SEE AND KNOW: YEA, THE FAITH WHICH IS BY HIM HATH GIVEN HIM THIS PERFECT SOUNDNESS IN THE PRESENCE OF YOU ALL.**
ACTS 3:16

The Apostle Peter makes it clear that it was not his, or Johns, own power or holiness that caused the lame man to walk, but faith in the name of Jesus Christ. Just like Peter, we simply *speak* God's Word in the name of Jesus Christ and *believe* that God will fulfill all that He has *spoken* and written for our edification and our blessing. It stands to reason that if: "without faith it is impossible to please God" – then conversely "with faith we can and do please God".

If we are truly servants of God, if God is our Father in heaven, we should strive to increase our faith. Faith cometh by *hearing* and hearing by the Word of God. We must *speak* and *hear* the Word of God continually.

#10 METHOD OF ATTACK: *MIRACLES AND PROPHECY STOPPED AFTER THE BIBLE WAS COMPLETED AND THE APOSTLES PASSED AWAY.*

**48)** AND IT SHALL COME TO PASS AFTERWARD, THAT I WILL POUR OUT MY SPIRIT UPON ALL FLESH; AND YOUR SONS AND YOUR DAUGHTERS SHALL PROPHESY, YOUR OLD MEN SHALL DREAM DREAMS, YOUR YOUNG MEN SHALL SEE VISIONS:

**49)** AND ALSO UPON THE SERVANTS AND UPON THE HANDMAIDS IN THOSE DAYS WILL I POUR OUT MY SPIRIT.

**JOEL 2:28-29**

This Prophecy in the Book of Joel makes it obvious that God intends to pour out His Spirit upon the Church in the last days. God is not finished with us yet! The Saints of God can still dream dreams, we can still have visions, and we can still prophecy. Do not let liars steal your blessings and gifts, which the Holy Spirit wishes to give you.

**50)** GO YE INTO ALL THE WORLD, AND PREACH THE GOSPEL TO EVERY CREATURE.

**51)** HE THAT BELIEVETH AND IS BAPTIZED SHALL BE SAVED, BUT HE THAT BELIEVETH NOT SHALL BE DAMNED.

**52)** AND THESE SIGNS SHALL FOLLOW THEM THAT BELIEVE; IN MY NAME SHALL THEY CAST OUT DEVILS; THEY SHALL SPEAK WITH NEW TONGUES;

**53)** THEY SHALL TAKE UP SERPENTS; AND IF THEY DRINK ANY DEADLY THING, IT SHALL NOT HURT THEM; THEY SHALL LAY HANDS ON THE SICK, AND THEY SHALL RECOVER.

**MARK 16:15-18**

This is the great commission. Was Jesus speaking only to the Apostles? Have all the demons been cast out? Have all the sick recovered? Has the gospel been preached to all the world?

Look around you, there is still plenty of work for everyone that believes in the authority and power of Jesus Christ, and God's Holy Word. If somebody asks you to pray for them, why not lays hands on them? Why not name the name of Jesus Christ? What will it hurt you or them? If they do not recover, they are in the same position they were in before you laid hands on them. Maybe you will look foolish to some people. Who cares? If they do recover, your faith and the faith of other witnesses will increase, glory to God in the highest!

Congratulations, if you can memorize these fifty-four verses written above, one (1) each week, in a little over one year you will lay a very strong foundation for your Christian walk and ministry. All mature Christians have a ministry because all mature Christians are servants of God. When you know these verses you will have a strong Biblical foundation. You will not be easily moved or led astray by false teachers and false prophets.

# CHAPTER 33

## BE A DELIVERER
## (THE SECOND YEAR)

God is searching the whole world for deliverers. The whole world is in darkness and bondage. The whole world needs to hear the gospel message because the gospel is the only thing that will bring light, liberty, life, and love to a fallen and lost world. However, remember it is not us that set people free, it is Jesus Christ (the Word of God) that sets the captive free.

Remember it is NOT our wisdom, or our knowledge, or our power, or our holiness, or our strength that draws people to Jesus Christ, it is the fruit of the Spirit. Therefore, we must start by cultivating our relationship with the Holy Spirit, so that He can produce fruit in our lives. We must begin planting and watering our own spirit by *memorizing* and *speaking* the Word of God. How do we cultivate a relationship with the Holy Spirit? We must get to know God by His Holy Word.

### FRUITS OF THE SPIRIT

**54)** **BUT THE FRUIT OF THE SPIRIT IS LOVE, JOY, PEACE, LONGSUFFERING, GENTLENESS, GOODNESS, FAITH;**
**55)** **MEEKNESS, TEMPERANCE: AGAINST SUCH THERE IS NO LAW.**
**GALATIANS 5:22-23**

It is not the branch that draws people to the vine, it is the fruit, which the branch bears, that draws people to the vine. If a branch does not bear fruit, it is pruned off of the vine to make room for more productive branches, and the unproductive branch is cast into the fire. Therefore, our chief aim, as a branch attached to the vine, should be to bear abundant fruit for the Lord. Paul is very specific when he writes to the Corinthians:

**56)** **BUT HIS I SAY, HE WHICH SOWETH SPARINGLY SHALL REAP ALSO SPARINGLY, AND HE WHICH SOWETH BOUNTIFULLY SHALL REAP ALSO BOUNTIFULLY.**
**2 CORINTHIANS 9:6**

The key to bearing fruit is *giving*. The more we give the more we will increase. I am not just talking about giving money. If God has blessed us with money, we need to be generous with our money, but God has blessed some people with position, like Esther and Joseph, or skill like Hiram, or wisdom, like Solomon, or understanding, like Abigail.

If we want to get, we must first give. If we want to reap a crop, we must first sow seed. If we want to receive spiritual fruit, we must give from our spiritual storehouse. The most important gift we can give to the lost world is the Word of God! Where is our spiritual storehouse, and what do we store there? The Word of God is the treasure that we have been diligently and patiently storing in our mind/heart (spiritual warehouse). If we want to reap spiritually, we must sow spiritually, and we must sow the Word of God in our mind/soul.

**BUT SANCTIFY THE LORD GOD IN YOUR HEARTS; AND BE READY ALWAYS TO GIVE AN ANSWER TO EVERY MAN THAT ASKETH YOU A REASON OF THE HOPE THAT IS IN YOU WITH MEEKNESS AND FEAR:**
**I PETER 3:15**

What is the answer we should be ready to give? Should our answer be from the newest and best selling relationship book, or psychology book, or financial book, or our favorite television talk show host? No, no, a thousand times NO!

The answer we must be ready to give is the Word of God. Receiving and believing the Word of God is the answer to all of mankind's problems. We will be ready to give an answer to every man that asks us only if we have God's Word memorized and stored away in our hearts. Even a Christian with no worldly wealth can give the Word of God and bless a lost and dying world.

## FIRST FRUIT = LOVE

God is Love. Therefore, the more we mature in the spirit, the more of His love will be manifest in our lives.

**57)** **A NEW COMMANDMENT I GIVE UNTO YOU, THAT YE LOVE ONE ANOTHER; AS I HAVE LOVED YOU, THAT YE ALSO LOVE ONE ANOTHER.**
**JOHN 13:34**

How can we tell if we love one another? Once again the answer is *giving*. How can we tell if God loves us? God *gave* His Son as a *propitiation* for our sins. *See* Romans 3:25

PROPITIATION. G2435. Hil-as-tay'-ree-on: an expiatory (place or thing) i.e. (concretely) an atoning victim, or (specifically) the lid of the Ark (in the Temple): - mercyseat, propitiation.

Jesus Christ is the mercy seat that covers the Ark of God. The Ark represents God's throne, His authority, His provision, His quickening life, and finally God's judgment proceeds from His throne. When the Ark was taken from the people of Israel by the Philistines, God smote the Philistine city of Gath. *See* I Samuel 5:9. When the men of Beth-shemesh looked into the Ark, over fifty thousand men died. *See* I Samuel 6:19.

Why? Because without the shedding of blood, without a propitiation for sin, or covering for our sins, God must judge sin and the judgment for sin is always death. The Jewish High Priest only entered into the presence of the Ark one time per year, after he was ritually cleaned.

When the priest entered the Holy of Holies, he sprinkled blood on the mercy seat for the remission of the nation's sins. However, Jesus made an eternal sacrifice by placing His body, as a propitiation (covering) for sin, between us and the judgment seat of God. All of God's judgment for all of our sins fell upon Him. Jesus *gave* everything for us. The Old French word for love is *charity*.

CHARITY. G26. Ag-ah'-pay: love, i.e. affection or benevolence; specifically (plural) a love- feast: - (feast of) charity (-ably), dear, love.

**58)** **AND ABOVE ALL THINGS HAVE FERVENT CHARITY AMONG YOURSELVES: FOR CHARITY SHALL COVER THE MULTITUDE OF SINS.**
**I PETER 4:8**

Charity has become synonymous with liberality to the poor, but it originally meant much more.

**Charity** means love; benevolence; affection; good will; that disposition of heart which inclines men to think favorably of their fellow men, and to do them good.

Charity is the feeling that should well up in our heart when we see someone we love who is sick, or hungry, or cold, or destitute, or in bondage. We naturally want to heal them, or feed them, or cover them, or lift them up, or set them free. As we mature in the spirit, our love will be manifest to a wider and wider circle of people, until finally we will have empathy and charity for all the people of the world. We will no longer be able to ignore the plea of the desperate, or take advantage of the simple, or grind down the poor.

## SECOND FRUIT = JOY

**59)** **A MAN HATH "JOY" BY THE ANSWER OF HIS MOUTH: AND A WORD SPOKEN IN DUE SEASON, HOW GOOD IT IS?**
**PROVERBS 15:23**

JOY. H8057. Sim-khaw: blithesomeness or glee (religious or festival): - exceeding (-ly), gladness, joy (-fulness), mirth, pleasure, rejoice (-ing).

A man hath joy (exceeding pleasure) by the answer of his mouth. How does a man have joy by the answer of his mouth?

ANSWER. H4617. Mah-an-eh': from 6030, a reply (favorable or contradictory); - answer, x himself.

Still a little confused? Let's look up the Hebrew word under number 6030.

SPEAK. H6030. Aw-naw: a primitive root; properly to eye or (generally) to heed, i.e. pay attention; by implication to respond; by extension to begin to speak; specifically to sing, shout, testify, announce; - give account, afflict (by mistake for 6031), (cause to, give) answer, bring low (by mistake for 6031), cry, hear Leannoth, lift up, say, x scholar, (give a) shout, sing (together by course), speak, testify, utter, (bear) witness.

Now we are getting somewhere. A man hath joy (*exceeding pleasure*) by the answer (*testimony, witness*) of his mouth.

**60)** **HOW BEAUTIFUL UPON THE MOUNTAINS ARE THE FEET OF HIM THAT BRINGETH GOOD TIDINGS, THAT PUBLISHETH PEACE; THAT BRINGETH GOOD TIDINGS, THAT PUBLISHETH SALVATION; THAT SAITH UNTO ZION, THY GOD REIGNETH!**
**ISAIAH 52:7**

The only joy that I can compare with *speaking* the Word of God is *hearing* the Word of God. When we are sick, or in distress, or in desperate circumstances, a messenger with the Word of God can truly lift our spirits. However, there is no greater joy than when we can personally deliver the gospel to somebody in distress, by speaking the Word of God and witnessing their deliverance.

**BUT SANCTIFY THE LORD GOD IN YOU HEARTS: AND BE READY ALWAYS TO GIVE AN ANSWER TO EVERY MAN THAT ASKETH YOU A REASON OF THE HOPE THAT IS IN YOU WITH MEEKNESS AND FEAR:**
**I PETER 3:15**

Remember the answer must be the right answer, and there is only one right answer to every problem: JESUS CHRIST (the Word of God). This is why it is so important for us to memorize God's Word. We receive the greater benefit when we testify about Jesus Christ, and tell what He has meant to us.

When I look back on my life, I cannot imagine accomplishing the things that I have accomplished without knowing Him. Oh, what a friend we have in Jesus! If you want true joy, be ready always to give an answer (*testimony*) to every man that asks you a reason of the hope that is in you. If we are saved, we should have a testimony that we can share with everyone.

**THIRD FRUIT = PEACE**

**61)** **THOU WILT KEEP HIM IN PERFECT "PEACE", WHOSE MIND IS STAYED ON THEE: BECAUSE HE TRUSTETH IN THEE.**
**ISAIAH 26:3**

PEACE. H7965. Shaw-lome': safe, i.e. (figuratively) well, happy, friendly; also (abstractly) welfare, i.e. health, prosperity, peace: - x do, familiar, x fare, favour, + friend, x great, (good) health, (x perfect, such as be at) peace (-able, -ably), prosper (-ity, -ous), rest, safe(-ly), salute, welfare, (x all is, be) well, x wholly.

*Peace* in Hebrew means far more than just relief from strife. Although it does mean relief from strife, it also means: health, prosperity, safety, perfect wholeness. Jesus Christ is the *Prince of Peace. See* Isaiah 9:6.

When a Jew in ancient Israel met another Jew, he said, "*Shalome*" (Peace). When two Jews parted in ancient Israel, they again said, "*Shalome*" (Peace). When they entered another person's home, they said, "Peace (Shalome) be in this house." Peace is essentially what God wants for everyone and there is only one way to attain Shalome. We must keep our minds *stayed* on God.

STAYED. H5564. Saw-mak': a primitive root; to prop (literally or figuratively); reflexively to lean upon or take hold of (in a favorable or unfavorable sense): - bear up, establish, (up-) hold, lay, lean, lie hard, put, rest self, set self, stand fast, stay (self), sustain.

We can only have health, prosperity, peace, safety, and perfect wholeness when our minds *lean* onto or hold fast onto God. How does our mind *lean* on God? Once again, we must *memorize* and *speak* His Word. Remember Joshua 1:8 and Psalm 1:2, we need to *meditate* on God's Word. We must *speak* God's Word over and over too ourselves. We must store God's Word in our mind. Our mind must *lean* on God's Word. I can personally testify that by leaning my mind on God's Word, I have enjoyed good health, prosperity, peace, safety and perfect wholeness. I also believe I have become smarter and wiser by leaning my mind on God's Word. If you do not believe me, why not try memorizing one Bible verse per week for a year or two and see what happens?

## FOURTH FRUIT = LONGSUFFERING

62) BUT, BELOVED, BE NOT IGNORANT OF THIS ONE THING, THAT ONE DAY IS WITH THE LORD AS A THOUSAND YEARS, AND A THOUSAND YEARS AS ONE DAY.

63) THE LORD IS NOT SLACK CONCERNING HIS PROMISE, AS SOME MEN COUNT SLACKNESS; BUT IS "LONGSUFFERING" TO US-WARD, NOT WILLING THAT ANY SHOULD PERISH, BUT THAT ALL SHOULD COME TO REPENTENCE.

2 PETER 3:8-9

LONGSUFFERING. G3115. Mak-roth-oo-mee'-ah: longanimity, i.e. (objectively) forbearance or (subjectively) fortitude :-longsuffering, patience.

Longsuffering is truly a fruit of the spirit and if you manifest this fruit, you are well on your way to being a mature Christian. Often times I look around at this sinful world, and wonder how God can allow all the horrors perpetrated by mankind to continue, but then this verse always comes back to me. What if God was not longsuffering? We would have all been cast into hell long ago.

We must also be willing to be longsuffering, if by the grace of God one more person can be saved from the eternal torment of hell. It is often said we must hate the sin, but not the sinner. Often times this is no easy task, especially when somebody is attempting to harm us or our loved ones. However, we must always remember, but for the grace of God, there go I.

We not only must be able to have empathy for others, and try to imagine walking in their shoes, but we must also try and remember what we were like prior to our own salvation. After a year of *speaking* God's Word, you will see a radical growth and

156

transformation in yourself. The same growth, year after year, and we will become totally different people.

We eventually are conformed to the image of Jesus Christ. An acorn cannot be compared to a mighty oak tree. We must be patient and longsuffering with the lost and with immature Christians. God is not done with them yet, and God is not done with us yet. Therefore, we must not become impatient with ourselves either. Eventually, in God's own good time, everything will reach fruition, both the good and the bad.

## THE FIFTH FRUIT = GENTLENESS

GENTLENESS. G5544. Khray-stot'-ace: usefulness, i.e. morally excellent (in character or demeanor): - gentleness, good (-ness), kindness.

**64)  THOU HAST ALSO GIVEN ME THE SHIELD OF THY SALVATION: AND THY RIGHT HAND HATH HOLDEN ME UP, AND THY "GENTLENESS" HATH MADE ME GREAT. PSALM 18:35**

GENTLENESS. H6038. an-aw-vaw': condescension, human and subjective (modesty) or divine and objective (clemency): - gentleness, humility, meekness.

Gentleness is a two way street. We can be treated with gentleness, and we can treat others with gentleness. We do not have to excuse other people's weaknesses, but we should pardon other people's weaknesses.

Why? Because that is what God does for us when we make mistakes. We do not expect a child to act like or perform like an adult, at least a mature adult would not expect a child to hold down a steady job, or support a family, or be wise as Solomon. We should also not expect the unsaved person, or carnal Christians to behave in a Christ like manner, or to produce all the fruit of the spirit. It is impossible for them to behave like a mature Christian until they become a mature Christian.

We need to be gentle with people, not because of who they are, but because of who they may be in the future. "Thy gentleness hath made me great." King David wrote Psalm 18 when he was delivered from his enemies and from King Saul. King David was looking back over all his troubles. He was remembering all his enemies, many people had persecuted him, and he recognized that he was able to accomplish everything he did because God overlooked his weaknesses.

God had delivered David and made him great. God new King David's potential before he was in his mother's womb. Remember before you blast someone, "Except for the *gentleness* and grace of God, there go I." Perhaps if we can remember that God is not done with any of us yet, the fruit of *gentleness* will eventually be formed in us all.

## THE SIXTH FRUIT = GOODNESS

65) **WHEREFORE ALSO WE PRAY ALWAYS FOR YOU, THAT OUR GOD WOULD COUNT YOU WORTHY OF THIS CALLING, AND FULFILL ALL THE GOOD PLEASURE OF HIS "GOODNESS", AND THE WORK OF FAITH WITH POWER:**

66) **THAT THE NAME OF OUR LORD JESUS CHRIST MAY BE GLORIFIED IN YOU, AND YE IN HIM, ACCORDING TO THE GRACE OF OUR GOD AND THE LORD JESUS CHRIST.**

**2 THESSALONIANS 1:11-12**

GOODNESS. G19. Ag-ath-o-soo'-nay: goodness, i.e., virtue or beneficence: - goodness.

GOOD means something good, specifically: worth; virtue; merit; benefit; advantage; something desirable or desired.

*Goodness* is a basic attribute of God's character and is manifest in all of His actions. God is good and everything God does is good. God wants us to be good, to be beneficial to others, and to contribute to His Kingdom. When we *walk in the spirit*, we cannot help but be virtuous.

All things were created for God's pleasure. *See* Revelations 4:11. It is God's pleasure for us to be good because that was His intention when we were created in His image. Only our rebellion against His perfect plan has caused all of the evil in the earth, all the vitriol, all the poison, all the disease and all the death.

When we *walk in the spirit*, we desire to build and not to destroy, we desire to help and not to hurt, we desire to love and not to be selfish. Most of all, we desire to glorify the name of Jesus Christ, so that everyone may know that we are in Him and He is in us.

## THE SEVENTH FRUIT = FAITH

67) **SO THEN "FAITH" COMETH BY HEARING, AND HEARING BY THE WORD OF GOD. ROMANS 10:17**

FAITH. G4102. Pis'-tis: persuasion, i.e. credence; moral conviction (of religious truth, or the truthfulness of God, or a religious teacher), especially reliance upon Christ for salvation; abstractly constancy in such profession; by extension the system of religious (Gospel) truth itself: - assurance, belief, believe, faith, fidelity.

Faith comes by *hearing* the Word of God! Hearing God's Word only once a week is not good enough. The more you hear the Word of God, the more your faith will increase. *Faith* is simply the end product of hearing and believing God.

Disbelieving God is what caused the fall of Adam and Eve, and it is the root of all mankind's individual and collective problems. If you are *walking in the spirit,* you will crave to *hear* the Word of God. Thank God, we do not have to go to a minister or buy C.D.'s to hear God's Word. We can speak God's Word to ourselves everyday and all day long if we want to.

**68)** B UT WITHOUT "FAITH" IT IS IMPOSSIBLE TO PLEASE HIM: FOR HE THAT COMETH TO G OD MUST BELIEVE THAT HE IS, AND THAT HE IS A REWARDER OF THEM THAT DILIGENTLY SEEK HIM.
H EBREWS **11:6**

If we believe God, we please God. If we disbelieve God, we displease God, and it is as simple as that. If you want to be a good Christian, if you want to *walk in the spirit*, you must spend time *hearing* God's Word every day. God is a *rewarder* of them that *diligently* seek Him!

Can it get any clearer than that? Christians spend all their free time watching television, or entertaining friends, or amusing themselves, and then wonder why they are sickly, poor and unhappy. Do you think it might be because they do not take a few minutes every day to seek God?

Could it be Christians are suffering because they do not really believe God's Word? Spend just a little time every day praying, reading God's Word, speaking God's Word, hearing God's Word, and see if your circumstances do not radically change in just a few short years.

## THE EIGHTH FRUIT = MEEKNESS

Meekness is always associated with greatness throughout the Bible. I have heard that being meek does not mean thinking less of yourself, being meek simply means not thinking of yourself at all. The truly meek person does not get indignant by real or imagined slights. The meek person puts other people's needs above their own needs. The meek person is always seeking to benefit other people.

MEEKNESS. G4236. Prah-ot'-ace: *Gentleness*; by implication *humility*: - meekness.

The Bible says that Moses was very meek, more than every man on the face of the earth. *See* Numbers 12:3. Jesus said:

**69)** C OME UTO ME, ALL YE THAT LABOUR AND ARE HEAVY LADEN, AND I WILL GIVE YOU REST.
**70)** T AKE MY YOKE UPON YOU, AND LEARN OF ME; FOR I AM "MEEK" AND LOWLY IN HEART: AND YE SHALL FIND REST UNTO YOUR SOULS.
M ATTHEW **11:28-29**

If we recognize who we are in Jesus Christ, it is easy to be meek. If someone insults us or abuses us, we simply let God take care of the situation. Sometimes we can become indignant over the most trivial slights.

We have to recognize if something is important, God will take care of the matter. If something is not important, we should not waste our time or energy being angry at somebody. Jesus tells us to pray for those who despitefully use us or persecute us. *See* Matthew 5:44.

Why do we need to love our enemies? First and foremost, I have noticed that when I pray for someone who I feel has slighted me, I do not toss and turn at night plotting my revenge. It helps me sleep at night and I need my rest. Praying for our enemies truly helps us forgive and forget.

Second, if you are a child of God and somebody comes against you, they are actually coming against God and they are in terrible danger. When Miriam and Aaron spoke against Moses, God caused Miriam to become a leper. *See* Numbers 12:10.

Probably the best reason we should be meek ourselves is because we do not know how much God esteems somebody who we might insult, and the consequences may be dire to our own health and welfare. Who knows how much sickness and death has come upon people throughout history because they have mistreated the wrong person or persons?

71) BUT THE "MEEK" SHALL INHERIT THE EARTH; AND SHALL DELIGHT THEMSELVES IN THE ABUNDANCE OF PEACE.
PSALM 37:11

Finally, we know how the Book ends. The meek are the final winners. The meek live in peace and plenty for the rest of eternity. It should be easy to be gracious and meek when you know God plans on giving you everything in the end.

## THE NINTH FRUIT = TEMPERANCE

Temperance or self-control is a hallmark of a mature Christian. When the whole world is terrified and hearts are failing because of fear, the mature Christian has the blessed assurance that Jesus Christ is still in control. Jesus will judge the quick and the dead. Jesus has all power (*authority*) in heaven and earth. We can comfort ourselves and others because we know Him.

72) ACCORDING AS HIS DIVINE POWER HATH GIVEN UNTO US ALL THINGS THAT PERTAIN UNTO LIFE AND GODLINESS, THROUGH THE KNOWLEDGE OF HIM THAT HATH CALLED US TO GLORY AND VIRTUE:

73) WHEREBY ARE GIVEN UNTO US EXCEEDING GREAT AND PRECIOUS PROMISES: THAT BY THESE YE MIGHT BE PARTAKERS OF THE DIVINE NATURE, HAVING ESCAPED THE CORRUPTION THAT IS IN THE WORLD THROUGH LUST.

74) AND BESIDE THIS, GIVING ALL DILIGENCE, ADD TO YOUR FAITH VIRTUE; AND TO VIRTUE KNOWLEDGE;

75) AND TO KNOWLEDGE "TEMPERANCE"; AND TO TEMPERANCE PATIENCE; AND TO PATIENCE GODLINESS;

76) AND TO GODLINESS BROTHERLY KINDNESS; AND TO BROTHERLY KINDNESS CHARITY.

77) FOR IF THESE THINGS BE IN YOU, AND ABOUND, THEY MAKE YOU THAT YE SHALL NEITHER BE BARREN NOR UNFRUITFUL IN THE KNOWLEDGE OF OUR LORD JESUS CHRIST.
2 PETER 1:3-8

TEMPERANCE.   G1466.   Eng-krat'-i-ah:   self-control   (especially   continence):- temperance.

It is through the *knowledge* of Jesus Christ (the Word of God) that all the fruit of the spirit eventually comes. It is the knowledge of Jesus Christ that brings temperance, patience and godliness. We know that He also suffered temptation; however, He overcame the world. We also overcome the world by faith in Jesus Christ (the Word of God).

There is a famine of the Word of God in the land. There is a famine of the fruit of the spirit in the Church. Those who know Jesus Christ, and know the Word of God, will bear spiritual fruit. Those who bear fruit will draw all those who are spiritually hungry to the vine. It is our duty as Christians to speak God's Word and to bear spiritual fruit. It is every Christian's duty to be fruitful and to multiply.

# CHAPTER 34

## SAVING LOST SOULS

Saving lost souls is the whole reason we are still dwelling upon the earth. Saving lost souls is the reason God does not send a fiery chariot to take us up into heaven after we are saved. We have work to do. We need to preach the gospel to a lost and dying world. We need to feed those that hunger and thirst after righteousness. We need to lead the lost out of the barren wilderness and into the Promised Land.

Do you know the gospel? Are you saved or are you just going through the motions? There is an interesting interaction between some un-named person and Jesus in the Book of Luke. Jesus was journeying through the villages of Israel and teaching the people. Jesus was journeying toward Jerusalem and His eventual crucifixion. Obviously, somebody was wondering what all of us have wondered at one time or another because they asked Jesus the following question: "Lord, are there few that be saved?"*See* Luke 13:32.

Jesus answered:

**STRIVE TO ENTER IN AT THE STRAIT GATE: FOR MANY, I SAY UNTO YOU, WILL SEEK TO ENTER IN, AND SHALL NOT BE ABLE.**
**LUKE 13:24**

Should we be afraid? There are many false teachers, false prophets, false religions and false churches in the world today. They are all inspired by the *rulers of darkness* to lead people away from our glorious liberty in Jesus Christ.

Apparently, false doctrines sprang up like weeds where ever the gospel was preached. Essentially, these false doctrines all preach and teach the same thing. They all teach that you make it into heaven by your own works and not by the grace of Jesus Christ. The message of justification by works always bears bad fruit and eventually leads to death and hell. The message of grace always bears good fruit and leads to eternal life and the Kingdom of God.

The works of the flesh are adultery (sleeping with another person's spouse), fornication (sleeping with anybody other than your spouse), uncleanness, lasciviousness, idolatry (image worship), witchcraft (drug use), hatred, variance (quarreling), emulations (jealousy), wrath, strife (contention), seditions (division), heresies (disunion), envying, murders, drunkenness, revellings (rioting), effeminate, abusers of themselves with mankind (homosexuality), thievery, covetousness, reviling, extortion, and such like. *See* I Corinthians 6:9-10 and Galations 5:19-21. If your churches founder(s) or your church leader(s) endorse or practice these types of works, you need to come out of that church organization. Jesus said:

BEWARE OF FALSE PROPHETS, WHICH COME TO YOU IN SHEEP'S CLOTHING, BUT INWARDLY THEY ARE RAVENING WOLVES.

YE SHALL KNOW THEM BY THEIR FRUITS. DO MEN GATHER GRAPES OF THORNS, OR FIGS OF THISTLES?

EVEN SO EVERY GOOD TREE BRINGETH FORTH GOOD FRUIT; BUT A CORRUPT TREE BRINGETH FORTH EVIL FRUIT.

EVERY TREE THAT BRINGETH NOT FORTH GOOD FRUIT IS HEWN DOWN, AND CAST INTO THE FIRE.

WHEREFORE BY THEIR FRUITS YE SHALL KNOW THEM.

MATTHEW 7:15-20

Therefore, I cannot stress this enough, please do some research on the founders of the church you are attending and ask people about the pastor, minister, preacher, priest or reverend of the church you are attending. If they are bearing good fruit, they can teach you how to bear good fruit, but if they are bearing bad fruit, they are most likely leading a lot of people to hell.

## WHAT IS THE GOSPEL?

78)  FOR I AM NOT ASHAMED OF THE GOSPEL OF CHRIST: FOR IT IS THE "POWER" OF GOD UNTO SALVATION TO EVERY ONE THAT BELIEVETH; TO THE JEW FIRST, AND ALSO TO THE GREEK.

79)  FOR THEREIN IS THE RIGHTEOUSNESS OF GOD REVEALED FROM FAITH TO FAITH: AS IT IS WRITTEN, THE JUST SHALL LIVE BY FAITH.

ROMANS 1:16-17

POWER. G1411. *Doo'-nam-is: force* (literally or figuratively); specifically *miraculous power* (usually by implication a *miracle* itself): - ability, abundance, meaning, might (-ily, -y deed), (worker) of miracle (-s), power, strength, violence, mighty (wonderful) work.

The Apostle Paul was explaining to the Romans why all the miracles were occurring around himself and the other followers of Jesus Christ. Miracles always follow the preaching of the *true* gospel. People are saved, sick people are healed, poor people are made rich, foolish people are made wise, and those bound, blinded and imprisoned by the rulers of darkness are set free. Have you seen any miracles lately? If you want to see miracles, maybe you should listen to somebody who is preaching the gospel, or maybe you should start preaching the gospel yourself.

80)  FOR I DELIVERED UNTO YOU FIRST OF ALL THAT WHICH I ALSO RECEIVED, HOW THAT CHRIST DIED FOR OUR SINS ACCORDING TO THE SCRIPTURES;

81)  AND THAT HE WAS BURIED, AND THAT HE ROSE AGAIN THE THIRD DAY ACCORDING TO THE SCRIPTURES;

I CORINTHIANS 15:3-4

The Apostle Paul explained to the Corinthians the gospel in a nutshell: 1) Jesus Christ died for our sins according to the scriptures, 2) He was buried and 3) He rose again on the third day according to the scriptures.

The first and most important part of the gospel is: Jesus Christ died for our *sins* according to the scriptures. Most unbelievers do not have a clue about sin. Most non-Christians, and probably many self proclaimed Christians will say something like this: "I'm not a sinner" or "I'm a good person", or "God does not send good people to hell." Unfortunately, according to scripture, everyone is a sinner.

**82)** FOR ALL HAVE SINNED, AND COME SHORT OF THE GLORY OF GOD;
ROMANS 3:23

Then they might ask something like this: "Isn't hell only for really bad people?" The Book of Revelations has a pretty long list of people cast into the lake of fire.

**83)** BUT THE FEARFUL, AND UNBELIEVING, AND THE ABOMINABLE, AND MURDERERS, AND WHOREMONGERS, AND SORCERERS, AND IDOLATERS, AND ALL LIARS, SHALL HAVE THEIR PART IN THE LAKE WHICH BURNETH WITH FIRE AND BRIMSTONE: WHICH IS THE SECOND DEATH.
REVELATION 21:8

The fearful, unbelieving and ALL liars are lumped in with murderers, pimps and sorcerers. It looks like nobody has a chance to escape the lake of fire, and that is the whole point. Everybody has been afraid, not believed and lied. Nobody has a chance without trusting in the grace and resurrection power of God. If God has the power to resurrect us from the dead, He also has the power to save us from our sin. However, we must *believe* in Jesus Christ and what He did for us!

There have been many people throughout history who have proclaimed themselves as savior or messiah, but Jesus is absolutely unique because He fulfilled the scriptures. No other self proclaimed savior or messiah has ever willingly and meekly laid down their life for the sins of mankind, and fulfilled Bible prophecy so perfectly.

**84)** ALL WE LIKE SHEEP HAVE GONE ASTRAY; WE HAVE TURNED EVERY ONE TO HIS OWN WAY; AND THE LORD HATH LAID ON HIM THE INIQUITY OF US ALL.
**85)** HE WAS OPPRESSED, AND HE WAS AFFLICTED, YET HE OPENED NOT HIS MOUTH: HE IS BROUGHT AS A LAMB TO THE SLAUGHTER, AND AS A SHEEP BEFORE HER SHEARERS IS DUMB, SO HE OPENED NOT HIS MOUTH.
**86)** HE WAS TAKEN FROM PRISON AND FROM JUDGMENT: AND WHO SHALL DECLARE HIS GENERATION? FOR HE WAS CUT OFF OUT OF THE LAND OF THE LIVING; FOR THE TRANSGRESSION OF MY PEOPLE WAS HE STRICKEN.
**87)** AND HE MADE HIS GRAVE WITH THE WICKED, AND WITH THE RICH IN HIS DEATH; BECAUSE HE HAD DONE NO VIOLENCE, NEITHER WAS ANY DECEIT IN HIS MOUTH.
ISAIAH 53:6-9

Pontius Pilate washed his hands saying, "I am innocent of the blood of this just person." Oh… if it was only that easy. However, Pontius Pilate, as the civil authority, did not find Jesus guilty of any crime, let alone a crime deserving the death penalty. Jesus did not demand His rights. Jesus did not tell His disciples to find the best defense lawyer available. Jesus did not conduct His own self defense. Jesus silently allowed Himself to be accused, and while He was nailed to the cross, He prayed that God would forgive His accusers and those who crucified Him.

Jesus died on a cross between two thieves and He was buried in a rich man's tomb. No other self proclaimed savior or messiah in history has fulfilled the ancient prophecy of Isaiah so perfectly.

The second part of the gospel is that Jesus was buried. Jesus died just like everyone on earth has died or eventually will die. No one gets out alive! Jesus Christ is God but He was also a man. He laughed, He cried, He worked, He played, He was born and He died. He was our perfect substitute. He was a man so He could suffer temptation just like we suffer temptation, but without sin.

Sacrificing a chicken, or a goat, or a cow will not pay for the sins of a human being. If somebody murders a man, the courts do not give the death penalty to a sheep. If somebody murders a man, the murderer must pay the ultimate penalty. Jesus did not commit any sin, but He paid the ultimate price, He gave up His own life.

Then the question is: How can one man pay the price for the sins of billions of people? The answer is: Jesus was not only man, but He is also the Everlasting Father and the Mighty God! Only Almighty God can pay for the sins of the entire world!

The third and final part of the gospel is Jesus Christ rose from the dead on the third day according to scripture. This part of the gospel message has definitely never been fulfilled by any other self proclaimed savior or messiah. The Apostle Paul testifies that over five hundred people saw Jesus alive after He was crucified and buried. *See* I Corinthians 15:6.

88) FOR THOU WILT NOT LEAVE MY SOUL IN HELL, NEITHER WILT THOU SUFFER THINE HOLY ONE TO SEE CORRUPTION.
PSALM 16:10

89) AND MANY OF THEM THAT SLEEP IN THE DUST OF THE EARTH SHALL AWAKE, SOME TO EVERLASTING LIFE, AND SOME TO SHAME AND EVERLASTING CONTEMPT.

90) AND THEY THAT BE WISE SHALL SHINE AS THE BRIGHTNESS OF THE FIRMAMENT; AND THEY THAT TURN MANY TO RIGHTEOUSNESS AS THE STARS FOR EVER AND EVER.
DANIEL 12:2-3

Jesus Christ fulfilled messianic Bible prophecy perfectly, up to and including rising from the grave, and we have been promised that if we confess with our mouth that Jesus

Christ is Lord, and believe in our heart that God has raised Him from the dead, we will also *live forever*! This is truly *good news*! If we turn many to righteousness, *they* will live forever, and we will be as the *stars forever and ever*!

91) **THE WORD IS NIGH THEE, EVEN IN THY MOUTH, AND IN THY HEART; THAT IS, THE WORD OF FAITH, WHICH WE PREACH; (SEE DEUTERONOMY 30:14)**

92) **THAT IF THOU SHALT CONFESS WITH THY MOUTH THE LORD JESUS, AND SHALT BELIEVE IN THINE HEART THAT GOD HATH RAISED HIM FROM THE DEAD, THOU SHALT BE SAVED.**

**ROMANS 10:8-9**

If you have memorized the first ninety-two Bible verses written above, you should be well grounded in your Christian faith, and you should be able to lead somebody to salvation. If you are privileged to lead somebody to a saving knowledge of Jesus Christ, you have a heavy responsibility in front of you.

You have the responsibility to make sure they become mature Christians. You must direct them to the Promised Land. You must direct them to the Word of God. The Apostle Paul was an evangelist to the gentiles, but he was not like some modern day evangelist, who appears in town for a week or two and then take off to the next city. The Apostle Paul spent several years in each city and built up the local Church. The Apostle Paul took responsibility for making sure that his early converts to the faith became mature Christians before he evangelized another city.

# CHAPTER 35

## LAST BUT NOT LEAST

I have a few more Bible verses that I believe every mature Christian should know. I think they are important because they give us hope and they increase our faith. First, I believe that Jesus Christ not only died for our sins, He suffered so that we do not have to suffer. Jesus not only took all our sins on the cross, He also took all our sickness.

**93)** **BUT HE WAS WOUNDED FOR OUR TRANSGRESSIONS, HE WAS BRUISED FOR OUR INIQUITIES: THE CHASTISEMENT OF OUR PEACE WAS UPON HIM, AND WITH HIS STRIPES WE ARE HEALED.**
**ISAIAH 53:5**

We know from the New Testament that this verse from the Book of Isaiah refers to our Lord and what He suffered for our sakes. *See* I Peter 2:24. It is written, "With His stripes we *are* healed." The Word does not say, we might be healed, or we are going to be healed. This healing Word of God is available to all Christians right now!

I used to be sick all the time, but after learning about the Word of faith I have not been sick in several years. I am not saying sickness does not try to get hold of me, but I refuse to let sickness get hold of me. If I feel some pain or an itching throat coming on, I immediately speak God's Word from Isaiah 53:5, and I keep speaking it until the symptoms are gone. Often times I speak it when somebody comes around me sneezing and coughing. Resist the devil and he will flee from you. You resist the devil by speaking God's Word.

I refuse to allow sickness in my body because my body is the temple of God. I believe vibrant health is an important part of my testimony. Do I really believe God's Word, or am I just going through the motions? Above all things, I do not want to be a hypocrite. I do not want to be an actor. I want to be the real deal.

Sometimes we do things that make us sick. If you are a heavy smoker or heavy drinker or heavy drug user, you cannot expect to have great health. You cannot expect to build up your health with God's Word while tearing your health apart with poisons at the same time.

Jesus said, "Thou shalt not tempt the Lord your God," when the devil tempted Him to cast himself down from the temple. *See* Matthew 4:7. The devil wants to use our pride to poison us, but we can resist any temptation with God's Word. Always go to the Word of God. God will never fail you and His Word is forever true. The Word of God can set you free from alcohol, drugs, cigarettes and every other addiction.

**94)** **THY WORD IS A LAMP UNTO MY FEET, AND A LIGHT UNTO MY PATH.**
**PSALM 119:105**

If you do not have God, you are like a ship without a rudder being blown off course by every trouble and storm. If you do not know God's Word you are spiritually blind and lost in darkness. The Word of God lights our way and keeps us from stumbling. The Word of God is a sure path leading us from glory to glory.

Psalm 119:105 is so very important to memorize for every new Christian, this verse will always lead us back to our rock and our foundation. Jesus said that whosoever heard, and did His sayings, was a wise man. Jesus promised neither rain, wind, flood, nor storms of life can move a house founded on this rock.

Whenever you are confused or bewildered, you must go back to the Word of God. He will provide you the answers to all your questions. Speaking His Word will calm all your fears. If you read God's Word, you will realize that all the mighty men and women of God were a type of Christ. Every faithful servant of God reflects the personage of Jesus Christ in some way or fashion. Every mature Christian will reflect the Lord if they will speak and believe His Word.

God is searching the world for true believers so He can show Himself mighty on their behalf. God wants the world to see the blessings He will pour out on His Church, if only we will trust in His Word.

**95)** **THE HEART OF THE WISE TEACHETH HIS MOUTH, AND ADDETH LEARNING TO HIS LIPS.**
**PROVERBS 16:23**

This whole book has been an attempt to illustrate the importance of *memorizing*, *speaking* and *hearing* God's Word. God has made some truly astonishing promises in His holy scripture. Long life, health, riches, peace and honor are promised to those who will *trust* Him. *See* Proverbs chapter 3. Miraculous power is promised to those who will *believe* Him. *See* Matthew 17:20.

All of God's promises are directly related to how we relate to Him. Do we *believe* His Word or not? If we are real "believers" we must believe that He is, and that He is a rewarder of those who diligently seek Him. *Walking in the spirit* and being *wise* is not something we do, it is what we are because we *believe* God.

If we see somebody lift a heavy weight, we say he is strong. If we hear somebody rattle off the correct answers to a quiz, we say he is smart. However, nobody is born strong, or wise, or heroes of faith, they all had to work to attain specific results. People have the mistaken idea that God picks people at random to become wise and mighty. However, if we read the Bible carefully, we will see that God seeks those who believe His Word. We see that the wise and mighty all went through trials, through tribulations, and all their trials taught them all one thing: they could rely on God and His Word. God's Word tells us that people are wise if they teach their mouth and add learning to their lips.

**96)** **"DELIGHT" THYSELF ALSO IN THE LORD; AND HE SHALL GIVE THEE THE DESIRES OF THINE HEART.**

**97)** "COMMIT" THY WAY UNTO THE **LORD**; TRUST ALSO IN HIM; AND HE SHALL BRING IT TO PASS.
**PSALM 37:4-5**

DELIGHT. H6026. Aw-nag': to be soft or pliable, i.e. (figuratively) effeminate or luxurious:- delicate (-ness), (have) delight (self), sport self.

COMMIT. H1556. Gaw-lal': a primitive root; to roll (literally or figuratively): - commit, remove, roll (away, down, together), run down, seek occasion, trust, wallow.

Delighting ourselves in the LORD is the same as a wife putting her total trust in her husband. She trusts that he will provide for her and love her. She is confident that he will defend her and fight for her. She knows that his desire is only for her comfort and safety. She leans on him and totally relies on him.

I know this may not be a very modern attitude, but it is the attitude God wants us to cultivate towards Him. God wants us to rest in His perfect providence and provision. When we trust in God to supply our needs, our heart's desires will begin to come alive. We will begin to dream dreams and see visions that ordinary people do not dare to dream or imagine. We will understand that nothing is impossible for God and none of our dreams are too big for Him.

At first our requests will be average. We will ask for a warm place to sleep and food in our stomachs. We will ask for safety and health. God will provide for all our basic needs. Our faith will be quickened by the Holy Spirit and our horizons will become much larger.

We will begin to ask for bigger things, we will ask for impossible things. We will begin to ask God for miracles. We will ask God to give sight to the blind and salvation to the lost. We will ask God to make the lame man to leap like a hart and the dead man to be raised from the grave. Our faith in God will move mountains and our trust will become as firm as the Rock of Ages. All of our cares will be rolled away from our shoulders because we will know God loves us. Trust in God's Word, and simply ask Him for the desires of your heart. He will bring it to pass.

**98)** THE ANGEL OF THE LORD ENCAMPETH ROUND ABOUT THEM THAT FEAR HIM, AND DELIVERETH THEM.
**PSALM 34:7**

I believe there are devils and demonic spirits trying to harm us, but I also believe that all Christians have guardian angels. Angels are ministering spirits sent to help us in our work and to protect us. When Jesus was going to be taken prisoner, Peter took out a sword and was going to defend Him. Jesus told Peter that if He prayed to His Father, God would give Him more than twelve legions of angels. *See* Matthew 26:53.

At the time of Christ a Roman legion consisted of approximately five-thousand (5,000) soldiers. Jesus was telling Peter that He simply needed to ask, and God would send over seventy-thousand (70,000) angels to deliver Him. You might say, "Well of course God would send a host of angels to protect Jesus, but I'm not Jesus."

There was another time in the Bible where God sent a host of angels to protect Elisha the prophet. *See* II Kings 6:16-17. When Elisha and his servant were surrounded by the Syrian army, Elisha told his servant not to be afraid because: **"They that be with us are more than they that be with them."** Elisha prayed that the Lord would open the eyes of his servant and his servant saw the mountain full of horses and chariots of fire round about Elisha.

You might say, "I am not Elisha either." We can be like the prophets, and we can be like the apostles, they were just human beings like us! James said that Elijah the Prophet was a man subject to like passions as we are and he prayed earnestly that it might not rain: and it rained not on the earth for three and one-half years. *See* James 5:17.

**99)** **TRUST IN THE LORD WITH ALL THINE HEART; AND LEAN NOT UNTO THINE OWN UNDERSTANDING.**
**100)** **IN ALL THEY WAYS ACKNOWLEDGE HIM, AND HE SHALL DIRECT THY PATHS.**
**PROVERBS 3:5-6**

I have saved the best verses for last. Not leaning on your own understanding may be one of the most difficult things we ever do, but it is also one of our major stumbling blocks when it comes to becoming spiritually mature. It is extremely difficult to start questioning the things we think we know. Often times we have preconceived ideas about how things work due to what we have been taught, or what we have experienced. For instance, we all know that we cannot walk on the water because we will sink. However, Jesus was able to walk on the water, and the Apostle Peter was also able to walk on the water too...for a short while at least. *See* Matthew 14:25-32.

All throughout the Bible there are instances where people experience things that most people believe are impossible. The Book of Hebrews speaks of the heroes of faith and lists their accomplishments:

Sarah bears a child at ninety years old, the Children of Israel pass through the Red Sea dry shod, Daniel stops the mouths of lions, women receive their dead raised to life again. The Bible is composed of events that are impossible for most people to believe. However, if we can believe God's Word, the Bible illustrates that people who trust in God will experience events beyond normal people's understanding.

The most important thing we will ever do besides accepting Jesus Christ as our savior is to start knowingly doubting our own senses, our own understanding, our own learning, our own experience and begin *believing* the Word of God. The only thing separating us from the heroes of faith is our doubt in God's Word. Miracles will happen for us if we can only believe God's Word.

**101)** **IF THOU CANST BELIEVE, ALL THINGS ARE POSSIBLE TO HIM THAT BELIEVETH.**
**MARK 9:23**

# CONCLUSION

Mankind is very unique. Unfortunately, familiarity breeds contempt. We spend so much time being around other people that we tend to discount each individual's importance in God's grand scheme of things. According to the Bible, if we overcome, we will rule and reign with Jesus Christ in the heavens and over the earth for all eternity.

I believe there are literally multitudes of angels and devils for every human ever born on the earth. Each person on the earth is a literal battlefield with a host of angels and devils battling for each soul. If we can intentionally begin agreeing with the Word of God, we can turn the tide of battle not only in our own favor, but in the favor of everyone around us.

I am a member of an Indian Tribe that owns a casino. When I was attending law school another law student asked me if I felt bad when I saw some old person dragging around an oxygen tank from slot machine to slot machine. I said, "No, when a person has one bad habit, they usually have a lot of other bad habits to go along with it." You usually won't find a heavy smoker that does not drink, or gamble, or doesn't pursue a lot of other self-destructive behaviors. If they are not literally possessed by demons, they are probably heavily influenced by devils.

Conversely, if you are a Christian, you can ask for God's angels to defend you from sickness, poverty, and any other enemy, human or spiritual, which might be coming against you. The problem with most people, even a lot of Christians, is that they do not realize they are involved in a spiritual battle every moment of their lives. Once you realize who and what you are, you can begin to cause the tide of battle to turn in your favor by *speaking*, *hearing* and *believing* the Word of God.

Now I am going to tell you how to turbo-charge your spiritual life. The most important thing you can do is start searching for other mature Christians. You need to find people who are like minded with you. You need to find people who also memorize the scriptures because they believe the Word of God. If you cannot find another mature Christian, ask God to send you one, or convert someone, but find somebody.

AGAIN I SAY UNTO YOU, THAT IF TWO OF YOU SHALL AGREE ON EARTH AS TOUCHING ANY THING THAT THEY SHALL ASK, IT SHALL BE DONE FOR THEM OF MY FATHER WHICH IS IN HEAVEN.
MATTHEW 18:20

Two mature Christians are truly an irresistible force. That is why it is so important NOT to be unevenly yoked with unbelievers. An unbelieving spouse, business partner, friend, doctor, or lawyer can literally kill you. I am not saying dump your spouse if they are not a Christian, I am afraid you are stuck with them, but that does not mean you should not try to convert them.

If you have a believing spouse, or business partner, or friend, or relative, you should cherish them. How do you *know* whether someone is a mature Christian? They will *know* and *believe* the Word of God!

Two believers together are exponentially more powerful than one believer alone. That is why God has ordained a husband and wife. That is why Jesus sent out His disciples two by two. That is why the Apostle Paul evangelized with a partner. That is why pastors should have an associate pastor.

Every person needs somebody to share their ideas and troubles with. Every person should have a prayer partner. Every person should have somebody to warn them when they stray from the truth. Moses had Aaron, Barak had Deborah, Ruth had Naomi, Esther had Mordecai, David had Jonathan, Paul had Silas and Barnabus, there are two witnesses in the Book of Revelation, and even Jesus had Peter, James and John. It will become ever more important to have other mature believers around you as the final days arrive upon the earth.

**AND LET US CONSIDER ONE ANOTHER TO PROVOKE UNTO LOVE AND TO GOOD WORKS: NOT FORSAKING THE ASSEMBLING OF OURSELVES TOGETHER, AS THE MANNER OF SOME IS; BUT EXHORTING ONE ANOTHER: AND SO MUCH THE MORE, AS YE SEE THE DAY APPROACHING.**
**HEBREWS 10:24-25**

There are a lot of good Churches, all over the world, that are full of mature Christians. There are also a lot of bad Churches full of unbelievers. How can you tell the difference? Good Churches *know* and *believe* the Word of God! Mature Christians "consider" one another to provoke each other unto love and good works.

CONSIDER.   G2657. Kat-an—o-eh'-o: to observe fully; - behold, consider, discover, perceive.

A mature Christian will take an interest in everybody around them. A mature Christian is always looking to serve others. A mature Christian wants to edify the Church. If you have attended a Church for years, and you have not taken the time to know anybody, and nobody has taken the time to know you, you are in trouble. Some people go to a church for their children's sake, or to socialize, or to find business contacts, or because their family has always attended that church. Do not be one of those people.

You want to attend a church because attending edifies your spirit and you can edify other believer's spirits. You want to attend a church because you are seeking the kingdom of God. When you are intimate with a group of mature Christians, and you are all seeking the kingdom of God together, everything else will fall into place.

**BUT SEEK YE FIRST THE KINGDOM OF GOD, AND HIS RIGHTEOUSNESS; AND ALL THESE THINGS SHALL BE ADDED UNTO YOU.**
**MATTHEW 6:33**

We are fast approaching the second coming of Jesus Christ. There are more people alive today than have ever lived throughout all the rest of earth's history. It is projected that the earth's population will reach seven billion by 2012. It is also projected within a few short years billions of people will have internet access via mobile internet devices (mib's). The Book of Daniel predicted that knowledge would increase at the time of the end.

**BUT THOU, O DANIEL, SHUT UP THE WORDS, AND SEAL THE BOOK, EVEN TO THE TIME OF THE END: MANY SHALL RUN TO AND FRO, AND KNOWLEDGE SHALL BE INCREASED. DANIEL 12:4**

Both Chapters 24 and 25 in the Book of Matthew are devoted to Jesus speaking about His second coming. He describes two different types of Christians in the last days, the wise and the evil. The wise servant is watching for His coming, but the evil servant is spiritually asleep. We do not want to be like the foolish virgins with no oil in our lamp.

Olive oil has always represented the Holy Spirit in the Bible. The Holy Spirit causes our light to shine in a dark and despairing world. It is our duty to make sure our lamp is full of oil (the Word of God).

How do we fill our lamp with oil? We need to *speak* God's Word. We need to *hear* God's Word. We need to *memorize* God's Word. We need to *believe* God's Word. The foolish virgins obviously did not believe the Lord when He told them He was coming back for them, and they did not prepare for His arrival.

Russell H. Conwell, the founder of Temple University, wrote a sermon called *Acres of Diamonds*. It is free on the internet as an e-book. His sermon tells us that we do not have to travel the world to find riches. Great wealth and opportunity are all around us if we have eyes to see. Truly, all around us are riches that will abound to our credit for all eternity. All we have to do is open our eyes, and start gathering our treasure as God directs us.

**AND THEY THAT BE WISE SHALL SHINE AS THE BRIGHTNESS OF THE FIRMAMENT; AND THEY THAT TURN MANY TO RIGHTEOUSNESS AS THE STARS FOR EVER AND EVER. DANIEL 12:3**

If by some chance, you have read this book and have not yet given your life to Jesus Christ, it is truly the easiest thing in the world.

1) Publically confess the LORD Jesus Christ, and
2) Believe that God has raised Him from the dead. *See* Romans 10:9
3) Repent from your dead works. *See* Hebrews 6:1

Then find other believers that *believe* the Word of God. Ask to be baptized to illustrate your death and resurrection with Jesus Christ. *See* Romans 6:4. You are born again! Start studying God's Word. Start *speaking* God's Word. Start *hearing* God's Word. Start *believing* God's Word. Do not let anybody rob you of all the riches that are yours by faith in Jesus Christ (the Word of God). You have health, you have wealth, you have wisdom, you have authority and you have Jesus Christ living within you.

**THEREFORE LET NO MAN GLORY IN MEN. FOR ALL THINGS ARE YOURS;**
**WHETHER PAUL, OR APOLLOS, OR CEPHAS, OR THE WORLD, OR LIFE, OR DEATH, OR**
**THINGS PRESENT, OR THINGS TO COME; ALL ARE YOURS;**
**AND YE ARE CHRIST'S; AND CHRIST IS GOD'S.**
**I CORINTHIANS 3:21-23**

I have listed 101 verses that you should memorize to prepare you to become a mature Christian, but you should not stop there. You should memorize at least one new scripture every week. Usually when I am reading the Bible, a scripture verse will jump out at me and I know that I should memorize it. I mark it down and begin the process as I have outlined in this book by repeating it over and over until it is stored up in my mind. Often times it is exactly the Word that I will need sometime in the near future.

God will always prepare us for the spiritual battle that is ahead by giving us His perfect Word, and He will prepare us for every battle if we will only listen and be sensitive to the Holy Spirit. You cannot fight the flesh with your will power. You cannot fight the flesh with the flesh. You cannot fight the Devil with the flesh. Unbelief in God's Word is the root of all mankind's problems, and belief in God's Word is the answer to all of mankind's problems. There is only one way to gain the victory.

SPEAK, HEAR AND BELIEVE THE WORD OF GOD!